God and Me!®

52 Week Devotional
for Girls Ages 10-12

HENDRICKSON
PUBLISHERS

ROSE
KiDZ

52 Week Devotional
for Girls Ages 10-12

Linda Washington
Jeannette Dall
Kathy Widenhouse

God and Me!® 52 Week Devotional for Girls Ages 10-12
Compiled from God and Me!® Devotions for Girls Ages 10-12 series, vols. 1-3 (©2012-2015)
Compilation ©2016 Rose Publishing, LLC

RoseKidz® is an imprint of
Rose Publishing, LLC
P.O. Box 3473
Peabody, Massachusetts 01961-3473 USA
www.hendricksonrose.com
All rights reserved.

Cover and interior design by Nancy L. Haskins
Illustrations by Aline L. Heiser and Dave Carleson

ISBN 978-1-58411-178-8
RoseKidz® reorder# L46839
JUVENILE NONFICTION/Religion/Devotion & Prayer

Printed in the United States of America
Printed May 2019

Table of Contents

Table of Contents

You Are God's Garden

Do you enjoy seeing gardens with beautiful flowers and healthy vegetables?

If you've ever helped care for a garden, you know it takes a lot of work to make it wonderful. The soil needs to be prepared, and the seeds and plants put in the ground. Rain and sunshine make the plants sprout and grow. Weeds need to be chopped out. Sometimes you have to rid the garden of bugs and other critters. But once everything is growing and looking great, you can relax and enjoy the wonderful smells, sights, and tastes of your garden.

Devotions with God are like growing a garden. First you plan what to plant. Then you gather everything you need. Finally, you calm your mind so you can hear what God has to say. That sometimes means getting rid of the "bugs" in your life, such as the TV and the Internet. The neat thing about spending time with God is you get to enjoy the sunshine of his love and the rain of his blessings.

Are you ready to begin this adventure packed with fun stories and activities to help you grow closer to God? (If you need help with any of the activities, check out the Scripture references and the puzzle answers at the end of the book.)

So, Get Ready to Grow in God's Garden!

You Are God's Child

[The Lord says,] "I have summoned you by name; you are mine."
– Isaiah 43:1

The Name Game

Maggie sat hunched over the kitchen table staring at a piece of paper. She frowned and chewed on her pencil. Wadded-up paper littered the floor.

Her dad took in the scene as he walked in. "Hi, Mags. What's up?"

"Not another one!" Maggie sighed as she wrote on the paper.

"Another what?" her dad asked.

"Another name for me," said Maggie. She explained that Miss Jason had given the class a special assignment—to write a short essay about what their names mean to them.

"That sounds interesting and fun," said Mr. Everts.

"I don't think so," replied Maggie. "I have too many names. You call me Mags and Mom calls me Maggie, except when she's mad, then it's Margaret Ruth. My brother calls me Magatron, and the baby calls me Ma-a. Grandma calls me Meg, and Uncle Ben calls me Peg."

"Hmm," her dad said. "I see your problem. And you forgot the very best name—God calls you his child. You are a Christian.

"Margaret Ruth, Maggie, Mags, Magatron, Ma-a, Meg, Peg, God's child, why don't you write about all your names?"

Your Turn

1. What is special about your name?
2. What is special about being God's child?

_____

_____

Prayer

Thank you that you have called me by name. Amen.

9

You Are God's Child

[The Lord says,] "I have summoned you by name; you are mine."
— **Isaiah 43:1**

You Remind Me Of...

When the Ramirez family arrived at the family reunion, a woman came up and hugged Mrs. Ramirez. The woman said, "Sally, I'm so glad to see you! Your daughter reminds me of you—same freckles, same color of hair. Catch you later." She hurried off.

"Cousin Rachel," Mrs. Ramirez explained.

A man came up and shook Jon's hand. "Welcome!" He looked at Clarise. "You sure look like your dad—same eyes, same nose."

"That's Uncle Pete," Mr. Ramirez told Clarise as the man left.

At noon, Clarise took her food and sat next to Grandma. "I'm tired of people saying I remind them of Mom or Dad," Clarise said. "I'm me!"

"Sure you are," Grandma replied. "But you're a little bit of your mom and dad—and even me. Every family member is alike in some way. Actually, all people are alike in one way. We are made in the image of God. That means we share his nature, so we can love and be wise, truthful, and thankful for our wacky relatives."

Clarise laughed and dug into her food.

Your Turn

1. Who do people say you remind them of?
2. Why is it important to know you're made in the "image of God"?

_____

_____

_____

Prayer

God, help me remind others of you when they see what I do and say. Amen.

You Are God's Child

[The Lord says,] "I have summoned you by name; you are mine."

– Isaiah 43:1

Your Actions Are Important

Amy was filling her backpack when Kelly called. "Let's go! Everyone's waiting."

When Amy and Kelly joined the group, Marian said, "Are you ready for your initiation into The Club?"

Amy said, "I guess so."

"It's so-o-o cool!" said Heather. "We'll have fun!"

Amy was nervous about joining The Club. Only the most popular sixth-grade girls were included. She told herself the initiation wouldn't be difficult.

"This is your initiation," Kelly explained. "We're going to the candy store. You need to sneak a candy bar out of the store without paying for it."

Remember who you are! The words seemed to be cranked at top volume in Amy's mind. She told the girls, "I can't do that. That's stealing. Count me out." Then she headed home and told her mother what had happened.

"Good for you!" said her mother. "That took courage."

"I remembered what Dad said," Amy replied. " 'When you face a problem, remember who you are.' I remembered that I am part of the Chen family and part of God's family, and we don't steal."

Your Turn

1. Why did Amy want to join The Club?
2. How do you think she felt after she said no?

_____

Prayer

Dear God, help me always remember who I am—your child. Amen.

You Are God's Child

[The Lord says,] "I have summoned you by name; you are mine."
– Isaiah 43:1

Gifts from God

Nevada entered the house and dropped her backpack.

"You don't look happy," Mrs. James commented.

"Mom, why did you name me Nevada?" she asked.

"Is that why you're miserable?"

"Not really. Mrs. Morgan picked Amy Johnson to play her violin at the assembly. I practice as much as she does. Why is she a better musician?"

"Honey, Amy is gifted musically. It comes naturally to her."

Nevada sighed. "I'm not good at anything."

At that moment, Walter, the family dog, limped into the kitchen.

"What's wrong, boy?" Nevada asked. She examined his paw and found a piece of glass in a pad. After taking it out, she stroked his fur. Walter wagged his tail.

"Nevada!" her brother Archie called. "Will you help me with math?"

"Okay. Be right up!" Nevada gave Walter a final pat.

Mrs. James smiled. "God gave each of us special abilities. I'd say he gave you the gift of a kind heart. Instead of wanting the gift someone else has, choose to be thankful for what God gave you."

Nevada smiled and Walter barked.

Your Turn

1. What abilities has God given you?
2. What do you think God wants you to do with your abilities?

_____

_____

Prayer

God, help me appreciate the gifts and talents you've given me. Amen.

You Are God's Child

[The Lord says,] "I have summoned you by name; you are mine."

– Isaiah 43:1

Every Gift Is Special

The excitement level was high in the fifth- and sixth-grade Sunday school class. The kids were planning to do a skit, complete with music.

Jasmine Huff looked troubled. What could she do to help? She couldn't act or sing very well.

"We'll need someone to work on the sets," said Kim, the college student who helped teach the class.

Well, that leaves me out again, Jasmine thought.

"We'll need people to sign up to help backstage—to move props and clean up."

Jasmine raised her hand, glad to have something to do.

One girl commented, "Those are the unimportant jobs."

Some of the kids laughed.

Mr. Upland, the teacher, called for silence. "There are no unimportant jobs," he said. "Just like there are no unimportant gifts or abilities. We all need to work together if we're going to do this skit. Helping out backstage is just as necessary as acting on stage." Mr. Upland turned to the girl who had made the remark, "Rebecca, I'll put you down to help on the clean-up crew so you'll discover every job is important."

Your Turn

1. What's a talent or ability you wish you had?
2. What can you do to bring glory to God using your abilities?

_____

_____

Prayer

Lord, you've blessed me with abilities and talents. I want to use them to glorify you. Amen.

You Are God's Child

Family Tree

Ask your mother, father, grandparents, uncles, and aunts to tell you about the relatives you don't know very well. You may hear some very interesting stories. Then have them help you create a family tree.

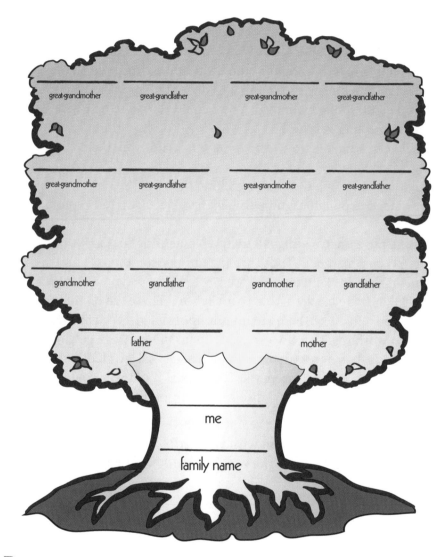

Prayer

Lord, thank you for my entire family. Amen.

You Are God's Child

Your Talent Résumé

Adults use résumés to list their experiences and abilities to find jobs. Create your résumé by checking the boxes and filling in the blanks. You can do a lot!

Name: _____

What I enjoy doing: _____

_____

What I can do:

☐ Teach others   ☐ Sing or dance   ☐ Write stories, songs, poems

☐ Help Mom and Dad   ☐ Other sports   ☐ Smile at others

☐ Skate or ski   ☐ Bake cookies   ☐ Other: _____

☐ Do science projects   ☐ Solve math problems   _____

My favorite things to do: _____

_____

What I would like to learn to do: _____

_____

What I want to do for God if given opportunities: _____

_____

Prayer

Dear God, thank you for making me who I am. Help me discover the special purpose you have for me. Amen.

God Gave You Family and Friends

Be devoted to one another in love.

– Romans 12:10

Brothers...

"Mom!" Melissa yelled. "Make Jimmy stay outta my room!"

"I wasn't in your room!" Jimmy yelled from his own room.

"Yes, you were! Why is your electronic pet thingy in here?" Melissa sighed. Brothers! What's the point of them? Why couldn't I be an only child?

Mrs. Samuels appeared in the doorway. "My happy family," she said, shaking her head.

"He started it!" Melissa said.

"Can't you guys go five minutes without all this arguing?"

"Sometimes I wish I didn't have a brother!"

Mrs. Samuels sat on the bed. "I don't think you'd really be happy if you didn't."

Melissa huffed, not wanting to agree with her mother. "I'd be happy if he'd quit sneaking into my room."

"I'll talk to him. Now will you at least try to get along?"

"Uh huh," said Melissa reluctantly.

Minutes later, Jimmy stood in the doorway. "I'm sorry." After a pause, he asked, "Wanna play the new game I got?"

"Okay." Melissa smiled. Maybe having a brother wasn't so bad after all.

Your Turn

1. Name a special thing about each family member.
2. What do you like about being part of your family?

Prayer

Jesus, thank you for my family. Amen.

God Gave You Family and Friends

Be devoted to one another in love.

– Romans 12:10

Saturday Appointment

"Hi, Mr. Potts!" Rachel said. She slid onto the park bench near an old man.

"You're late," Mr. Potts said with a chuckle. He handed Rachel a small sack of cracked corn.

Every Saturday, Rachel and Mr. Potts fed the ducks together. Mr. Potts lived in a retirement home a few blocks away. After she'd met him, she introduced him to her parents. Rachel's grandfathers were dead, so Mr. Potts was like a grandfather to her.

A cluster of ducks quacked around their ankles. Rachel and Mr. Potts laughed as thy watched the ducks.

Mr. Potts smiled at Rachel. "I look forward to these Saturday outings. I felt lonely and sorry for myself until you came along." He looked at his watch. "Well, I'd better get back. See you next week?"

Rachel thought a moment. God had brought Mr. Potts to be her friend. "Mr. Potts, could I call you Grandpa?"

Mr. Potts' wrinkled face lit up. "I would be honored!"

Your Turn

1. Who do you feel close to at school? At church? In your neighborhood?
2. How do you let those people know they are special to you?

_____

_____

Prayer

Thank you, Lord, for the people you've given me to love. Amen.

God Gave You Family and Friends

Be devoted to one another in love.

– Romans 12:10

Grandpa Louie

Grandpa tapped at Selena's open bedroom door. "Janice, I baked some of those cookies you like. You and your friend are welcome to try some."

"Thanks, Grandpa Louie," Selena said.

Grandpa smiled and shuffled away.

After he left, Selena's friend Katie said, "Why does he call you by your sister's name?"

"Sometimes he forgets," said Selena.

"Your grandpa's pretty old," Katie said.

"Yes," agreed Selena.

Katie paused. "Does he have that Alzheimer's disease?" she asked.

"Well, he forgets some things," answered Selena, "but he doesn't have Alzheimer's. Even my mom calls me Janice sometimes!"

"Do you ever obey what he says?" asked Katie. "My grandma tells me what to do when we visit her. But I ignore her, like my parents do."

Selena shook her head. "I don't ignore my grandpa! I respect him. Even when he calls me by my sister's name, I love him! Besides, God says to honor him."

Your Turn

1. How did Selena show respect for her grandfather?
2. How do you show respect for people older than you?

Prayer

Show me how to be respectful to adults, Lord. Amen.

God Gave You Family and Friends

Be devoted to one another in love.

– Romans 12:10

The Book Report

Jessica's brown eyes stared at her book report. She couldn't believe it. A big, red "D" looked back at her. Angry tears sprang to her eyes.

When the bell rang, Mrs. Leonard called Jessica to her desk. "Jessica, I gave you that 'D' because you didn't do your best work."

Jessica had to admit that Mrs. Leonard was right. She hadn't read much of the book because she'd gone to friend's sleepover instead.

"Jessica, you're a bright girl. I know you can do better than this. I'll tell you what. I'll throw out this grade if you read a different book and write a better report."

Jessica nodded, but she wasn't happy. When she got home, she reluctantly showed her mother the paper and shared what her teacher had said.

"Mrs. Leonard really seems to think a lot of you," said Mrs. Branson. "Some teachers wouldn't give you another chance.'"

"Now I have to do the whole thing over," Jessica grumbled.

"God has put a special teacher in your life," Mrs. Branson went on. "It's great that she cares about you."

Your Turn

1. Who are the people in your life who challenge you the most?
2. Who is the best teacher you've had? Why?

_____

_____

Prayer

Dear Lord, thank you for the teachers and leaders in my life. Amen.

God Gave You Family and Friends

Be devoted to one another in love.

– Romans 12:10

Who Is Your Neighbor?

Shelli and her friend Renee swung lazily back and forth on Shelli's front-porch swing. "Who's the weird woman on that porch?" Renee asked, pointing to the house across the street.

"That's Mrs. Fields," Shelli replied.

Renee laughed. "Where'd she get that outfit? A garbage bin?"

Shelli laughed and shrugged.

Everyone on Shelli's block knew Mrs. Fields had been having financial problems after her husband's death. She was also a little strange. Shelli's mother had mentioned that Mrs. Fields had to take medication every day. Sometimes Shelli's mom had to remind Mrs. Fields to take it.

Shelli didn't think any more about Mrs. Fields until she was in Sunday school. Her class had just read the story of the Good Samaritan. During discussion time, the teacher asked, "Who is your neighbor?"

Shelli thought about people she liked or would want to help. A sudden thought came to her: Mrs. Fields is my neighbor. Shelli made a promise to God and herself that she would talk to her mom and then help Mrs. Fields.

Your Turn

1. Who are your neighbors?
2. What can you do to show love to your neighbor?

Prayer

Lord, help me be kind to my neighbors, no matter who they are or how they behave. Amen.

God Gave You Family and Friends

Family Love

Being devoted to one another, as Romans 12:10 says, takes time and effort. Go through the maze to discover ways you can show love to the people in your life. To get through the maze, you'll need to unscramble some words. If the unscrambled word is a good thing to do, you're on the right path. If it's a bad thing, you've hit a dead end.

Prayer

Lord, I love my family, but sometimes I forget to show them. Please give me ideas of how to show my love. Amen.

God Gave You Family and Friends

Family Album

The Bible reveals many family connections. Answer the questions by filling in the correct names of people using the list.

David Esau Jesse Jesus Ruth

Who was David's father?
(Matthew 1:6)

_____

Who was Boaz's wife?
(Matthew 1:5)

_____

Who was Jesus' ancestor?
(Matthew 1:17)

_____

Who was Jacob's brother?
(Genesis 25:26)

_____

David, Boaz and Jacob were part of the family line of this important person: _____
(Matthew 1:2, 5, 16)

Prayer

Heavenly Father, I know relationships are important. Help me show my love to my family and friends. Amen.

God Helps You Face Fear

I will instruct you and teach you in the way you should go;
I will counsel you with my loving eye on you.

– Psalm 32:8

Fear of Failure

"I can't do it!" Sarah stated. She stared at the pommel horse in despair.

"Try it again," her gym teacher said.

Sarah was tired of trying and failing. She'd tried twice before. A fall had resulted each time. She didn't have the courage to keep trying.

"Have you prayed about it?" the teacher asked. He was also the music leader at Sarah's church, so he knew she was a Christian.

Sarah shrugged and said, "What if God decides not to answer? That's what I'm afraid of. What if I fall again?"

"When we're afraid, God wants us to trust him," the teacher said.

Sarah sighed before whispering a quick prayer for courage. She knew her teacher was right. After a while, she returned to the starting point. She ran toward the pommel horse, gave a great leap, touched the horse with her hands, and landed on her feet.

"I did it!" she cried triumphantly. She smiled as she reconsidered what she'd said. "Umm…I mean God helped me do it!"

Your Turn

1. What are you afraid to try?
2. What would you like to tell God about your fears?

_____

_____

Prayer

Lord, sometimes I'm afraid to try again. I'm also afraid you won't help me. Take my fear, Lord. Please give me your courage and strength. Amen.

23

God Helps You Face Fear

*I will instruct you and teach you in the way you should go;
I will counsel you with my loving eye on you.*

– Psalm 32:8

Never Alone

Alyssa glanced around fearfully as she waited just inside the doors for her mother to pick her up from swim class. The neighborhood around the YMCA wasn't very safe, and Alyssa was afraid. *I wish Mom would hurry up.*

The sun had set and it was dark. There were still a number of people at the gym, but Alyssa was still nervous. She prayed silently, Jesus, I'm scared. Will you help me? Let me know I'm not alone.

Sirens wailed outside, followed by the loud laughter of a passing group of teenagers. Alyssa didn't feel as afraid as she had earlier. Thank you, Lord, she prayed.

Within minutes, she saw a familiar car. She dashed outside and got into the car beside her mother.

"Honey, I'm sorry I was late picking you up," her mother said.

"That's okay, Mom. I was scared, but I prayed. I knew God was with me."

Your Turn

1. Who or what do you turn to when you're afraid?
2. How does God help people who are afraid?
3. How can you help people who are afraid?

Prayer

God, when I'm afraid, help me remember you're with me. I'm glad I can count on you for love and protection. Amen.

God Helps You Face Fear

I will instruct you and teach you in the way you should go;
I will counsel you with my loving eye on you.

– Psalm 32:8

Too Quick to Accuse

As soon as Aaron looked at his broken music player, he only thought one thing: It was Holly's fault. With that thought in mind, he walked into his sister's room, waving his player.

Holly lay across her bed reading a book.

"You broke my music player!" Aaron accused.

Holly looked at him. "No, I didn't."

"You had it last."

"So? That doesn't mean I…"

"Don't ever touch my stuff again!" Aaron yelled. He stormed out of her room. As he started down the stairs, his mom was coming up.

"Oh," she said, "I meant to tell you that I caught Felix chewing your music player." Felix was the family's new puppy. "I know you love that player, so I'll buy you a new one."

Holly poked her head out of her room. She stared at Aaron, a hurt look on her face.

Aaron felt horrible for being so mean. He said, "Holly, I'm sorry."

Your Turn

1. What should Aaron have done instead of yelling at Holly?
2. Have you been quick to get angry? What happened?
3. Look up and write out James 1:19.

_____

Prayer

God, help me be quick to listen and slow to get angry. Amen.

God Helps You Face Fear

I will instruct you and teach you in the way you should go;
I will counsel you with my loving eye on you.

– **Psalm 32:8**

Holding a Grudge

"I'll never speak to Rebecca again!" Kennedy vowed, slamming the door.

Her older brother, Cal, looked up from his work and said, "Some people say 'hello' when they come into a house." Kennedy ignored him. She seethed, "I hate it when people talk about me behind my back!"

"What happened?" Cal asked.

"I found out that Rebecca told Kelli I flunked the science test. All Rebecca, did was say, 'I'm sorry.'" Kennedy said. "Humph! As if that should stop me from being mad at her."

"But shouldn't it?" Cal asked quietly.

Kennedy started to talk, but changed her mind.

"Isn't Rebecca your best friend? Do you like holding a grudge more than you like being friends?" Cal shrugged. "If you keep that up, you won't have any friends."

"Who asked you?" Kennedy growled. She knew he was right, but she wanted to stay mad at Rebecca.

Your Turn

1. Find and copy Ephesians 4:26-27. What makes you hold a grudge?
2. What can you do instead of holding a grudge?

Prayer

Lord, help me avoid staying angry with someone. Give me the courage to forgive. Amen.

God Helps You Face Fear

I will instruct you and teach you in the way you should go;
I will counsel you with my loving eye on you.

– Psalm 32:8

The Empty House

Jasmine didn't look up as the car stopped in front of Grandpop's house. *Maybe I can pretend everything is the same.* "I think I'll stay in the car," she said.

Her mom squeezed Jasmine's hand. "Come in when you feel like it."

I'll never feel like it! Jasmine sobbed as she remembered Grandpop's funeral. His house wouldn't be the same without his smile and bear hug.

When Jasmine got out of the car, she walked to the garden. Flowers were blooming, and the tomatoes were ripe. The garden was Grandpop's favorite place. Jasmine kicked the dirt and cried.

She stepped onto the back porch and saw her grandfather's gardening shoes right where he usually took them off.

When her mom came out, she found Jasmine holding the shoes.

"It helps me feel better to hold Grandpop's shoes," Jasmine whispered. "I miss him so much!"

Her mom hugged Jasmine. "I know, honey. And it's okay to cry and feel sad. You loved Grandpop. I'm sad too. But things are different for him too. He's happy because he's in heaven with Jesus."

Your Turn

1. Has anyone you loved died? How did you feel?
2. What do you think heaven is like?

Prayer

Lord, please help me when I'm sad. Also help me comfort people who are sad. Amen.

God Helps You Face Fear

Fruit of the Spirit

If you have trouble with anger, you probably need to take a fruit break. Sound crazy? This fruit is probably not what you are thinking of. Instead of apples and oranges, check out Galatians 5:22-23 NLT: "The Holy Spirit produces this kind of fruit in our lives: love, joy, peace, patience, kindness, goodness, faithfulness, gentleness, and self-control." The Holy Spirit helps you keep your cool.

Circle the nine fruit of the Spirit in this word search.

Love	**Patience**	**Faithfulness**
Joy	**Kindness**	**Gentleness**
Peace	**Goodness**	**Self-Control**

T	S	S	E	N	E	L	T	N	E	G	S	S
E	E	R	E	L	T	O	U	E	R	Y	T	I
L	C	S	E	L	S	E	L	S	A	O	I	M
F	A	I	T	H	F	U	L	N	E	S	S	P
W	E	O	L	E	T	C	Y	E	T	S	S	L
E	P	E	A	A	L	Q	O	T	E	T	E	I
Z	E	A	T	L	O	Y	J	N	K	V	N	C
G	E	T	T	T	H	A	D	U	T	I	D	L
H	C	O	J	H	S	N	J .	O	E	R -	O	I
T	E	C	N	E	I	T	A	P	Q	V	O	T
S	R	I	S	K	J	O	I	C	E	R	G	L

Prayer

Dear Lord, help me memorize the fruit of the Holy Spirit so I will think about them and put them into practice. Amen.

God Helps You Face Fear

Heaven Is a Wonderful Place

Think of the most beautiful and happiest place you've ever experienced. Heaven will be a thousand times better. Use the key to find out more about heaven.

Heaven is...

— — — — — — —
Ω Ø ® + √ + ®

— — — — — —
π + ® Ω + % $

— — — — — —
Δ Ø ¥ Ω * æ

— — — — — — — —
π + @ % + Ω * æ

.filled with — — — — — —.
@ # © + æ ß

— — — — — — — — — — —
μ @ © # & Ω & % + # $

where we will see — — — — —
Δ + ß * ß

where we will be — — — — — — and — — — — — God.
ß @ & # $ ß   π ® @ & ß +

KEY			
A @	G ©	N #	T $
C %	I &	O Ø	U *
D ∂	J Δ	P π	V √
E +	L æ	R ®	W Σ
F Ω	M μ	S ß	Y ¥

Prayer

Lord, I know heaven is a wonderful place because you are there! Amen.

God Helps You Overcome Sadness

[There is] a time to weep and a time to laugh.

– Ecclesiastes 3:4

Fifth-Grade Warriors

"What if…" Heather Banks paused to look at her friend Katie. "What if nobody likes us? What if we end up the nerdiest kids in the entire fifth grade? What if we can't do geometry?"

"That's why we've got to plan now—so we will be happy being ourselves," Katie said firmly. "Let's make a list of what we're worried about. Then we can plan what to do."

"But we can't plan everything. We don't know what's going to happen."

"Are you girls still worried about starting fifth grade?" Mrs. Banks asked as she entered the family room.

"Worried?" Heather waved her arm trying to brush her mother's words aside. But she had to admit they were true. "Well, maybe a little."

"Everyone worries about the unknown," Mrs. Banks said. "God doesn't want you to waste time doing that. Instead, he wants you to trust that he's in control of your future. He's already got everything worked out for your best."

Your Turn

1. What are you worried about?
2. Do you worry about the future? Why or why not?

_____

_____

_____

Prayer

Lord, I gladly give my worries to you. Amen.

God Helps You Overcome Sadness

[There is] a time to weep and a time to laugh.

– Ecclesiastes 3:4

Erase Worry

Faith looked glum as she glanced over the work her tutor had given her.

"You've been awfully quiet today, Faith," Mr. Samuels said.

"I'm worried about my dad," Faith replied. "I couldn't sleep last night." Her eyes filled with tears. "He had a heart attack five days ago."

"I'm sorry." Mr. Samuels closed his book. "How is he now?"

"The doctor says he's getting better. He's still in the hospital."

"My wife and I will pray for your family," said Mr. Samuels.

Faith mumbled a tear-filled thank you and added, "I'm so worried."

Mr. Samuels patted Faith's hand. "I know you're worried, but worrying won't help your father or you." He wrote "worry" on a piece of paper. Then he took an eraser and erased the word. "God promises to help you erase worry. He wants you to depend on him. He will help you through any and all problems. May we pray together right now?"

Your Turn

1. When you're facing a problem, what do you usually do?
   ☐ I worry until I make myself more upset.
   ☐ I talk it over with God and with a friend or family member.
   ☐ I try to ignore it.
2. Do you worry that God doesn't care about you or your problem? Look up and write out Psalm 32:8.

_____

Prayer

God, you know the problem that's worrying me right now. Please take care of it and remind me that you're in charge. Amen.

God Helps You Overcome Sadness

[There is] a time to weep and a time to laugh.

– Ecclesiastes 3:4

The Assembly

"I can't believe I have to do this in front of the whole school!" Melanie wailed. "Why did Miss Austin pick me to square dance with Tyler?"

The arts assembly was in two days. Melanie's class was demonstrating square dancing. Melanie worried she'd look stupid and get teased. She worried so much she got a stomachache.

Beth, Melanie's older sister, nodded sympathetically. "I know how you feel. Remember when I had to get up in front of the whole school and read a poem? I'd just gotten my braces. My mouth was a mess. I was so worried!"

Melanie nodded. She remembered.

"I thought everybody would make fun of me too," Beth said. "I was so upset, I got a stomachache."

Melanie touched her own stomach. "Me too."

"Well, instead of worrying about what could happen, I asked God to help me do my best." Beth said. "I felt better immediately! Try it, Melanie!"

Your Turn

1. Do you worry about looking silly in front of everyone? What do you do?
2. Trusting God will help you erase worry. What are you trusting God for today?

Prayer

Jesus, when I worry, please remind me that you are with me. Amen.

God Helps You Overcome Sadness

[There is] a time to weep and a time to laugh.

– Ecclesiastes 3:4

One Day at a Time

Vanessa asked her best friend, Trisha, "Did anybody buy anything?"

"One lady ordered some wrapping paper," Trisha said. "How about you?"

"Mr. James in my building ordered some magazines."

The girls had watched other kids walking through the apartment complex. Each one carried a form like ones Vanessa and Trisha clutched. Vanessa and Trisha decided to give up for the day.

"Today was awful!" Vanessa complained to her dad. "Everybody from school was out trying to sell the same stuff."

"Well, you're all trying to raise money," Mr. Clark said.

"Three people yelled at me," Vanessa admitted. "One man threatened to sic his dog on me. I don't think I can go through another day like this."

"I'll take off work early and go with you," offered Mr. Clark. "Don't worry about tomorrow. You've had enough trouble for one day."

Vanessa smiled. "I recognize that! It's from the Bible—Matthew 6:34."

Your Turn

1. Look up and write out Matthew 6:34.
2. What can you do instead of worrying about tomorrow?

_____

_____

Prayer

Lord, sometimes I worry about tomorrow. Help me look to you for help and confidence instead. Amen.

God Helps You Overcome Sadness

[There is] a time to weep and a time to laugh.

– Ecclesiastes 3:4

Feeling Miserable

Sonia pulled the covers up. She was totally miserable.

Her older sister, Kris, poked her head around the door that was ajar. "Better get a move on. We're needed at the shelter in an hour." She looked at Sonia's long, unsmiling face. "What's wrong?"

"I feel miserable," Sonia mumbled. "I'll never be happy again."

"Uh-huh," Kris said. "And why is that?"

Sonia took a deep breath. "Yesterday we tried out for parts in the fifth-grade play. I wanted a main part, but all I got was one line. Then we had a spelling contest, and I missed an easy word. And, worst of all, Megan is moving to another state. Now I'll have no best friend."

"I can see why you feel down," Kris said. "You may feel sad for a while, but you'll be happy again. I'll tell you one thing that works for me when I'm sad." Kris walked to the bed and put an arm around Sonia. "I help someone else, and then I forget about me and my worries. So let's go help some people today."

Your Turn

1. How do you get over feeling sad?
2. How can God help you when you're sad?

_____

_____

Prayer

God, thanks for being with me all the time, even when I'm miserable. Amen.

God Helps You Overcome Sadness

Ancient Worriers

People in Bible times worried too. Use your Bible to solve these crosswords. The first puzzle tells who worried. The second puzzle tells what happened.

PEOPLE

People Clues

Across

1. _____ prayed when he was worried about being attacked by enemies. (2 Chronicles 20:4-6)

3. _____ worried because he was too short to see Jesus. (Luke 19:1-3)

Down

2. _____ worried about her sister not helping her. (Luke 10:38-40)

4. _____ worried about not having children. (Genesis 30:1-2)

5. _____ worried about being sent to Pharaoh. (Exodus 4:10-13)

SOLUTIONS

Solutions Clues

Across

1. God defeated the Israelites' _____ . (2 Chronicles 20:27)

3. Jesus found him in a _____ tree. (Luke 19:4)

Down

2. Jesus said that _____ was right to listen to him. (Luke 10:41-42)

4. God gave her a _____ . (Genesis 30:22-24)

5. God promised to send _____ along to Pharaoh as a companion. (Exodus 4:14)

God Helps You Overcome Sadness

Worry Advice

Color the shapes to discover the best solution to worry.

Prayer

Heavenly Father, thank you for watching over me and teaching me the way I should go. Amen.

God Wants You to Be Humble

I have learned the secret of being content in any and every situation,
whether well fed or hungry, whether living in plenty or in want.
I can do all this through him who gives me strength.

– Philippians 4:12-13

Me, Me, Me!

Veronica was proud of her voice. In two days she would sing her first solo in front of everyone at church.

All week, she practiced her scales. But when Sunday came, Veronica's throat felt scratchy. "Mom, something's wrong with my throat."

Mom sighed. "Honey, I think you've been practicing too much."

"I just want my voice to be perfect," Veronica sighed. "Sonya is so jealous."

"Honey, God gave you a wonderful gift. But he didn't mean for you to act proud about it," said Mom.

Veronica nodded, although she wasn't really listening. Her throat was so sore.

At church, Veronica began singing well, but soon her voice disappeared. Laryngitis! Embarrassed, she rushed to sit by her parents.

"I sounded awful!" Veronica whispered to her mom.

"Honey, it's okay," her mom replied. "Your voice will get better. But I hope something else will get better, too—your humility."

Your Turn

1. Look up and write down the definition of "humility."
2. How do you act when you're really good at something?

Prayer

Lord, help me be humble and give you credit for my gifts and abilities. Amen.

God Wants You to Be Humble

I have learned the secret of being content in any and every situation,
whether well fed or hungry, whether living in plenty or in want.
I can do all this through him who gives me strength.

– Philippians 4:12-13

Real Love

"I love you for what you do for me-e-e-e!" Maria Vasquez sang along to the song playing in the car. She heard a grunt from her father.

"What's wrong, Dad?" Maria grinned.

"That's your favorite song?" Dad asked, glancing at her.

Maria nodded yes.

"Are those words true?"

Maria smiled. "I just like the music."

"I love you 'cause you're beautiful!" blared out of the speakers.

Dad asked, "Do you believe that loving a person is because of what he does for you or for how he looks?"

Maria shrugged. "Some people say that."

"That's not real love. Real love isn't about what we get. We love people because God loves us. We choose to love regardless of what they do for us or what they look like." Dad smiled. "That's why I love you, even when you are grouchy in the morning!"

Your Turn

1. What can you tell people about "real love"? (Read 1 Corinthians 13:4-7 for help.)
2. Is it possible to love people you don't like very much?

Prayer

Lord, I don't always want to love people. Help me choose to love anyway. Amen.

God Wants You to Be Humble

*I have learned the secret of being content in any and every situation,
whether well fed or hungry, whether living in plenty or in want.
I can do all this through him who gives me strength.*

– Philippians 4:12-13

Love Yourself

"I am so stupid!" Paige growled.

Her twin sister Patti overheard. "Don't be so hard on yourself."

"Don't be so nosy!" Paige snapped.

"Ex-cu-u-u-u-se me!" Patti huffed.

"I keep messing up this dumb report," groaned Paige.

"If I made the same mistakes, would you call me stupid?" asked Patti.
"You know you wouldn't. Would you call Mrs. Barnes stupid?" Mrs.
Barnes was a friend the twins had adopted as their grandmother.

"Of course not!" exclaimed Paige.

"If you don't treat anyone else like that, why treat yourself that way?"
Patti asked. "You can't love others well if you don't love yourself."

Paige opened her mouth to say something sassy, but she couldn't
think of anything. So she smiled instead.

Patti grinned too and tackled her twin in a bear hug.

Your Turn

1. How can you show love to your neighbors and to yourself?
2. Read Romans 12:3. Can you love yourself too much?

_____

_____

Prayer

Lord, help me love myself as you love me. I want to love people with
your love. Amen.

God Wants You to Be Humble

*I have learned the secret of being content in any and every situation,
whether well fed or hungry, whether living in plenty or in want.
I can do all this through him who gives me strength.*

– Philippians 4:12-13

Love Your Enemies

"Hey, look!" Sabrina pointed to a story in the newspaper in front of her.

Her brother, Mark, quickly skimmed the first paragraph. "Wow, I didn't know Bruce Peterson's house burned down."

Bruce was one of the toughest kids in the neighborhood. Sabrina remembered how he and his brother had once started a fight with Mark and his friend.

"They lost everything in the fire," Mark said.

"I'll bet half the stuff they had was stolen," Sabrina said. "Remember how Bruce stole my music player? He claimed he didn't, but everybody knows he's one of the biggest thieves at school."

Mark said, "Well, that might be true, but they need help now. They don't have anything left. Maybe we can give them some clothes, and food, and stuff."

"The Petersons?" said Sabrina, surprised. "They've been nothing but trouble to this neighborhood ever since they moved in!"

"Yes, I know," admitted Mark. "But if our house burned down, wouldn't you want people to help us?"

Sabrina looked at Mark. "I hate it when you're right." Then she smiled.

Your Turn

1. Do only people who are kind and loving deserve your compassion?
2. How can you show compassion to someone?

Prayer

Jesus, please show me how I can help someone this week. Amen.

God Wants You to Be Humble

I have learned the secret of being content in any and every situation, whether well fed or hungry, whether living in plenty or in want. I can do all this through him who gives me strength.

– Philippians 4:12-13

The Old Man

While walking with her friends one day,
    Regina Todd saw an old man.
His clothes hung in rags, a haunted look in his eye,
    As he quietly looked through a garbage can.
Her friends laughed as they saw the old man.
They nudged one another with winks.
"Look at that guy," one of them said.
    "It's not only the garbage that stinks."
The other kids laughed, but Regina looked sad,
What would Jesus do? she questioned herself
    As she watched the old man look for food
She held out her hand and gave him a look,
    Which she hoped showed that she cared.
The old man looked her way and gave a soft sigh,
    Then came forward as much as he dared.
She smiled as he took her hand.
Her heart felt a joy that she knew:
    If Jesus were here, he would probably smile,
    Because I'm doing what he wants me to do.

Your Turn

1. Have you felt compassion for someone? What did you do?

Prayer

God, open my eyes to see people who need compassion. Amen.

God Wants You to Be Humble

A Message for You

Unscramble these words. In the order they appear, put the circled letters on the lines to find an important message from God to you.

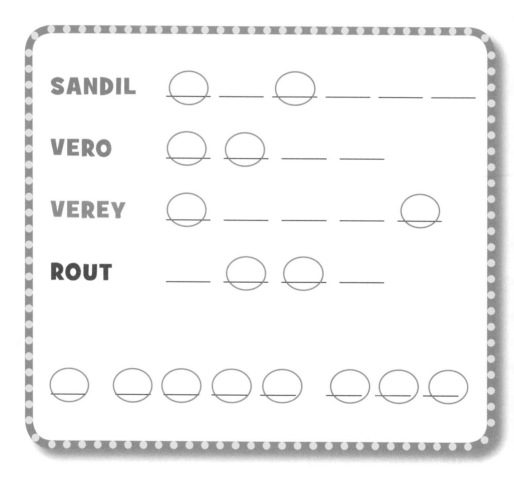

SANDIL

VERO

VEREY

ROUT

Prayer

Heavenly Father, your Word teaches me to love people like I love myself. Help me to have and show that kind of love. Amen.

God Wants You to Be Humble

C-A-R-E

Congratulations! You've been drafted as an agent of CARE—Compassion Awareness Reaching [out to] Everyone. Here are your first two cases.

Case # 96007

Subject: Roberto Muñoz **Age:** 10

Hobbies: Playing computer games

Needs: Other kids make fun of him because he stutters.

What would you do?

_____

_____

Case # 96008

Subject: Mona Whines **Age:** 12

Hobbies: Taking lunch money from second graders

Needs: Parents just divorced. Some kids are scared of her. She really needs a friend.

What would you do?

_____

_____

Prayer

Lord, open my eyes to see people who need kindness. Show me what I can do for them. Amen.

God Gives You Joy

Stand firm. Let nothing move you.
– 1 Corinthians 15:58

Committed or Not?

"Time to practice your violin, Monique!" Mom called from upstairs.

Monique grumbled as she switched off the TV. "Stupid violin!" she said as she snatched her case from its place in a corner of the family room.

Mom came downstairs just as Monique was setting up her music stand and still complaining.

"Remember how you begged me to let you learn the violin?" Mom asked. " 'I'll stick with it,' you said. Remember?"

Monique recalled saying that, but she didn't answer her mother. A few minutes later, she asked, "May I just practice half an hour today? There's a show on TV I want to watch."

Instead of answering, Mom played a song from her classical playlist on her phone. Soon the room was filled with the music of a master violinist—one of Monique's favorites.

"I wish I could play like her," Monique said.

"If you want to play better, you need to be committed to practicing," said Mom, turning off the music. "Commitment keeps you going even when you're tired."

Your Turn

1. "Standing firm" means being committed. To what or to whom are you committed?
2. Why do you think being committed to a task is important?

Prayer

Lord Jesus, help me remain committed to what I have to do, even when I sometimes don't want to do it wholeheartedly. Amen.

God Gives You Joy

Stand firm. Let nothing move you.
– 1 Corinthians 15:58

Abuela

Thoughts of her *abuela,* (her grandmother) always filled Rosa with quiet laughter—the kind of laughter that bordered on tears. How she missed Abuela! Abuela used to sing to her in a mixture of Spanish and English while she prepared dinner for the family. That seemed like a long time ago. Rosa was eight years old then, and now she was ten.

Rosa told her mother of the quiet laughter that bubbled inside her as she thought of how wonderful Abuela was. "How can it be," she wondered, "that I feel sad and happy at the same time?"

"Thinking about how much Abuela meant to you makes you feel joy, even though you're sad because she's no longer here," her mother said. "Joy lasts even in sad times."

"I miss Abuela. Is it wrong to not be sad all the time when I think of her?" Rosa asked.

Her mother shook her head. "You can have joy even when you're sad because joy goes deeper than the way you feel. Joy is something God gives you. So you can be joyful even when you're sad."

Your Turn

1. Can you think of a time when you felt joyful? What was happening?
2. Which is more lasting: feelings of happiness or of joy?

_____

_____

_____

Prayer

God, thank you for the joy you give me. Amen.

God Gives You Joy

Stand firm. Let nothing move you.

– 1 Corinthians 15:58

God's Presence

As the youth group sang the final verse of the closing praise song, everyone clapped and cheered to the Lord.

"I love that song!" Kristy yelled to her friend Sharon.

"Me too." Sharon added her voice to the sounds of praise filling the gym.

"Are you glad you came tonight?" Kristy whispered, once the shouting died down. The girls gathered their Bibles.

"Yeah. I was feeling kinda down before," said Sharon. "The worship time really picked me up."

Kristy nodded. "That's what my mom always says. 'Being in the presence of God makes us joyful.' It's contagious."

"I wonder why we don't feel like this all the time?" Sharon asked.

Kristy thought about that for a moment. "Maybe we do. We just don't pay attention to it sometimes. Remember what Pastor Harvey said tonight? 'With Jesus in our lives, we have lasting joy.' That's what he said, right?"

Sharon nodded. "So that means whether we feel joyful or not, it's there if we want to find it."

Your Turn

1. What does "joy" mean to you?
2. Can you be joyful without being aware of it? Explain.
3. What have you been joyful about?

_____

_____

Prayer

Jesus, you are the joy in my life. Amen.

God Gives You Joy

Stand firm. Let nothing move you.

– 1 Corinthians 15:58

Ready, Willing, and Committed

"Eight doors shut in our faces," Shelby said. "Is that a record?"

"Nine," her friend Kim corrected. "Bobbie said she had ten doors slammed in her face. That's the record. I'm ready to quit while we're behind."

The girls' Sunday-school class had divided into teams to go door-to-door in the neighborhood and pass out information about Jesus and their church. It was a hot day. Kim and Shelby were discouraged after numerous people refused the gospel tracts and said they weren't interested. Some people had been rude.

"Want to quit?" Kim asked.

"Yes," Shelby answered. She looked at her watch. "But we can't. Not for fifteen more minutes. We promised we'd go until three."

"Seems a waste of time," complained Kim. "Nobody wants to hear about Jesus."

"That sure seems true today. But we still believe!" Shelby said. "Besides, we're the ones who suggested doing this. If we don't stay committed, nobody at youth group will take us seriously again."

Kim sighed. "Okay, let's go. Maybe this time the person will be interested...or we'll break Bobbie's record."

Your Turn

1. What were the girls committed to do?
2. How do your actions show your commitment to Jesus?
3. When difficulties come, what can you do to persevere?

Prayer

Dear Lord, help me remain committed to you no matter what happens. Amen.

God Gives You Joy

Stand firm. Let nothing move you.

– 1 Corinthians 15:58

Perseverance

"I can't do it! I just can't stop biting my nails!" Amelia Anderson wailed. She nibbled on a fingernail, as if to prove her point.

Her mother smiled. "Now, now. It takes three 'P's' to break a bad habit."

"Three 'P's'?" Amelia asked.

"Practice, patience, and perseverance," explained Mrs. Anderson.

The first two Amelia understood, but that last word was new. "Perseverance?"

"Yes," her mother said. "Perseverance is that 'stick-to-it attitude' that keeps you going. Remember how long it took your dad to quit smoking?"

Amelia laughed. "He quit six times."

"Yes, but he persevered is what I'm getting at," Mrs. Anderson emphasized. "He hasn't smoked in two years."

Amelia nodded. She was beginning to grasp this new concept.

"Perseverance starts with prayer," her mother added. "God will help you keep going, especially when you've got the 'I can't do its.'"

Together, Amelia and her mother prayed that God would help Amelia persevere.

Your Turn

1. What do you have trouble stopping or continuing to do?
2. When are you most tempted to give up doing what's right?

_____

_____

Prayer

Jesus, I need your help today. I depend on you to help me keep moving forward. Amen.

God Gives You Joy

Who Stayed Committed?

Jesus had twelve disciples. One of them betrayed Jesus by showing the Romans where he was. Which disciples stayed committed to Jesus? Make a photocopy of this page or trace the shapes on another piece of paper. Cut out the pieces and then put them together to form a fish. You'll find one piece that doesn't fit. On it is the name of the disciple who betrayed Jesus.

Prayer

Lord, help me stay committed to you no matter what. Amen.

God Gives You Joy

Weird Words

Look at these pictures. Can you figure out the familiar phrases they represent? For example, the first phrase means "joy in times of sadness."

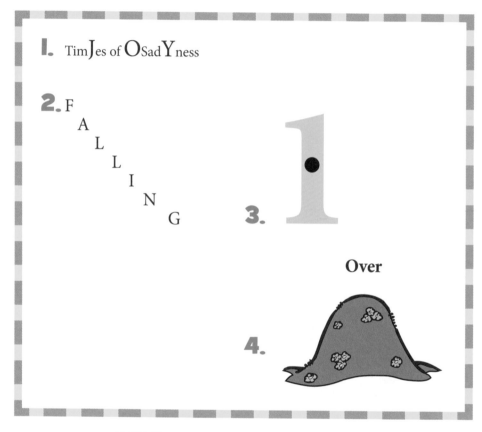

I. TimJes of OSadYness

2. F
  A
   L
    L
     I
      N
       G

3. 1 •

Over

4.

Bonus:

HELPING   HELPING

Prayer

Lord, help me remember that even when I'm feeling sad or unhappy, I still have your joy inside me. Amen.

You Can Always Trust God

We trust in the name of the Lord our God.
– Psalm 20:7

Who Can You Trust?

"I'm on the basketball team!" Keesha yelled. She twirled around the kitchen pretending to dribble a basketball.

"Way to go, girl!" her mom said.

Keesha's dad held up his hand, and Keesha gave him a high-five.

She caught her breath. "Now, I need just the right basketball shoes. I'll get the ads I saved from last Sunday's newspaper." As she read the ads, she frowned. They were confusing. "Best shoe for serious players," read one. "Voted best shoe by players and coaches," said another. "Our shoe beats out the competition," claimed yet a third ad. Keesha threw up her hands in frustration. "Who can I believe?" she asked. "Every company says they have the best shoe."

Her dad chuckled. "That's advertising, Keesha. Each company wants you to buy its product. You're right, you can't completely trust any of them. There's only one name you can trust totally all the time. That's God. We can believe everything he says, and he always keeps his promises. I'm sure glad of that, aren't you?"

Keesha nodded as she tossed aside the newspaper.

Your Turn

1. Who and what do you find hard to trust?
2. How do you react when you find out someone can't be trusted?
3. Why can you always trust God?

_____

_____

Prayer

God, I trust you in every situation no matter how scary or uncertain I feel it is. Thanks for being completely trustworthy. Amen.

You Can Always Trust God

We trust in the name of the Lord our God.

– Psalm 20:7

The Risk of Respect

Julie led her cousin to the pew occupied by some of her friends. She was nervous about Angelica visiting her church. Her cousin was from New York City, and she acted differently than the kids in Julie's small Midwestern town. Angelica was only a year older, but to Julie it seemed like a lot more.

Julie wanted her cousin to think she and her friends were cool. During the last part of the service, Julie and her friends made fun of the people around them. During a moment of prayer, Julie started to whisper to Angelica. Suddenly she noticed Angelica's head was bowed.

At the end of the service, Angelica told Julie how much she'd enjoyed the service. "But I have a question. Don't you respect God? I wondered because you kept talking during the service."

Julie was embarrassed. "I was showing off so you'd think I was cool."

Angelica smiled. "Respect for God is cool." Angelica put her arm around Julie. "And you're always cool with me."

Your Turn

1. How did Angelica show respect for God and the people in church?
2. Look up "reverence" in a dictionary. Why is reverence for God important?

_____

_____

_____

Prayer

Lord, I want to show my respect for you. Help me to listen and be considerate. Amen.

You Can Always Trust God

We trust in the name of the Lord our God.
– Psalm 20:7

Everybody's Doing It

Serena drank her chocolate milk and half-listened to the conversation at the lunch table. Some kids were swearing and using bad language. The bell rang, signaling the end of lunch. Serena and Dolores walked to their classroom.

"I never hear you using curse words," Dolores said. "How come?"

"Because I respect God," Serena answered. "I don't want to use bad words or misuse his name."

"But everybody curses," Dolores said.

"Not everybody. I don't," Serena said.

"My dad curses," Dolores said. "He's a lawyer. He says if it's not written down, it's not legal. Where does it say in the Bible not to curse?"

"One of the Ten Commandments is to 'not misuse the name of the Lord,'" Serena said. "I'm sure there are verses that say we should be kind when we talk."

Dolores shook her head. "You can't even prove God exists."

Serena was tired of arguing with Dolores. She didn't think her friend wanted to know what was right or wrong. She just wanted to do what she wanted without guilt.

Your Turn

1. Do you think Serena is right about Dolores' attitude?
2. If your friends misuse God and his name, what do you do?

Prayer

God, show me how to respect you and stand up for you. Amen.

You Can Always Trust God

We trust in the name of the Lord our God.
– Psalm 20:7

Trust

Up and down the sidewalk they went. Sadie felt like she'd been running a marathon. Her hair was wet with sweat, and her shirt was sticking to her back. She half-expected her arms to drop off any moment. Teaching a five-year-old to ride a bike wasn't easy.

"Hold tight, Sadie," Robbie said. "Don't let me fall!"

"Okay! Sit straight and pedal, Robbie."

Robbie's short legs pumped up and down. Sadie held the handlebars and the back of the seat. When the bike got going in a straight line, Sadie slowly let go of the handlebars.

Suddenly Robbie noticed what she'd done. "No, Sadie! I'm gonna fall!"

"You're doing fine," Sadie said. "Trust me! I won't let you fall."

Carol, Robbie's mom and Sadie's aunt, brought out some lemonade, and they all sat under the maple tree. Eleven-year-old Sadie was thankful for the rest.

"I can almost ride, Mom. Sadie helped me. Did you see me go?" asked Robbie.

"You're doing super, Robbie," said his mom. "Sadie, it's great you're helping. He trusts you completely."

Your Turn

1. List the people you trust. Why do you trust them?
2. What do you trust God to do for you?

_____

_____

Prayer

Dear God, thank you for always keeping your promises. Help me trust you in every situation. Amen.

You Can Always Trust God

We trust in the name of the Lord our God.
– Psalm 20:7

Loyalty

"It's not true!" Iris cried. "Why would I take your bracelet?"

Ivy stared at her. "Skip said he saw it in your locker."

"Ivy," Iris pleaded, "you're my best friend. I wouldn't steal from you."

"C'mon, Iris. A joke's a joke, but this isn't funny." Ivy frowned.

Iris gave up and walked away.

When Ivy arrived home, she heard her mother say, "I'll have Ivy there. Thank you."

"Have me where?" Ivy asked after her mother put down the phone.

"That was the police. They have a bracelet that belongs to you. Thankfully we had your name inscribed on it. It was with some stolen stuff in a boy's locker at your school. Somebody named Skip. Do you know him?"

Shocked, Ivy sank down on a chair. "I thought he was a friend. He told me Iris took my bracelet. I believed him."

"I thought you trusted Iris. She's been a loyal friend." Her mother put her hand on Ivy's shoulder. "And a true friend knows when to admit she was wrong."

Your Turn

1. What is your definition of "loyalty"?
2. How do your friends know you are a loyal friend?

_____

_____

_____

Prayer

Jesus, help me be loyal to you and to my family and friends. Amen.

You Can Always Trust God

A Psalm to God

David wrote many songs to show his love and respect for God. Take a look at Psalms 27, 37, and 38. Now pour out your feelings about God in your own psalm. For help, use the sentence starters. If you prefer to draw a picture, that's okay too. God loves your creativity!

God, you are...
When I think of you, I...
Because I know you are holy, I...

Prayer

God, I want to show *you* every day how much I respect and love you. Amen.

You Can Always Trust God

Trust God

To discover an important truth, follow these directions.

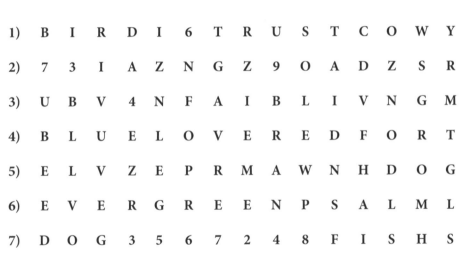

Cross out the last letter of each line.

Cross out all the numbers except 2, 5 and 8.

Cross out the As and Zs in line 2.

Cross out animal names in lines 1 and 7.

Cross out colors in lines 4 and 6.

Cross out the Bs and Vs in line 3.

Cross out every other letter in line 5.

Circle the leftover letters and write the words they make on the lines below.

1)	B	I	R	D	I	6	T	R	U	S	T	C	O	W	Y
2)	7	3	I	A	Z	N	G	Z	9	O	A	D	Z	S	R
3)	U	B	V	4	N	F	A	I	B	L	I	V	N	G	M
4)	B	L	U	E	L	O	V	E	R	E	D	F	O	R	T
5)	E	L	V	Z	E	P	R	M	A	W	N	H	D	O	G
6)	E	V	E	R	G	R	E	E	N	P	S	A	L	M	L
7)	D	O	G	3	5	6	7	2	4	8	F	I	S	H	S

____ _____ ____ _____

_____ _____

____ _____ ____ _____.

_____ ____ : ___

Prayer

Heavenly Father, I trust you completely. Amen.

Be Loyal to God

[Lord,] keep their hearts loyal to you.

– 1 Chronicles 29:18

A Loyal Friend

Sandra reviewed her plan of action as she walked down the school hall. "First, I'll ask Candice if she believes in God. Then I'll invite her to church. No, wait. Maybe I should…" She saw Candice coming toward her. Behind Candice were two of the most popular girls in the sixth grade—Sue and Jillian. *I'll wait to talk to Candice until Sue and Jillian leave,* Sandra decided.

Candice said, "We were looking for you, Sandra. Sue, Jillian, and I were just talking about something. You go to church, right?"

Sandra took a deep breath. "Yes…"

Candice continued. "Jillian's dad says there is no God. Can you prove there is?"

"Umm, well, you see…" Sandra started. With Jillian watching her closely, Sandra was nervous. She wanted to be friends with all three girls.

"Why do you go to church?" Sue asked suddenly.

"Well, my parents make me go," Sandra mumbled, trying to be casual.

Jillian looked satisfied. "Want to hang out with us? We're going over to my house."

Sandra nodded, but she felt terrible inside.

Your Turn

1. Why do you think Sandra felt terrible?
2. What helps you to be loyal to God?

Prayer

Lord, help me be loyal to you even when it's hard. Amen.

Be Loyal to God

[Lord,] keep their hearts loyal to you.
– 1 Chronicles 29:18

A Cheerful Giver

Dara Wilkins counted the money in her hand once more. She had $40. Forty whole dollars! Her relatives had been generous with birthday money this year. She couldn't wait to get to the mall and spend it.

"Now, remember what we agreed on," her mother said. "Ten percent goes into your bank account."

Dara quickly did the math. Four dollars. She wasn't happy about that, but she nodded.

"And don't forget to give to the Lord," Mrs. Wilkins added.

"Do I have to?" Dara asked. "If I keep giving my money away, I won't have much left."

Mrs. Wilkins said, "Dara, what did you have before your birthday?"

"Nothing, but…"

"Do you really think four dollars is too much to give to God when he's given you so much?" her mother asked.

"No…" Dara said glumly.

Mrs. Wilkins placed her hand on Dara's shoulder. "Second Corinthians 9:7 says, 'God loves a cheerful giver.' I won't force you to give what you don't want to. But think about what I said."

Your Turn

1. How did Dara feel about giving?
2. Why do you think *cheerful* giving is important to God?

_____

_____

Prayer

Lord Jesus, help me be cheerful in my giving and sharing. Amen.

Be Loyal to God

[Lord,] keep their hearts loyal to you.

– 1 Chronicles 29:18

A Generous Heart

When Traci entered the family room, her dad said, "I just heard from Connie Webber. Fred's had a heart attack."

"Oh no!" Traci said.

The Webbers were their next-door neighbors. Mr. and Mrs. Webber didn't have children, so they "adopted" the kids in the neighborhood. Whenever Traci needed help with homework and her parents weren't available, she would go to the Webbers' house.

"Don't worry," Dad said. "I hear Fred's already getting better."

Traci wanted to do something nice for Mr. Webber. Suddenly an idea came. She would make him a card and get everyone in the neighborhood to sign it.

Days later, she presented the card to her father to sign and to take to Mr. Webber. She'd collected more than fifty get-well greetings from kids and parents.

"This is great!" Traci's dad said. "Fred will love this." He looked the card over. "You did a great job on this card."

"Mr. Webber has always been nice to me, so I wanted to give something back."

Your Turn

1. When someone is generous to you, does that inspire you?
2. Do generous people always receive something in return?

Prayer

Lord, help me not to give to receive, but to give because I love you. Amen.

Be Loyal to God

[Lord,] keep their hearts loyal to you.
– 1 Chronicles 29:18

Loyal Doesn't Always Mean Instant

It was Saturday morning, and Amanda's parents were away. She and her seventeen-year-old brother, Eric, were home alone.

Amanda popped instant oatmeal into the microwave and put bread in the toaster. In less than two minutes, her breakfast was ready. She ate while she watched her favorite cartoon. After she finished, she looked for Eric. Amanda found him in the garage, his feet sticking out from under his old car.

"Hey, Eric, whatcha doin'?" Amanda said.

"Looking for an oil leak," he answered as he emerged.

"Will you take me to the mall this morning?"

"Nope," Eric said. "Maybe next Saturday."

"Next Saturday! That's forever. Come on, Eric!"

"No can do," Eric said. "This weekend I need to work on my car. I'm sure there will be a pair of shoes left next Saturday."

"I can't wait that long," Amanda insisted.

"Well, I wish I could find this oil leak instantly too," he said. "We both have to be patient. Looking forward to something can make getting it more fun." He crawled under the car.

Maybe I'll bake some cookies, Amanda decided.

Your Turn

1. What are some disadvantages of getting things immediately?
2. How did Amanda handle having to wait?

Prayer

God, thanks for being patient with me. Help me learn patience. Amen.

Be Loyal to God

[Lord,] keep their hearts loyal to you.

– 1 Chronicles 29:18

I'll Do It!

Sharon, twelve, and Susie, seven, were spending a rainy afternoon with their neighbor Mrs. Wilkens.

"Mom's birthday is tomorrow. Can we make something special for her?" Sharon asked Mrs. Wilkens.

"Great idea!" Mrs. Wilkens replied. "You two can make a birthday cake."

Soon the ingredients for a chocolate cake were assembled. Sharon measured the flour. Susie carefully put sugar in a measuring cup, one teaspoon at a time.

"Hurry up! I need it now!" Sharon barked. After putting in the sugar, she put in one egg. She impatiently waited for Susie to crack open the other one. Sharon grabbed the egg. "You're taking too long!"

"I quit!" Susie said and started to cry.

"Time out!" Mrs. Wilkens said. "Sharon, relax. We aren't in a hurry. You need to remember you're five years older than Susie. She can't do things as quickly as you can. You need to be patient."

Sharon put her arm around Susie. "Hey, sis. I'm sorry. You can stir all the stuff together, okay?"

"All right!" Susie whooped as she grabbed the mixing spoon.

Your Turn

1. What makes you impatient?
2. What do you do when you lose your patience?
3. How can you stay patient?

Prayer

God, help me be more patient with people and situations. Amen.

Be Loyal to God

The Secret of Loyalty

Do you want to know the secret to being loyal to God? Come closer…
closer…closer… Wait! That's too close! Ah, that's better. The secret to
being loyal to God is…hidden in the puzzle. All you have to do to find it
is solve multiplication problems. Color the areas where the answers are
even numbers.

Prayer

Lord, help me be loyal to you always. Amen.

Be Loyal to God

Patience, Patience

How much patience would you have in these situations? Check the patience level that fits. It may take patience to do this activity!

	Lots	Some	Little	None
Waiting for your turn in a game				
Waiting at the dentist's office				
Waiting for your parents to decide if you can do something you want				
Waiting for your little brother or sister				
Waiting for a big math test				
Waiting for a special trip or holiday				
Waiting to mow the lawn				
Waiting to find out if you made the team				

Prayer

Dear Lord, please help me be patient, especially when I have to wait. Amen.

Ask God for Wisdom

If any of you lacks wisdom, you should ask God,
who gives generously.

– James 1:5

Ask for It

Trudy emptied her cow-shaped bank on her bed. Only three dollars were left from the forty-five dollars she'd received for her birthday two months ago. Suddenly the things she'd spent her money on seemed silly. Now she barely had anything to take on the field trip to historic Williamsburg, Virginia.

Her mother had warned her. "You'd be wise to not spend so much. Remember, you can ask God for wisdom."

Trudy had replied, "Yeah, okay," and then forgot about it.

"Mom, I hardly have any money left," Trudy complained.

"I won't say I told you so," her mom said, looking as if she wanted to. "Your father and I have agreed to loan you some money to take with you. But keep in mind that this is a loan. You have to pay it back."

Trudy groaned but nodded.

"Remember when I said to ask God to help you be wise?" Mom said. "I didn't say that because I wanted to hear myself talk. Wisdom will help you avoid making some mistakes."

Your Turn

1. Was Trudy wise in the way she handled money?
2. Why is asking for wisdom important?

_____

_____

_____

Prayer

Lord, give me wisdom to know how to follow you and live your way. Amen.

Ask God for Wisdom

If any of you lacks wisdom, you should ask God,
who gives generously.

– James 1:5

Miss Goody Two-Shoes

"Goody Two-Shoes!" Kyle muttered as his sister left. His brother grinned.

"Wanda is a tattletale," Kyle said. "She told Mom I broke the garage window. She always acts like she's so perfect."

"Wanda is trying to stay on Mom's good side so she can go to a skating party," Jason said.

"Kyle, come here!" Mom called.

Kyle stomped toward the kitchen. His mother sat at the kitchen table, a laptop in front of her.

"Why didn't you tell me about the garage window?"

Kyle hung his head. "I was going to, but Miss Goody Two-Shoes beat me to it. She always acts like she's perfect."

"Kyle, we're not talking about your sister. You're grounded. Now, tell Wanda I want to see her."

Wanda came into the room. "You wanted me?"

"Yes. You can't go to the skating party."

"Why?" Wanda exclaimed. "I've been good."

"You wanted to get your brother in trouble so you would look better," Mom stated. "Your father and I have tried to teach you that true goodness comes from God. It includes being kind to others."

Your Turn

1. Look up "goodness" in a dictionary. How do you define it?
2. Goodness is a fruit of the Holy Spirit. Why does God think it's so important?

Prayer

Lord, please let the fruit of goodness grow in my life. Amen.

Ask God for Wisdom

If any of you lacks wisdom, you should ask God,
who gives generously.

– James 1:5

Good Character

Amelia Taylor wiped her eyes as the pastor said the eulogy at her aunt's funeral.

"Most of all," he said, "we knew her to be a woman full of goodness and mercy."

Amelia agreed with that. Her Aunt Nancy was a wonderful person. Amelia couldn't understand why God had allowed her to die so young—she wasn't even forty. After the funeral, Amelia slowly walked to the car with her mom. "There were a lot of people at the funeral," Amelia said.

Mrs. Taylor nodded. "Everyone loved Nancy. She had a truly good heart."

"That's what Pastor Henry said," Amelia said. "But my Sunday-school teacher once said that no one was good. She said that's why we're not able to get to heaven on our own."

"I don't think that's what she meant," Mrs. Taylor answered. "None of us is good enough to get to heaven based on our own actions, but when we join God's family, we grow to be more like Jesus. As we follow him, he helps us be kind to others."

Your Turn

1. How would you describe a kind and good person?
2. Can a person be good enough for heaven on her own?

_____

_____

_____

Prayer

Lord Jesus, thank you for helping me be good so I can please you. Amen.

Ask God for Wisdom

If any of you lacks wisdom, you should ask God,
who gives generously.

– James 1:5

The Party

Andrea sighed. What should she do about Jeneta's party? Everyone wanted to go. But Andrea had heard through the school grapevine that the party wouldn't be supervised. She knew her parents wouldn't allow her to go. Andrea had also heard some seventh-grade boys planned to crash the party and sneak in beer.

I want to go, Andrea thought. Maybe I'll tell Mom that Jeneta's parents will be there. Andrea glanced at her Bible. Hadn't she just read the Ten Commandments? "You shall not lie" was one of them.

The phone rang. It was Jeneta.

"Are you coming to my party?" Jeneta asked. "My parents will be gone, so we'll have the house to ourselves."

Andrea sighed. "I can't come. My parents won't let me go to an unsupervised party."

"So don't tell 'em," Jeneta suggested.

Andrea thought for a moment. "I won't lie. That's not right."

"Well, it's your loss," said Jeneta just before hanging up.

Andrea hung up. She knew she'd made a wise decision.

Your Turn

1. How do you think Andrea felt about not going to the party?
2. What wise choices can you make, even if it's hard?

Prayer

Lord, help me use your wisdom and live by your rules. Amen.

Ask God for Wisdom

*If any of you lacks wisdom, you should ask God,
who gives generously.*

– James 1:5

An Attitude of Thankfulness

"Isn't it wonderful?" Ingrid's eyes shone as she took a bite out of the cotton candy. "Thanks for inviting me to the circus."

"Twenty-seven," Rhea said.

"What?" Ingrid asked.

"You've thanked me twenty-seven times," Rhea grinned.

"I'm glad you're enjoying yourself," Mrs. Bernard said, smiling at Ingrid. "It's nice that someone is having a good time."

Mrs. Bernard glanced at her youngest daughter, Jill. Jill had been complaining ever since they arrived. She grumbled about having to wait in a long line to buy a program. She didn't like the location of their seats.

"Mom, may I get some more cotton candy?" Jill asked.

Mrs. Bernard shook her head. "You've already had some. You don't need any more sugar."

Jill snorted.

"Jill, you begged to go to the circus. But you keep complaining." Mrs. Bernard said. "It's time for you to be thankful, like Ingrid is."

Jill sat back in her seat and pouted.

Your Turn

1. How was Ingrid's attitude different from Jill's?
2. Who do you think is more pleasant to be around—someone with a thankful attitude or someone who complains? Explain.

_____

_____

Prayer

Lord, teach me to have a thankful attitude. Amen.

Ask God for Wisdom

A Good Verse

Use the code to figure out the words in this great Scripture verse.

. Psalm 23:6

Prayer

Heavenly Father, help me be good toward others. I know that pleases you. Amen.

Ask God for Wisdom

Wisdom from Above

The commandments of the LORD are right, bringing joy to the heart. The commands of the LORD are clear, giving insight for living.
- Psalm 19:8 NLT

Suppose you were the host of a radio call-in show. How would you use the above Scripture to help the caller make a wise choice? For more insights, read Acts 4:19 and Romans 13:9.

Caller: Uh, hi. My friend Craig and I were trying to get in with the cool kids at school. But the cool kids pick on younger kids. They also steal things for fun. What should I do?

You: _____

_____

_____

_____

_____

Prayer

Dear Lord, help me memorize the fruit of the Holy Spirit so I will think about them and put them into practice. Amen.

Express Your Thanks

Give thanks in all circumstances.

– 1 Thessalonians 5:18

Volunteer Work

"Pass the carrots," Jonathan said.

His sister, Tara, practically flung the carrots at him. "Some people are just insensitive!" Tara said.

"What are you mad at me for?" Jonathan asked.

"If you have to ask, then forget it. May I be excused, Dad?"

Dad sighed and nodded. He looked inquiringly at Jonathan.

"I don't know what's wrong with her, Dad," said Jonathan. "All I did was come home from Steve's and wash up for dinner."

"Hmm. Who set the table?" Dad asked. "Tonight was your night."

"Oh, I guess Tara. I forgot." Jonathan realized he was in trouble.

"And you thanked your sister for doing your job?" asked Dad.

Jonathan looked embarrassed. "I just forgot, that's all. Besides, I didn't ask her to do it. She obviously volunteered."

"If a person volunteers to do something, she shouldn't be thanked? Jesus voluntarily died for our sins. Does that mean we shouldn't thank him?" Dad asked.

Jonathan shrugged. "I guess I haven't thought about it much."

Dad wrapped an arm around Jonathan. "I think it's time you did."

Your Turn

1. Have you ever forgotten to thank someone? How do you think that person felt?
2. What has God done for you that you want to thank him for?

_____

_____

Prayer

Lord, remind me to be thankful and to show I'm thankful. Amen.

Express Your Thanks

Give thanks in all circumstances.

– 1 Thessalonians 5:18

The Entire Truth

"Deena, why are you so late getting home?" Mom asked.

"We stopped for fries. I'm going to my room." Deena responded quickly. She sighed as she flopped onto her bed. At the mall, her friend Lisa was caught shoplifting. The store's security team had questioned them both. Deena was cleared but felt guilty and embarrassed. She didn't want to talk.

Minutes later, Mom stood in the doorway. "You weren't completely honest with me. Lisa's mother called. She said something about talking to mall security. What happened?"

Deena spilled out the story in one big gush.

Her mom was calm, but firm. "Deena, you know how I feel about lying."

"But I didn't lie to you," Deena said.

"You didn't tell me the entire story when I asked you, did you?" asked her mother. "Keeping back part of the truth is a type of lying."

"I thought you'd be mad at me because of Lisa," said Deena.

"I'm not mad at you for Lisa," answered Mom. "I don't like it when you keep things from me. Next time, be completely honest."

Your Turn

1. Why do you think Deena withheld part of the truth?
2. Why is not telling the entire truth the same as lying?

_____

_____

Prayer

Lord, help me tell the entire truth, even if it is uncomfortable or gets me in trouble. Amen.

Express Your Thanks

Give thanks in all circumstances.

– 1 Thessalonians 5:18

An Honest Answer

After her mother told her to stop lying, Deena was honest all week. Now Lisa was mad because Deena told her that her new vest was ugly. Deena's math teacher, Mrs. Ralston, got angry when Deena told her the homework assignment was a waste of time. Her mother got mad when Deena complained about dinner one night.

"Mom, you told me to be honest," Deena said. "Now everybody's mad at me."

"Honesty is important," said Mom. "But it's also important to be respectful and kind."

Deena was frustrated. "Does that mean I shouldn't tell the truth? When I told Lisa her new vest was ugly, that was the truth."

"Did she ask what you thought?" Mom questioned.

"Yes, she asked me if I liked it," Deena said.

"You can be honest and gentle. You could have just told Lisa no and left it at that. You don't want to deliberately hurt someone's feelings."

Deena said, "This honesty thing is complicated."

Her mom patted her hand. "You can always ask God for help in what to say."

Your Turn

1. What does "honesty" mean to you?
2. How can you be honest yet give a gentle answer?

_____

_____

Prayer

Lord, I want to be honest, but I don't want to hurt people's feelings. Give me your wisdom. Amen.

Express Your Thanks

Give thanks in all circumstances.

– 1 Thessalonians 5:18

Forgive Again?

"That's the third time you've borrowed my stuff without asking!" Melissa yelled. "Look what you did! You got nail polish all over my sweater!"

"I'm sorry!" her twin sister, Melanie, said.

"You're not sorry!" Melissa shouted.

"I am!" Melanie insisted, tears building up. "Don't you believe me?"

Melissa shook her head as Melanie left. *I'm tired of forgiving Melanie for the same thing over and over.*

Seconds later, their mother stood in the doorway. "Melissa, where's the umbrella you borrowed from me?"

Melissa looked around the room. "Oh no! I lost it! I'm sorry, Mom."

"That's the third umbrella you've lost!" her mother stated.

"I said I was sorry!" Melissa answered. "Don't you believe me?"

Her mother folded her arms. "Did you believe your sister when she said she was sorry? Yes, I heard you two arguing. So, would you like me to forgive you?"

"Yes," Melissa said sheepishly.

Her mother hugged Melissa. "When we don't forgive, honey, God won't forgive us."

Melissa pulled away. "I'm going to find Melanie so I can forgive her."

Your Turn

1. Read the parable found in Matthew 18:21-35.
2. Why does forgiving others affect whether you're forgiven?
3. What happens when you don't forgive?

Prayer

Lord, sometimes I don't want to forgive. I need your help to soften my heart. Amen.

Express Your Thanks

Give thanks in all circumstances.

– 1 Thessalonians 5:18

Forgiving

Amy passed the basketball to Nina. "When's the last time you saw your dad?"

Nina shot the ball. It bounced off the rim. "Two months ago. Since he moved, I don't see him much."

"You must hate him for leaving you," Amy said as she took a shot. Amy knew the feeling. Her father had left when she was in grade school.

"I forgave him," Nina said she ran for the ball.

Amy looked at Nina as if she'd spoken gibberish.

"I just don't hate, and you shouldn't either," said Nina.

"But you told me your dad has never said he was sorry," Amy questioned. Amy stopped bouncing the ball. "So, he walks back into your life, and you're supposed to forget what happened?"

"I don't like what he did. I didn't want to talk to him, at first. But God helped me forgive him. That doesn't mean I forget, it means I choose to put what he did behind me. If I didn't, the hurt would stay. Besides, this way I see him every once in a while."

Your Turn

1. Why did Amy forgive her father?
2. Has God helped you forgive someone? What happened?
3. Are you supposed to forgive people only if they ask?

_____

_____

_____

Prayer

Lord, I need your help to forgive. Thank you for your grace to do it. Amen.

Express Your Thanks

Attitude of Gratitude

If you want an attitude of gratitude, think about what makes you thankful. For each letter, write one thing you're thankful for.

T _____

H _____

A _____

N _____

K _____

Y _____

O _____

U _____

G _____

O _____

D _____

Prayer

Thank you, God, for your gifts of salvation and love. Amen.

Express Your Thanks

Something to Avoid

Proverbs 6 lists six things the Lord hates. One of them is in the puzzle. Use the "hours of the clock" code to figure it out.

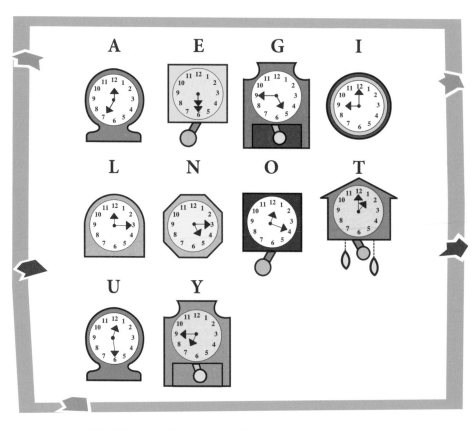

12:35   12:15   6:45   9:00   5:15   4:45

____   ____ ____ ____ ____

1:00 12:20   5:15   4:45   12:30 6:30

____ ____ ____ ____ ____ ____

Prayer

Lord, help me understand how to be honest and kind at the same time. Amen.

Growing in Responsibility

[Jesus said,] "We must do the works of him who sent me."
– John 9:4

A Big Responsibility

Anita stood and stretched. "Whew! Why don't we take a break?"

Her friend Tai also stood. "Yeah, let's take a short one. Then we've got to finish the rest of these weeds. Mrs. Winchell's counting on us."

Anita looked at her watch. "We've been working for hours. I've got a skating party to go to this afternoon."

Tai stuck a spade in the earth. "We could've asked Mrs. Winchell if we could pull her weeds next weekend. Why didn't you say something earlier?"

Anita shrugged. "I'm going home."

"But we're not done yet!" Tai waved a hand toward the rest of the garden.

"Mrs. Winchell will never know we didn't finish," Anita answered. "She barely notices anything in this garden."

Tai was insistent. "Well, we'd know we didn't finish. Besides, we're responsible for doing a good job. Colossians 3:23 says, "Whatever you do, work at it with all your heart, as working for the Lord."

Anita pulled off her gardening gloves. "I'm going. Are you coming?"

Tai shook her head. "I'm going to keep my promise."

Your Turn

1. What are your responsibilities?
2. How can you work at them "with all your heart"?

_____

_____

Prayer

Lord, thank you for the tasks you've given me. I will do my best with your help. Amen.

Growing in Responsibility

[Jesus said,] "We must do the works of him who sent me."
– John 9:4

Ready for Responsibility?

"Are you sure you're ready to babysit the Wheeler twins?" Mom asked.

Regina sighed. "Mom, I've watched kids before. Besides, I'm almost thirteen!"

"Yes," Mom replied, "but you've never watched two kids by yourself. Babysitting two children is a big responsibility."

"I can handle it," Regina said as she grabbed her jacket.

"Well, call home if you need help." Mom said.

"I'm sure I won't need any help," Regina muttered as she left.

By four that afternoon, Regina had called home four times and her mother had stopped by to help her. Regina looked glum when she got home. "I thought I could handle it myself. I was wrong."

"Well, both kids had the sniffles. That made them both a little cranky. I think the Wheelers weren't aware that the boys weren't feeling well." Mom put her arm around Regina's shoulders. "I'm proud of you. You did your best. Having a big responsibility doesn't mean you can't ask for help. If the kids hadn't been sick, I think you could have handled them fine by yourself."

Your Turn

1. What responsibilities have you been given?
2. How can you show your trustworthiness?

Prayer

Jesus, give me the desire and the skills to be trustworthy. Amen.

Growing in Responsibility

[Jesus said,] "We must do the works of him who sent me."
– John 9:4

The Dare

"C'mon! Are you chicken?" Brenna held the beer in front of Charlene. The four other girls in the basement had each taken a sip.

Charlene looked at the beer. She knew drinking was wrong, but Brenna had dared everyone to drink some. And Brenna was one of the coolest kids in the fifth grade. Charlene had been so excited about being invited to a sleepover at Brenna's house. Now she wasn't so sure.

Jesus, I don't have the courage to say no, Charlene silently prayed. *Please help me.*

Brenna gently wiggled the bottle. Charlene sighed before shaking her head. "I don't want any," she said quietly.

"She's scared!" one girl said and sneered.

Charlene nodded. "Yes, I'm scared. My grandfather was an alcoholic. I don't want to drink. It's wrong."

Two girls laughed, which made Charlene blush. But Brenna didn't laugh. Instead, she looked thoughtful. "This game is boring anyway." Brenna left to pour the rest of the beer into the bathroom sink.

Your Turn

1. If you were Charlene, what would you have done?
2. What do you need courage to do? Ask God to help you.

_____

_____

_____

Prayer

Dear God, I need courage to stand up for you and your principles. Help me do what's right. Amen.

Growing in Responsibility

[Jesus said,] "We must do the works of him who sent me."

– **John 9:4**

Gifts from God

Marcia pouted. "Why do I have to learn to swim?" she asked.

"What's wrong with learning to swim?" her older sister, Brianna, asked. "Everybody in the family's had to learn. Don't you want to go swimming with us on vacation?"

"Not really," said Marcia.

"You lie!" Brianna poked Marcia in the stomach and glanced at her watch. "It's almost three. Get ready. Mom said I can drive you to the pool."

Marcia's eyes grew wide. "I can't go. I think I'm getting a cold." She faked a cough.

Brianna laughed. "There's nothing to be afraid of."

"That's easy for you to say," Marcia replied. "You know how to swim."

"Listen, squirt. I was afraid when I first learned. But I prayed and asked Jesus for help to face what I was afraid of. He helped me," Brianna said.

"Well, maybe I should pray for help to face the way you drive," suggested Marcia with a smile. "That's scary enough!"

Your Turn

1. What fears do you need to face?
2. What will you do about being afraid?
3. How did God give you the courage to face other fears you've had?

Prayer

Jesus, with you in my corner, I don't have to be afraid. Thank you for giving me courage. Amen.

Growing in Responsibility

[Jesus said,] "We must do the works of him who sent me."
– John 9:4

Why Me?

Cassie liked Uncle Toby, but she was upset that he was staying with her family for two months. "Why me?" she complained. "Why do I have to give up my room? Why can't Uncle Toby sleep on the sofa-bed?"

"He can't climb stairs," her mother explained.

Cassie grumped as she moved many of her things into the family room. She hardly said a word to Uncle Toby when he arrived.

One evening while Cassie was doing her homework, Uncle Toby sat opposite her. "Thanks for giving up your room."

"I didn't want to," Cassie mumbled. "It didn't seem fair."

"I know how you feel," her uncle replied. "When I was in the hospital, I kept thinking, 'Why me? Why did I get into an accident? Why do I have five broken bones?' Finally, a friend asked, 'Why not you?' I thought about that. I realized life isn't fair. Careful people have accidents, good people get cancer, and hard workers lose jobs. The world isn't fair, but God always is. I trust him."

Cassie considered that. She smiled and said, "Sorry I was such a grump."

Your Turn

1. How do you react to unfairness?
2. What's the difference between "fairness" and "justice"?
   (Look up both words in a dictionary.)

_____

_____

Prayer

God, I'm happy you're always fair. Help me be fair too. Amen.

Growing in Responsibility

Ripe or Not

Some people trust God and are "ripe" for responsibility. Others are more cautious and aren't quite ripe so they refuse to accept full responsibility. Look up these people in the Bible. Circle the ripe apples that have names of a people ready for responsibility. Put a square around those who weren't ready to trust God wholeheartedly.

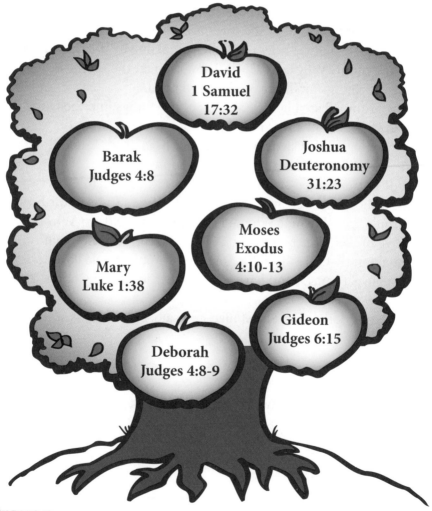

David
1 Samuel
17:32

Barak
Judges 4:8

Joshua
Deuteronomy
31:23

Mary
Luke 1:38

Moses
Exodus
4:10-13

Gideon
Judges 6:15

Deborah
Judges 4:8-9

Prayer

Father God, please work in my heart so that I am ready for responsibility. Amen.

Growing in Responsibility

Courage Under Fire

God gave his people courage to face trouble and challenges. Can you find these courageous people in the word search?

Shadrach	Joseph
Abednego	Mary
Daniel	Meshach
David	Nehemiah
Deborah	Paul
Esther	Peter
James	Silas
John	

L	J	H	C	A	R	D	A	H	S
I	U	A	L	M	E	C	P	S	N
F	D	H	M	B	K	E	L	A	E
E	I	G	O	E	S	U	E	L	H
S	V	R	U	O	S	V	I	I	E
T	A	C	J	J	O	H	N	S	M
H	D	H	O	L	Y	R	A	M	I
E	B	I	D	N	U	O	D	C	A
R	O	G	E	N	D	E	B	A	H
Z	R	E	T	E	P	A	U	L	S

Prayer

Dear God, I want to be like the courageous people in the Bible and do what is right. I know you will help me. Amen.

What God Wants from You

Whatever you do, work at it with all your heart,
as working for the Lord, not for human masters.

– Colossians 3:23

The Missing Pieces

When Dad opened the kitchen garbage can, fruit flies darted. The smell wasn't pleasant either. He glanced at the counter stacked with dirty dishes. He summoned the twins in his "you better come running" voice.

"Hi, Dad. What's up?" asked Jordan and Jenny together.

"Apparently not your sense of responsibility," said Dad. "The garbage is smelly and full of bugs. The counter is overflowing with dirty dishes."

"I was going to do dishes," explained Jenny, "but Chris called."

"I hate taking out the garbage," said Jordan. "I decided to wait until the can was really full. Save some trips that way."

Their dad told them to wait. He returned with an easy jigsaw puzzle. He asked the twins to help him put it together. When they were finished, they realized two pieces were missing!

"This puzzle is like our family," Dad explained. "Unless we all do our jobs, there are gaps. Each must do a part." Dad gave the twins the missing pieces and they completed the puzzle.

Your Turn

1. How did the twins' neglect affect their family?
2. What responsibilities do you have in your family?
3. How is your family affected when you don't do your jobs?

_____

_____

_____

Prayer

Heavenly Father, thank you for putting me in a family. Help me do my part so my family is strong and runs smoothly. Amen.

What God Wants from You

*Whatever you do, work at it with all your heart,
as working for the Lord, not for human masters.*

– Colossians 3:23

Family Harmony

With five kids, the Bradford family home wasn't quiet. Music, talking, laughing, and ringing phones blended together into a family-life melody. But sometimes this melody was out of tune.

Jim teased Cindy, so Cindy yelled, "Mom, tell Jim to leave me alone!"

Toddler Jeremy got into the older kids' rooms. He was chased out, doors were slammed, and Jeremy cried.

Greg and Linda argued over who had to do every job.

Cindy thought she should have the same privileges as her older brother.

The older kids thought Jeremy was spoiled.

One night their dad said, "I want to tell you a story about the early church. The older people thought they were better than the younger people. They fought about it constantly. Men and women argued about whose job it was to spread the Good News, so nobody did it. Everyone thought the little kids were pests, so they were told to buzz off. They never learned about Jesus."

Mr. Bradford paused. Then he said, "Aren't you glad this isn't a true story? People worked together and Christianity spread."

Your Turn

1. What was causing disharmony in the Bradford family?
2. How does your family resolve arguments?

Prayer

God of peace, help me live in harmony with you and my family. Amen.

What God Wants from You

Whatever you do, work at it with all your heart
as working for the Lord, not for human masters.

– Colossians 3:23

The Poster Contest

"Wow! Twenty dollars!" Laurie Marsh said. As she turned her head, she caught sight of her twin brother, Laurence.

"Didn't you promise to help Jenny make a poster for this?" he asked.

"That was before I knew that there was a cash prize." Laurie had a dreamy look on her face. "I could use that twenty dollars."

"You're pretty good at art," Laurence agreed. "Much better than Jenny, huh?"

Laurie nodded. She wondered what her brother was trying to say.

"With friends like you, who needs enemies?" asked Laurence as he left.

Humph, Laurie thought. *He's just mad because he can't draw well enough to win the contest.* Then she remembered Jenny couldn't draw either . That's why Jenny had asked for her help. As she went to the refrigerator to grab a bottle of juice, Laurie saw a magnet her mother's best friend had given her. It said, "A friend loves at all times."

I did promise Jenny, Laurie acknowledged. She considered all the times Jenny had helped her. She grabbed her phone to see if Jenny wanted to start that afternoon.

Your Turn

1. Why is keeping a promise to a friend important?
2. Look up and write out Proverbs 17:17. What does it mean to you?

_____

_____

Prayer

Help me, Jesus, to be a loyal, faithful friend. Amen.

What God Wants from You

Whatever you do, work at it with all your heart,
as working for the Lord, not for human masters.

– **Colossians 3:23**

Portrait of a Friendship

Maia and Judith had been best friends since preschool. They called themselves "the VIPs" (**V**ery **I**mportant **P**eople). Now that they were in fifth grade, they didn't think anything could ever separate them.

Then Jillian arrived. She moved to their town from a different state. As soon as she started going to their school, Jillian wanted to be friends with Maia. Jillian didn't seem to like Judith. That feeling was mutual.

Maia liked Jillian, and she couldn't understand why Judith didn't like Jillian.

Jillian spread bad rumors about Judith.

Maia even believed them at first. But then she remembered what she'd learned in Sunday school about Jesus. Jesus was *always* a faithful friend to his disciples. He never dropped or betrayed a friend. She remembered how much she cared for Judith.

Maia went to Judith and asked forgiveness. And that's what Judith did. After all, what are friends for?

Your Turn

1. Have you been in a situation like Maia and Judith's? What happened?
2. How do you handle conflicts in your friendships?

_____

_____

_____

_____

Prayer

Lord Jesus, teach me to be loyal and forgiving in my friendships. Amen.

What God Wants from You

Whatever you do, work at it with all your heart,
as working for the Lord, not for human masters.

– Colossians 3:23

God's Family

"Now, let's talk about the body of Christ," Mrs. Christianson said. "The head of the body is Christ. We're all part of the body. Some of us might be arteries because of the gifts God gave us. Some of us might be big toes."

Everyone in the Sunday-school class laughed, especially Sammi. She could never think of herself as a big toe! That wasn't very flattering. She wanted to be something important, such as an arm or a leg.

Mrs. Christianson continued. "No matter who and what we are, we're important to Jesus. Being part of his body is being in a loving family. He helps us love one another and help one another. Sammi, you like to draw. You make posters for church events, like the skit next month. Katie, you and Tyler helped write the skit. Sidney, you usually volunteer to help clean up after events. Nat and Ron, you are the main actors. You have an important part to play in your family, your home, your church, and your school. You have an important role in God's family."

Your Turn

1. What did you do to join your family?
2. Are you part of God's family?
3. If you want to be, pray today's prayer and then tell your parents or another Christian adult.

Prayer

Dear Jesus, I believe you love me, you died for me, and you rose from the dead so I can live with you forever. Please forgive my sins and come into my life. Be my Lord and Savior. Thank you! Amen.

What God Wants from You

A Promise for a Friend

Because he loved his best friend, Jonathan, David wanted to do something kind for someone in his family. Solve the crossword to find out who David helped. (For additional help, read 2 Samuel 9.)

Across

1. David wanted to help Jonathan's son _____.

4. David returned all of the _____ that belonged to his family.

5. The man of 1 across was the grandson of _____.

6. The man of 1 across was _____ in both feet.

Down

2. Saul's servant _____ told him about the man of 1 across.

3. The man of 1 across was allowed to live in _____ as if he were a king's son.

Prayer

Lord, help me make good friends. I want friends who know you and love you. Amen.

What God Wants from You

The Job Jar

What family chore do you dislike the most? Probably everyone in the family, including Mom and Dad, has jobs they really hate doing. Try making the Job Jar and trading responsibilities for a week.

What You Need

- Large jar with lid
- Index card
- Pencils
- Clear tape
- Slips of paper
- Colored markers
- Stickers

What to Do

1. Clean a large jar and lid.

2. Write "Job Jar" on the index card in big letters. You can use the markers to decorate the label. Tape the label to the jar. The rest of the jar and the lid may be decorated with stickers.

3. Give each family member two or three slips of paper and ask them to write a detested job on each slip. Fold the papers in half and put them in the Job Jar.

4. Once a week, have each family member pick a job from the jar and do it. If you get your own job, go ahead and do it. You'll probably get a different job next week. You may find you don't mind doing a job someone else detests.

Prayer

Lord, thank you for my family. Teach me new ways to help them. Amen.

Everyone Is Special

For you are all one in Christ Jesus.

– Galatians 3:28

Part of the Family

Beverly sank under the covers, feeling miserable. In a way, she was relieved to have the flu. Being sick gave her an excuse not to go to Bible Club. That night a lot of the kids were performing a skit. Beverly had wanted to participate, but she couldn't think of anything she could do. *Why do I have to be the only person who can't do anything?* she wondered. *I guess no one will miss me.*

She heard the doorbell ring, followed by several loud whispers. Seconds later, her mother entered her room carrying a bouquet of balloons. "Twenty kids from your Bible Club were outside," said Mom. "They wanted you to have this."

Beverly read the card: "Hurry up and get well!" It was signed by everyone in the club. "I can't believe they did this!"

"They wanted you to know you're missed," Mom said.

"I don't see why. I never do anything special." Beverly pouted.

"That's certainly not true!" her mom exclaimed.

Your Turn

1. How did Beverly's friends help her feel better?
2. How do you help your family and friends?

_____

_____

_____

Prayer

God, show me what I can do as a member of your family. Amen.

Everyone Is Special

For you are all one in Christ Jesus.

– Galatians 3:28

Miss Molly

Emily's Sunday-school class was on their way to sing and visit at a nursing home. *This is a waste of time. What can I talk about with those people?* Emily thought.

While singing, Emily watched the people. Some sat there motionless, some clapped, and some tapped their feet. One tiny lady in a wheelchair smiled.

After the class had finished singing, Mr. Sanford directed Emily to the small woman in the wheelchair. "Emily, meet Miss Molly," he said. "Miss Molly, Emily."

Miss Molly smiled and held out a gnarled hand. Speaking slowly in a whispery voice, she said, "I'm glad to meet you, dear. You have a beautiful voice. I played piano and sang professionally. Now, tell me about you."

Soon Emily was having a great time visiting with Miss Molly. Miss Molly didn't feel sorry for herself, and she laughed a lot.

When it was time to leave, Emily asked Miss Molly, "May I come back Saturday?"

"I'd be honored!" Miss Molly smiled. "We can play checkers. Better practice—I'm a mean player."

Emily laughed as she waved good-bye.

Your Turn

1. How do you feel about elderly people?
2. How do you feel about people who are sick, injured, or chronically ill?
3. Do you ever feel unlovable?

Prayer

God, thank you for loving everyone. Help me do the same. Amen.

Everyone Is Special

For you are all one in Christ Jesus.
– Galatians 3:28

Lonely Leeza

It was almost time for class to start. The fifth graders were bustling around sharpening pencils, whispering to friends, and digging into their desks. Everyone paid attention when Miss Garrett came in. "Boys and girls, this is your new classmate, Leeza."

She looks scared, thought Donna. Leeza's clothes looked two sizes too big and were old-fashioned. Her hair was pulled back into a braid, and she wore big, dark-rimmed glasses. Some of the girls snickered as Leeza walked to her desk.

The morning didn't get any better for Leeza. She was so nervous she could barely read aloud. She tripped over Jim's foot when she walked past his desk. Donna noticed the new girl looked ready to cry.

At recess, Donna hung out with her friends but noticed Leeza standing by herself. "Leeza looks lonely," Donna remarked.

"Who cares? She's so weird," Kate said.

At lunch, Donna took a deep breath and walked to Leeza. "Hi, my name is Donna. Would you like to eat lunch with me?"

"Oh, yes!" said Leeza with a shy smile.

And that made Donna smile too.

Your Turn

1. Do you know someone new or shy? How can you help her?
2. Who has helped you when you felt awkward or lonely?

Prayer

God, help me care for people even when it feels awkward. Amen.

Everyone Is Special

For you are all one in Christ Jesus.

– Galatians 3:28

What Are My Rights?

"Look at this!" Carmen pointed to a magazine article. Her two friends, Teresa and Lupe, glanced at it. The article mentioned a group of fifth- and sixth-graders in a neighborhood who had organized a protest to get more allowance.

"Wow. They all said their parents didn't take them seriously until they got organized," said Carmen.

"Maybe we should organize," Teresa said.

"To do what?" Lupe asked.

Carmen shrugged. "To get more allowance maybe?"

Teresa folded her arms. "Too bad we can't vote or something. Kids like us need more rights."

"For real! My mom won't let me stay up late," said Carmen.

"I can't wait until I'm sixteen and can drive!" Teresa said.

"I like things the way they are," Lupe said.

Teresa looked surprised. "Why? Kids our age don't get any respect."

"I wasn't thinking about that," said Lupe. "I'm content. God takes care of me. I like my house, my neighborhood, and my school. My church is cool. My family loves me. I don't have any complaints."

Your Turn

1. Describe your environment. What do you like about it?
2. Do you ever feel unhappy with your world? What can you do?

Prayer

Lord, sometimes I feel overlooked. I'm glad you are my friend. Amen.

Everyone Is Special

For you are all one in Christ Jesus.
– Galatians 3:28

The Move

Lydia stormed to her room, determined never to speak to anyone again. How unfair life was! Why did her father have to get a job in a different state? Why did they have to move again? She'd told her friends how happy she was here. She didn't want things to change.

She glanced at the clock. Time to read her daily devotional. She grabbed it from the top of her Bible and yanked it open. Lydia was still angry at her father and a little mad at God. After all, God could have done something to prevent this whole situation.

She read the first sentence. "Wherever you are, God is." The thought was comforting and calming. "Wherever you are, God is. At least I'll know somebody in the place we're moving to," she said to herself. She chuckled. *Leave it to you, God, to get my attention and help me change my attitude.* Lydia felt a little better. *Maybe the new town will be nice, like Dad said. Thanks, God. You are right beside me.*

Your Turn

1. What do you wish would never change about your place in the world?
2. How do you know God cares about what happens to you?

_____

_____

_____

_____

Prayer

Lord, as long as you're a part of my world, I won't worry about changes. Amen.

Everyone Is Special

Everyone Is Special

Jesus often associated with people that no one else wanted to be around. He truly loved the unlovely—and he still does. To find out who some of these people were, solve the puzzle.

Cross out every G, H, J, Q, U, V, W, Y, Z. Write the leftover words on the lines.

G	Z	S	I	U	V	N	Y	Y	N	E	J	R	Q	S
T	Z	W	A	J	U	X	V	Z	M	H	E	Y	G	N
W	D	Z	V	E	H	G	A	F	L	U	A	M	Z	E
G	H	L	J	Q	U	E	V	P	E	Y	Z	R	S	H
Z	U	B	H	W	L	Z	Z	J	I	Q	J	N	D	V
Q	P	O	Y	Z	O	U	R	S	W	I	J	C	Z	K
G	G	I	H	N	J	Q	S	U	A	V	N	E	W	Z

_____   _____

_____   _____

_____   _____

_____   _____

Prayer

Lord, it's easy to love people who are like me, but it's not as easy to love people who are different or difficult. Help me love all people. Amen.

Everyone Is Special

The Least of These

Unscramble the Bible verse by carefully following these directions. Each letter is only changed once.

1. Change K to a letter that sounds like a part of your face.
2. Change O to H; V to K; Z to A; Q to P; D to M.
3. Change P to a letter that sounds like a personal pronoun.
4. Change W to a letter that sounds like the opposite of out.
5. Change J to R; Y to D; R to G; T to F; A to V.
6. Change M to a letter that sounds like a drink from China.
7. Change F to a well-rounded letter.
8. Change H to a letter that sounds like the Spanish word for yes.
9. Change B to the twelfth letter of the alphabet.
10. Change X to the sound a snake makes.
11. Change C to a letter that asks a question.
12. If you have followed the directions carefully, seven L's should remain. Change them to E.

I was ___ ___ ___ ___ ___ ___, and you ___ ___ ___ me.
   O   P   W   R   J   C   T   L   Y

I was ___ ___ ___ ___ ___ ___ ___, and you gave me a ___ ___ ___ ___ ___.
   M O K J X M C   Y J K W V

I was a ___ ___ ___ ___ ___ ___ ___ ___, and you
   X M J Z W R L J

___ ___ ___ ___ ___ ___ ___ me into your ___ ___ ___ ___.
K W A K M L Y   O F D L

I was ___ ___ ___ ___ ___, and you gave me
   W Z V L Y

___ ___ ___ ___ ___ ___ ___ ___. I was ___ ___ ___ ___, and
H B F M O K W R   X K H V

you ___ ___ ___ ___ ___ for me. I was in ___ ___ ___ ___ ___ ___,
   H Z J L Y   Q J K X F W

and you ___ ___ ___ ___ ___ ___ ___ me. (Matthew 25:35-36 NLT)
    A K X K M L Y

God Directs Your Path

Your word is a lamp for my feet, a light on my path.
– Psalm 119:105

Light for a Dark Path

Cindy and her friend Meg giggled as they followed the path. Their flashlights lit the path, their friends, and hike leaders, Karen and Mike.

After a few minutes, Karen stopped. "Is everybody enjoying our night hike?"

After the cheering died down, Karen said, "Remember talking around the campfire about reading God's Word? None of you really knew why it was important."

"Okay, lights out everybody!" Mike said.

As the flashlights clicked off, the area grew pitch dark. Cindy's elbow made contact with Meg, who let out a yip.

Once the excitement died down, Mike asked, "If we continue our hike this way, how well would we find our way?"

"No way!" someone said.

"I can see okay," someone else said.

"Tim, you'd get lost in a phone booth!" yelled another.

Karen cut in. "We could fall into a hole or trip if we don't have light. Finding our way in life can be just as hard as walking along a dark path. God's Word is like a flashlight that reveals the path. It helps us avoid trouble and stay safe."

Your Turn

1. In what ways has reading God's Word helped you?
2. How can you make reading God's Word part of your day?

Prayer

Lord, thank you for the Bible. I'm glad you love me and want to help me. Amen.

God Directs Your Path

Your word is a lamp for my feet, a light on my path.
– Psalm 119:105

Oh, How I Love Jesus?

Cam and her friends Joan and Brandon walked through the mall toward the food court. Several kids from their school were already there. Cam wondered how Joan and Brandon would act. At church, the three of them had talked about how much they loved God. But around school friends, Joan and Brandon sometimes used language that didn't honor God.

A group of kids were in the middle of a discussion when they walked up. "And Sydney stole that?" one girl said.

Sydney proudly showed the virtual pet he must have stolen.

Cam, Joan, and Brandon exchanged glances.

"Isn't this cool, Cam?" Sydney asked.

Cam shook her head. "No. Stealing is wrong."

"I knew you'd say that," Sydney said. He looked at Brandon and Joan. "You guys want to hang out at the arcade?"

The other kids got up.

"See you later, Cam," Joan said, looking apologetic just before they all left.

"Yeah, see you," Cam said. She walked toward the meeting place with her mother.

Your Turn

1. Why were Joan and Brandon reluctant to support Cam's position?
2. How do your friends know you believe in Jesus and follow him?

Prayer

Lord, I don't want to follow you sometimes. I want to follow you all the time. Amen.

God Directs Your Path

Your word is a lamp for my feet, a light on my path.
– Psalm 119:105

God's Messages

"Why should we read God's Word?" Mr. Abercrombie asked.

Sherri stared at her Sunday-school teacher as if he'd suddenly grown a third eye. She'd just asked herself the same question that very morning. During her quiet time with God, Sherri had flipped to a random passage in the Bible. It was about an Old Testament prophet she'd never heard of. The passage was full of warnings to Israel. *Boring,* she'd thought.

"Because we're supposed to?" one kid across the table from Sherri announced.

"Why are we supposed to?" Mr. Abercrombie asked.

Nobody came up with an answer.

"How do you communicate with a friend who's far away?" Mr. Abercrombie asked.

"Through e-mail," someone said. Another kid said, "Telephone."

Mr. Abercrombie smiled. "As Christians, we're God's children. He talks to us through our prayers, his Word, and his Holy Spirit, who lives in each of us."

Sherri made a pact with herself that she would re-read that morning's Scripture when she got home. She didn't want to miss out on anything God had to say.

Your Turn

1. How do you choose what's right and what's wrong?
2. What will you do this week to find out more from God's Word?

Prayer

Lord, thank you for your Word. Help me understand it so I can follow you. Amen.

God Directs Your Path

Your word is a lamp for my feet, a light on my path.
– Psalm 119:105

You *Can* Do Something!

Laura looked worried as she scanned the news headlines. Her social studies assignment was to read the front section of the newspaper every day for a week and discuss it in class. "I don't like doing this," Laura said to her dad.

"You're a good reader," he said. "You shouldn't have any trouble. If you need help understanding something, let me know."

"That's not the problem. The stories make me angry, or scared, or sad. I hate reading about murder, wars, famines, earthquakes, and sickness. Sometimes I feel like screaming and ripping up the paper, but I know that wouldn't do any good."

"Well, you're right," her father answered. "Tearing up the paper or yelling won't improve anything. As long as there's sin in the world, terrible things will keep happening. But you can do something."

"What's that?" Laura asked.

"You can pray for people in trouble. God promises to hear your prayers and help those in need. Let's pray for some of these 'front page' people right now."

Your Turn

1. How do you feel when you hear or read distressing news?
2. How can you help people you don't know?
3. Do you pray for leaders in your city, state, and federal governments?

Prayer

Merciful Father, please help people who may feel helpless. Let them know you care. Amen.

God Directs Your Path

Your word is a lamp for my feet, a light on my path.
– Psalm 119:105

Is God Listening?

Marianne stripped off her backpack and slumped in a kitchen chair. "Today was the pits! I tried out for cheerleading and wasn't picked. And after all that practice."

Her mom stopped working. "I'm sorry."

Marianne continued. "I prayed for weeks I would make the squad. Didn't God listen?"

"God always hears our prayers," Mom said.

"Why didn't he give me what I asked for?"

Just then baby Casey crawled into the kitchen. He pulled himself up with the table leg. He gibbered and pointed to the knife Mom held.

"Should I give Casey the knife?" Mom asked Marianne.

Marianne was startled. "Of course not! He would hurt himself."

"But he really wants it," Mom said as Casey threw a tantrum.

"Mom, you know he can't have a knife!"

Mom said, "Of course I do. I know what's good for Casey. I hear him screaming, but I'm not giving him what he wants. That's the way God is. He hears us, but he doesn't always give us everything we want because he knows what's best."

Marianne considered that. "Okay, I feel a little better."

Your Turn

1. Does God always hear your prayers? How do you know?
2. Does God answer your prayers the way you want?

Prayer

God, thanks for always listening and for knowing what's best for me. Amen.

God Directs Your Path

Prayer Power

Hooray for prayer! You can pray anytime, anywhere, and for anything. Find out when, where, or for what these Bible-time people prayed.

Exodus 15:22-25
Where was Moses? _____ What did he pray for?_____

Joshua 10:12-14
What did Joshua pray for?_____

1 Samuel 1:9-11
What did Hannah pray for?_____ Where was she? _____

Jonah 2:1
Where was Jonah when he prayed?_____

Daniel 6:10
Where did Daniel pray?_____ When? _____

Matthew 14:23
Where did Jesus go to pray?_____

Luke 5:12
Who prayed?_____ What did he pray for?_____

Acts 16:22-25
Who prayed?_____ Where were they? _____

When do you pray? _____

Where do you pray? _____

What do you pray for? _____

Prayer

Dear Lord, remember to pray, anytime, anywhere, and for anything. Amen.

God Directs Your Path

Command Code

Morse code was invented in the 1840s to transmit messages via telegraph. It was cutting edge technology until the telephone, fax machines, computers, and the Internet revolutionized communication. Morse code is a set of dots and dashes for each letter in the alphabet. Use Morse Code to figure out what God says about his commands.

A	B	C	D	E	F	G
•—	—•••	—•—•	—••	•	••—•	——•

H	I	J	K	L	M	N
••••	••	•———	—•—	•—••	——	—•

O	P	Q	R	S	T	U
———	•——•	——•—	•—•	•••	—	••—

V	W	X	Y	Z
•••—	•——	—••—	—•——	——••

•—— •••• ——— • •••— • •—•   •••• •— •••

____ ____ ____ ____ ____ ____ ____   ____ ____ ____

—— —•—— —•—• ——— —— —— •— —• —•• •••

____ ____ ____ ____ ____ ____ ____ ____ ____ ____

•— —• —•• —•— • • •——• •••

____ ____ ____ ____ ____ ____ ____ ____ ____

— •••• • —— •• •••

____ ____ ____ ____ ____ ____

— •••• • ——— —• • •—— •••• ———

____ ____ ____ ____ ____ ____ ____ ____ ____

•—•• ——— •••— • •••   —— •

____ ____ ____ ____ ____   ____ ____ . **John 14:21**

Praise and Worship God

Great is the Lord and most worthy of praise.
– Psalm 145:3

Alleluia!

Karina liked Sundays. The family went to church and often stopped at a restaurant for lunch. Sunday afternoons were good for reading and relaxing. This Sunday was special because Aunt Sue was visiting.

After lunch, Karina listened to her mom and Aunt Sue. Every once she'd join the conversation.

Bam! The door banged open and Lori marched in. "Alleluia, alleluia, alleluia, alleluia!" she sang in her loudest, four-year-old voice. Around and around the room she marched, each "alleluia" getting louder. Conversation stopped, and Karina covered her ears.

"Enough already!" Karina said. "My ears hurt."

Lori stopped, put her hands on her hips, and frowned. "We learned in Sunday school that God is happy when we sing to him. I'm singing loud so God will hear me."

"Honey, it's a nice song," said Aunt Sue. " Alleluia is sort of like saying hooray to God." She leaned forward and whispered, "And God has really good ears. He can even hear soft alleluias."

Lori marched out of the room whispering, "Alleluia, alleluia."

Your Turn

1. How do you praise God? For what do you praise God?
2. Why does God deserve your praise?

_____

_____

_____

Prayer

Alleluia, Lord! Alleluia, alleluia, alleluia. You are great! Amen.

Praise and Worship God

Great is the Lord and most worthy of praise.
– Psalm 145:3

Worship 24/7?

"I don't get it," Marsha muttered. "How can I answer that question? I think they made a mistake."

Her mom turned off the blender. "Were you talking to me?"

"Not really," Marsha answered. "Guess I was talking to myself. But now that you asked, maybe you can help me."

"I can try," Mom said as she came over to Marsha. "What's the problem?"

"I'm doing a page in this workbook for Bible Club," Marsha explained. "We've been talking about worship. This question asks, 'How do you worship God every day?' We only have church services two days a week, so how can I worship him every day?"

"You don't have to be in church to worship God," her mother explained. "You worship him every time you pray, and you worship him when you sing praise songs. God is even worshiped when you obey him and do what pleases him. Church services lets everyone worship God together, but each of us worships him alone too."

"So worship is not a 'Sundays only' activity," Marsha said. "It's a 'seven days a week' thing."

Your Turn

1. How do you worship God in church?
2. How do you worship God when you're not in church?

_____

_____

Prayer

Dear God, help me worship you everywhere I go. Amen.

Praise and Worship God

Great is the Lord and most worthy of praise.
– Psalm 145:3

A Sorry Sight

"Are you sure your mom won't get mad?" Willow asked. Her friend Marti nodded. "All I have to do is say I'm sorry."

"Yeah," said Willow, "but this is the third time you've been late coming home. I know my mom would be mad."

Marti shrugged. Just as they reached Marti's house, the family's new puppy crept out of the bushes in front of the house. The puppy walked slowly with his head down. "Uh-oh," Marti said. "Prince must've done something bad."

"How can you tell?" Willow asked.

"Because of the way he looks. This is his 'sorry' act." Sure enough, Marti soon discovered that Prince had chewed up one of her new ballet shoes.

"Prince, I'm sick of you always acting like you're sorry!" Marti exploded. "You're not sorry! You keep doing the same thing over and over. I wish you'd stop chewing things. Then I'd know you're really sorry."

Willow laughed. "Hey, your dog acts just like you do."

Her remark hit home. "Yes, I guess so." Marti wasn't laughing.

Both Willow and Prince had given her a lot to think about.

Your Turn

1. Have you acted like Marti? What happened?
2. How can you keep from repeating bad choices?

Prayer

Dear Jesus, I want to mean it when I say I'm sorry. Help me turn away from wrongdoing. Amen.

Praise and Worship God

Great is the Lord and most worthy of praise.
– Psalm 145:3

The End Is Near

Rita nudged her friend Jennifer and pointed to the man walking toward them. He was wearing a T-shirt with a message that read: "Repent. The end is near."

"That's from that new space movie," Rita said.

The girls had just passed a movie theater where a large movie poster had proclaimed the space movie's theme: "The end is near!"

Jennifer nodded. "That's also in the Bible. And it's no joke. The world we know will come to an end someday. No one knows when except God. The Bible says we've all sinned against God, and we need to turn away from our sins. That's why Jesus came—so we can get his forgiveness and live with him forever."

Rita rolled her eyes. "You sound like those weird guys in the movie."

Jennifer shrugged. "It's still true."

Your Turn

1. Why should you turn from sin?
2. Why does God offer salvation to everyone? How do they hear about it?

_____

_____

_____

_____

Prayer

Lord, I accept the salvation you offer. I believe you died for me. Thank you for forgiving me. Amen.

Praise and Worship God

Great is the Lord and most worthy of praise.
– Psalm 145:3

Hanging with the Hendersons

Lucie liked hanging out at her best friend Carrie's house. The Hendersons were a lot of fun. They had one weird rule. If you spent Saturday night at their house, you had to go to church with them Sunday morning. Lucie didn't mind going with them.

That Saturday night, Lucie spent the night at Carrie's house. "Mrs. Walters will be glad to see you," Carrie said. Mrs. Walters was her Sunday-school teacher.

"I've got a question I've wanted to ask," Lucie said. "What does 'abiding in Christ' mean?"

Carrie was surprised. "What made you think of that?"

Lucie looked embarrassed. "I've been thinking about it ever since I first heard it at your church. Your family acts differently than mine. You are all so friendly, and you seem to believe what they talk about at your church."

"I can tell you what it means," Carrie said. "It means having a personal relationship with Jesus. It means loving him, following him, and loving people in his name."

"Oh!" Lucie said. "That must be why I enjoy hanging out with you."

Your Turn

1. What do you know about Jesus?
2. How often do you talk with him?

_____

_____

Prayer

Dear God, I want to stick with Christ. Show me how. Give me the courage to follow him with all my heart. Amen.

Praise and Worship God

Psalm 100

Psalm 100 is a song of giving thanks, worshipping, and praising God. See if you can fit the highlighted words into the puzzle.

Shout for joy to the LORD, all the earth.
Worship the LORD with gladness;
Come before him with joyful songs.
Know that the LORD is God.
It is he who made us, and we are his;
we are his people, the sheep of his pasture.
Enter his gates with thanksgiving and his courts with praise;
give thanks to him and praise his name.
For the LORD is good and his love endures forever;
his faithfulness continues through all generations.

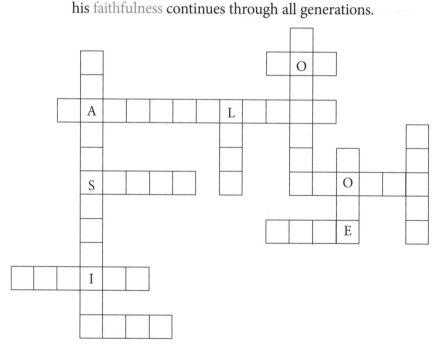

Prayer

Lord, you are my Shepherd. Thank you for guiding me always. Amen.

Praise and Worship God

Praise Poster

One way to praise God is through your creative talents. This praise poster will remind you to thank God for all he does. It will also be a witness to your friends that you love God.

What You Need

- 18" x 24" poster board
- colored construction paper
- broad-tipped markers in bright colors
- scissors
- glue

What to Do

1. Plan what you want to say on your praise poster. Some ideas: "Praise the Lord," "God Is Great," "My God Is Awesome."

2. Cut the letters for the words out of colored construction paper. Make the letters big and use bright colors.

3. Glue the words to the center of the poster board.

4. Use markers to decorate the rest of the poster. Make the poster look bright and cheerful.

5. Hang the poster on your bedroom wall or someplace where you will see it every day.

Prayer

Lord, I love you! I will praise you and worship you all the days of my life. Amen.

Abiding in Christ

If you remain in me and I in you, you will bear much fruit;
apart from me you can do nothing.

– John 15:5

As He Is

Heather frowned as she entered the family room. "Why didn't God answer my prayer? I prayed for Grandma to get better, Dad, but she died."

"God has his reasons, honey," Dad said as he placed a hand over Heather's. "Besides, he did answer your prayer. He told you 'no.' "

Heather folded her arms. "Well, I'm not asking him for anything soon."

"Now, didn't you tell me last week that you wanted to be closer to Jesus?"

Heather looked down. "Well, yes, but not if he's gonna act like this."

"So that means you're not going to talk to God?" asked Dad.

Heather was defiant. "I don't know if I even want to."

"Suppose I got mad at you because you didn't do what I wanted?"

"You did get mad at me, Dad," Heather replied. "Last week, in fact."

"I didn't break off contact with you," said Dad. "I love you too much to do that, no matter what you do. God loves you even more than I do. He wants you to stick with him whether times are good or bad."

Your Turn

1. Do you get angry and quit talking to family and friends?
2. Why do you think God wants you to accept his control?

Prayer

Help me, Lord, to accept—even welcome—your control in my life, especially when life doesn't go the way I planned. Amen.

Abiding in Christ

If you remain in me and I in you, you will bear much fruit;
apart from me you can do nothing.

– John 15:5

All Together Now

Astrid folded her arms, trying to ignore what her father was saying.

"Won't you at least try to get along with Denise?" he asked. "We're all going to live together."

Denise was the daughter of Astrid's soon-to-be stepmother. After the wedding next week, Denise would be moving into Astrid's room. Astrid thought Denise was a whiny busybody, always prying into her business and asking questions. Astrid didn't want to be sisters, much less friends. After all, she was a sixth-grader, and Denise was a lowly fourth-grader,

"Don't you agree life would be easier if we all got along?" Dad said.

Astrid shrugged. She was used to having her father all to herself since her mother's death. Now two strangers were coming to live in her house.

Her father finally left her alone, but his sad look made Astrid feel guilty. She felt even worse when she saw her Sunday school take-home paper. It was titled "Family Peace." Astrid sniffed. She didn't want to be nice, but she knew God wanted her to be.

Your Turn

1. What do you think Astrid could do to get along with her stepsister?
2. What do you do to get along with your family members?

_____

_____

_____

_____

Prayer

Lord, help me live in harmony with others. Amen.

Abiding in Christ

If you remain in me and I in you, you will bear much fruit;
apart from me you can do nothing.

– John 15:5

Family Problems

The overhead projector flashed a big headline across the wall: "Boy sues parents over punishment." Some of the kids in the Sunday-school class laughed while they read the article. Wanda was particularly interested. Her mother had grounded her for a week over one teensy little lie.

"Can kids really sue their parents?" Wanda asked.

"In special cases, yes," Mr. Wilmington replied.

"What about a sister?" one girl said. "Mine's driving me crazy."

Once the laughter died down, Mr. Wilmington asked, "What do you think the problem is?" He pointed to the article on the wall.

"Maybe his mom shouldn't have punished him so hard," Wanda suggested.

"This kid sounds like a real brat," one boy said. "He was just mad because his mother took away his phone and games."

"What would it take for the parents and son to live together in harmony?" asked Mr. Wilmington. "Living in harmony means working to get along, even when we're irritated. It means loving the other people more than wanting your own way."

"Maybe they need God," a girl suggested.

Your Turn

1. What irritates you about your family members?
2. How can you live in harmony with your family?

Prayer

Lord, I want to get along with my family. Help me live your love. Amen.

Abiding in Christ

If you remain in me and I in you, you will bear much fruit;
apart from me you can do nothing.

– John 15:5

Sharing Jesus

Yolanda and her friend Margaret looked at the church pamphlets scattered on the sidewalk.

"What a waste," Yolanda said.

"I don't really like tracts," Margaret said. "Somebody gave me one once—just shoved it in my hand without talking to me or asking if I wanted one."

"Then I guess you don't want to go door-to-door inviting people to our church," said Yolanda. "The youth group is doing that on Saturday."

"You're right!" Margaret exclaimed.

Yolanda was surprised. "Don't you want to tell people about Jesus?"

"Yes, but I'd rather do it the way you did," explained Margaret.

"Me?" Yolanda looked surprised again.

"You took the time to talk to me and to be my friend," Margaret said. "Remember when I first moved to this neighborhood? You were so nice to me, and your mom brought cookies over. I could tell you guys weren't phony. You and your family is why I first wanted to know about God."

Yolanda smiled and hugged her friend.

Your Turn

1. Who do you want to tell about Jesus?
2. What does your life tell people about Jesus?

_____

_____

_____

Prayer

Dear God, may my life show that Jesus is my Savior. Amen.

Abiding in Christ

If you remain in me and I in you, you will bear much fruit;
apart from me you can do nothing.

– John 15:5

Tell All About Him

Stacey and Makita were walking home after school. Stacey tried to get a word in edgewise, but her friend Makita rambled on and on. "She's soooo cool! I can hardly believe I get to meet Dorinda Marlowe!"

Stacey held up her hand. "You've said that twenty times already!"

"I know," answered Makita, "but I can't help it. I'm so excited that my uncle got backstage passes for her concert!"

"That is cool," said Stacey with a smile. "So, are you coming with me to church tomorrow?"

Makita's eyes glazed over. "You always talk about church."

"Not half as much as you talk my ear off about your favorite singer!" Stacey said. "I know she's important to you because you like her albums. Jesus is important to me, so that's why I invite you to church."

Makita hesitated.

"C'mon," Stacey encouraged. "You'll like my Sunday-school class. Besides, I said I'd go to the Dorinda Marlowe concert with you. And you know I don't like her music."

Makita didn't answer. Instead, she nudged Stacey and smiled.

Your Turn

1. What do you think of how Stacey shared Christ with her friend?
2. How do you show that Jesus is important to you?

_____

_____

Prayer

Lord, I want people to know you. Give me the courage and words to let your love shine through me. Amen.

118

Abiding in Christ

Read the Rebus

Here's a rebus for you to solve. Some of the words are sound alikes.

Live in  – **i** + – **e**

with **1** another.  – **e**

 + SHUN + 8.

_____

_____

_____

_____

_____

Prayer

Lord, please help me to be kind and get along with others. Amen.

Abiding in Christ

Do-It-Yourself Tract

Create a special card you can use to talk to someone about Jesus.

What You Need

■ Photocopy of page   ■ Pen with festive ink   ■ Clear tape

What to Do

1. Cut out the top card along the solid lines. As shown, fold the two sides inward; fold the top and bottom downward.

2. Open the flaps and write a message inside—perhaps a Bible verse or something special about God.

3. Fold the card up, secure with a small piece of tape. Pray about who to share the card with, and then do it.

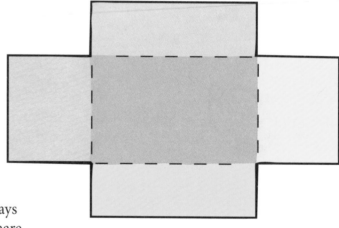

Prayer

Lord, help me always look for ways to share about you. Amen.

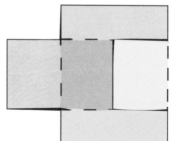

Fold in sides.   **Tape together.**

God—The Great Creator

The earth is the Lord's, and everything in it,
the world, and all who live in it.

– Psalm 24:1

Stormy Inside and Out

"What a yucky thunderstorm!" Caitlyn complained, glancing up.

"Cumulonimbus clouds or maybe nimbostratus," her younger brother said. He looked proud. "Nimbus and nimbostratus clouds are rain clouds."

"So, Brainiac?" replied Caitlyn. She didn't like when Samuel showed off.

"Do you want to know about the earth?" Samuel asked. "Or are you too busy reading dumb magazines? Just yesterday you said you wanted to learn more about God. God created the world, didn't he?"

Caitlyn couldn't argue with that, even though the storm had ruined her plans. "What did you call those clouds?"

Samuel pouted and didn't respond.

"Sam?" Caitlyn asked again. "I'm sorry I called you Brainiac. I've sorta been in a bad mood. I wanted to pick strawberries at Grandma's farm today."

"Me too," agreed Samuel. "Hey, you want to go look at a rainbow? I saw one out back."

When Caitlyn saw the rainbow, she felt a little better. "If it hadn't rained, we wouldn't see this."

A sudden roll of thunder was followed by a flash of lightning that lit up the sky. "Wow!" Caitlyn and Samuel said in unison.

Your Turn

1. What do you appreciate most about God's creation?
2. Is there always something interesting to see in God's creation?

Prayer

Lord, you're awesome! Everything in creation points to you. Amen.

God—The Great Creator

The earth is the LORD's, and everything in it,
the world, and all who live in it.

– **Psalm 24:1**

All God's Creatures

"This is one of my favorite places," Michelle said as she looked around. Her family was spending the day at the zoo.

Randy headed down the path to the giraffes. The twins piped up with, "First, let's see the dolphins." Michelle said, "I like the big cats." Their dad stopped, put two fingers in his mouth, and gave his famous ear-splitting whistle. All four children stopped in their tracks. "Listen up!" Dad said. "We'll see everything, but we're going to stay together. We'll start with Mom's favorites—the bears."

The family spent the day laughing at the monkeys, being amazed by the gigantic elephants, and admiring the beautiful birds. At the zoo hospital, they watched workers care for sick and injured animals. They saw baby animals in the nursery.

On the way home, Michelle said, "I think it's great God made all the animals different."

Mom agreed. "God gave us all of the animals, but he doesn't want us to just look at them or use them. He wants us to take care of them."

"We'd take care of a dog," the twins said hopefully.

Your Turn

1. Why did God create animals?
2. How can you help care for animals?

Prayer

God, thanks for making all the wonderful animals and letting me help care for them. Amen.

God—The Great Creator

The earth is the LORD's, and everything in it,
the world, and all who live in it.

– Psalm 24:1

Weeds, Weeds, and More Weeds

"We must have been crazy to say we'd do this," Kim complained.

"Not crazy," Jamie said. "This is how we get to church camp."

The sisters were weeding Uncle Luke's garden. Uncle Luke was paying each of them five dollars per week to do the work.

Kim tugged at a stubborn weed. "These roots must go to China!" She gave a mighty yank. The weed gave way, and Kim plopped in the dirt.

Jamie cracked up. "What a babe," she teased. "Sitting in weeds, sweat running down your nose, and dirty streaks all over your face."

"You don't look so great either!" Kim laughed.

Just then Uncle Luke called, "Take a break and have some lemonade!"

"I think I hate plants!" Kim announced.

"We wouldn't survive without them," Uncle Luke said. "They provide food, clean air, and oxygen. They hold soil in place and keep us cool. They also give us lumber, medicine, and paper. God created thousands of plants, which means millions of seeds. That way plants keep reproducing."

Kim sighed. "I wish weeds would reproduce somewhere else."

Your Turn

1. Have you taken care of plants? What did you do?
2. Why do we need to protect plants?

Prayer

Lord, thank you for giving us so many plants. Even though they are work to take care of, they provide many important things. Amen.

God—The Great Creator

The earth is the LORD's, and everything in it,
the world, and all who live in it.

– Psalm 24:1

A Big God, a Big Creation

"What's this?" Dinah pointed to the red circle on the book page. She nudged her friend Liz, who was seated next to her at the kitchen table.

"The mantle." Liz didn't bother raising her head from her arms.

"And this?" Dinah asked.

"The inner core," Liz sighed. "Why should we care about this stuff?"

"Because it'll be on the test tomorrow," Dinah said. "Now it's your turn to ask me questions."

Liz wasn't interested. "Got anything to drink in the fridge?"

"That's not going to be on the science quiz tomorrow," Dinah declared.

"But I'm thirsty!" Liz exclaimed.

Dinah pulled two juice boxes out of the refrigerator and found a bag of cookies. "Or would you prefer milk?" she asked Liz.

"Depends on the cookies," Liz glanced at the bag. "Chocolate chip, huh?

That calls for milk." She sat up, looking more awake.

"I don't mind learning this stuff," Dinah said, quietly. "Mainly because God created everything. Learning about the land reminds me how big he is."

Liz was convinced. "I like that reason for studying. Let's get back at it."

Your Turn

1. What are some of the biggest things in creation?
2. What are some of the smallest things in creation?

Prayer

Lord, when I look at the world, I see your hand everywhere. Amen.

God—The Great Creator

The earth is the LORD's, and everything in it,
the world, and all who live in it.

– Psalm 24:1

Caretakers of the Planet

Jerri took the wrapper off of her candy bar and tossed it on the ground as she climbed on her bike.

"Hey, pick that up!" her friend Tammy said.

"What difference does it make?" Jerri said. "Look at all the trash blowing around here. Who are you anyway, Smokey Bear?"

"Smoky Bear talks about forest fires," Tammy said, disgusted.

"Whatever." Jerri picked up the wrapper and crammed it into her pocket. "There! You happy?" She jumped on her bike and pedaled off down the street.

"Don't you care about what happens to the planet?" Tammy yelled, as she followed on her own bike.

"One candy bar wrapper won't kill the planet," called Jerri. "Hey, let's stop at the Burger Beehive for a shake."

The girls soon had frosty shakes in front of them.

"Aren't foam cups supposed to be bad for the planet?" Jerri asked with a mischievous grin. She cradled the cup containing her shake in her hands.

Tammy looked guiltily at her own cup.

Jerri laughed. "Don't worry. I won't hold it against you."

Your Turn

1. What things are harmful to God's creation?
2. Why do you think God wants us to take care of his creation?

Prayer

Lord, help me be a careful caretaker of your creation. Amen.

God—The Great Creator

An Abundance of Animals

God must have had a great time creating all the different animals. Find the names of the animals in this word search.

```
T C Z E B R A R B M A L
N R N I H P L O D O G A
A H E A O S T R I C H E
H I P P O P O T A M U S
P N E I R H O L I O N T
E O A G A A T S Y N O P
L C C A G W T H B K T T
E E O L N K E A E E N A
L R C A A Q R R A Y A O
K O K O K A Y K R H O G
O S R K N U M P I H C T
```

Ant	Goat	Lion	Rhinoceros
Bear	Hawk	Monkey	Seal
Chipmunk	Hippopotamus	Ostrich	Shark
Dog	Hog	Otter	Yak
Dolphin	Kangaroo	Peacock	Zebra
Elephant	Koala	Pig	
Elk	Lamb	Pony	

Which of these animals would you like for a pet?

_____

How would you take care of it?

_____

Prayer

Lord, your creation is amazing! Amen.

God—The Great Creator

Bible Plants

The Bible mentions many plants. Look up these verses to find some of them. Use a New International Version (NIV) Bible.

1. Numbers 11:5: _____

2. Deuteronomy 11:15: _____

3. Deuteronomy 23:24: _____

4. Ruth 1:22: _____

5. 1 Samuel 14:2: _____

6. 2 Samuel 6:19: _____

7. 2 Samuel 7:2: _____

8. Proverbs 7:2: _____

9. Song of Songs 2:1: _____

10. Jeremiah 24:2: _____

11. Hosea 14:8 _____

12. Joel 1:12: _____

13. Matthew 6:28: _____

14. Luke 3:17: _____

15. Luke 17:6: _____

16. Luke 19:4: _____

17. Hebrews 6:8: _____

18. James 3:12: _____

Prayer

Lord, you have filled the earth with such beauty. I am a willing caretaker of this planet. Amen.

Choosing to Cooperate

Let us not love with words or speech but with actions and in truth.

– 1 John 3:18

Important Guests

"Wow! They're really coming! When will they be here? How long will they stay? Where will they sleep?" Bree bounced around her mom, who was reading a letter from Bree's grandparents.

"Calm down, girl," Mom said. "I can't answer until I finish reading."

Grandma and Grandpa Brooks had been working in a foreign country for a year. Bree had talked to them, e-mailed them, and gotten gifts from them, but she'd really missed them.

"Okay, here's the scoop," her mom said. "They'll arrive next Friday and are staying for three weeks. So we need to clean the spare room."

"Oh, yuck, that room's a disaster," Bree replied. The spare room was where all of the "what do we do with this?" stuff was stashed.

"If everyone works together, we can get it in great shape. You kids start sorting through things. Either toss it or store it in the garage. Let's get going!"

By Friday, after a lot of hard work, the room was ready for Bree's grandparents. As she watched for the taxi to bring them from the airport, she sang, "They'll be comin' round the mountain when they come."

Then her brother Eric sang, "The spare room is all cleaned so they can come."

Your Turn

1. Why is it important for a family to cooperate?
2. What are the advantages of cooperating?

Prayer

Lord, help me to cooperate with my family members. I know it is how you want me to behave, but it can be difficult. Amen.

Choosing to Cooperate

Let us not love with words or speech but with actions and in truth.
– 1 John 3:18

The Study Group

Caroline pouted, "I hate my study group. I'm with Simon Winkler!"

"Bummer," said Libby. "He's a loser. Who else is in your group?"

"Camille Patterson and Wesley Bernard," answered Caroline.

"At least they're cool," Libby said. "Maybe you can get rid of Simon."

Caroline knew talking bad about Simon was wrong, but Libby was right. "We can't unless all of us vote him out," Caroline said. "My teacher says we have to have a very good reason for voting someone out."

All that week, Caroline noticed how hard Simon worked. Camille and Wesley barely contributed. Caroline decided to talk to Simon about Camille and Wesley. Before she could say anything, Simon said, "I know you want me out of the group. I heard you and Libby talking about me last week."

Caroline was mortified. She mumbled an apology, and then said, "Actually, I've been thinking we should vote Camille and Wesley out. They're not cooperating at all."

"Maybe we should give them another chance," suggested Simon.

Caroline smiled. "I'm glad we're part of the same group, Simon!"

Your Turn

1. What are some ways you can be cooperative at school?
2. Who do you find difficult to work with?

_____

_____

Prayer

Lord, sometimes I don't want to be cooperative. Help me have a better attitude. Amen.

Choosing to Cooperate

Let us not love with words or speech but with actions and in truth.

– 1 John 3:18

A New Wendy

Usually Wendy planned ways she could interrupt the class. Once, in a move that went down in history as the biggest prank at Elmwood Elementary, she clogged all the toilets in the girls restroom.

But today Wendy sat in class quietly doing her work. When called on, she gave the right answer instead of saying something funny. She wasn't sent to the principal's office, and her parents weren't called.

Mr. Lacey asked, "Are you feeling okay, Wendy?"

"Yes," Wendy said.

The kids stared at one another. What had happened to Wendy? Why was she being so cooperative? At recess, they surrounded Wendy, demanding to know what was going on.

"Jesus is my Savior now!" she announced. That means I want to follow Jesus and make God happy."

"Does that mean you're going to act this way all the time?" a girl asked.

Wendy nodded. "I needed to anyway. My dad says if I'm not more cooperative, he'll ground me for the rest of my life."

"I guess that means no more practical jokes, huh?" a boy said.

Wendy laughed. "Well, I can't give up everything, y'know!"

Your Turn

1. Why did Wendy become more cooperative?
2. How did the kids know Wendy was a new person in Jesus?

_____

_____

Prayer

Dear God, show me ways to cooperate. Amen.

Choosing to Cooperate

Let us not love with words or speech but with actions and in truth.

– 1 John 3:18

Cooperation Sunday

Everyone was excited. Ideas on what to do for the church's "Cooperation Sunday" flew fast and furious—and all at once.

"One at a time, please!" Mrs. Cody said loudly.

Anne raised her hand. "We could collect the offering."

"No!" one boy said. "I want to play my violin. I just learned a new piece."

"What are the rest of us going to do? Stand there and stare?" Anne said.

"For people talking about cooperation, I don't think we're being very cooperative," Mrs. Cody said. "Cooperation Sunday is everyone taking part in the Sunday worship service. That's a way of giving God thanks. The adult Sunday school class chose a speaker. The teens are leading the singing. So what would you like to do? We could sing a song."

No one was in favor of that.

"We could collect the offering," Anne suggested again.

"That's not very important," complained one boy.

"Giving is a very important," corrected Mrs. Cody. "Through the offering we collect, we send out missionaries, buy food for people, and pay church bills."

Several voices spoke at once: "Let's collect the offering!"

Your Turn

1. What are some jobs at your church that require cooperation?
2. What can kids your age do together to help people at church?

_____

_____

Prayer

God, help me to be joyful in cooperating with others. Amen.

Choosing to Cooperate

Let us not love with words or speech but with actions and in truth.

– 1 John 3:18

Learning to Cooperate

"Tess, what's this I hear about you disrupting your Sunday-school class?" Mom asked.

Tess wrinkled her nose. "I was only telling the latest jokes I'd heard. I can't help it if everyone laughed."

"Your teacher feels you weren't cooperating very much," said her mother. "I've decided that for the next two Sundays you can help out in the nursery."

"Why?" Tess whined.

"The nursery needs volunteers," Mom explained. "You're twelve now, so you're old enough to help out with the toddlers."

"Aw, Mom!" Tess grumbled all week. She didn't want to help out by working. But after the first Sunday in the nursery, she found she liked being with the kids for the most part.

"They laughed at all my jokes, too," she bragged to her mother. "But some of them were so bratty they didn't listen to a word I said."

"Now you know how your teacher felt." Mom grinned. "It's important to cooperate, isn't it? And taking care of the children allows their parents to participate in worship. That's a way to cooperate with others."

Your Turn

1. How did Tess learn the value of cooperation?
2. How can you use your talents to work with others at church?

Prayer

Lord, help me cooperate with others. Amen.

Choosing to Cooperate

Living in Unity

Solve the clues and fill in the indicated blanks to find some good advice about cooperation.

1. Fifth month of the year
2. Another word for "one" that rhymes with "peach"
3. Opposite of "out"
4. What you say when you're in trouble
5. Rhymes with "rod"
6. Sixth book in the New Testament
7. Opposite of "incomplete"
8. Add a "w" to the front of "it" and an "h" to the end
9. Number of disciples plus three
10. Rhymes with "mother"
11. 10 – 5
12. Opposite of "me"
13. Add "ony" to the end of a word that means "hurt"
14. Replace the "f" in "five" with an "L"

_____ _____ . . . _____ _____
   1   5   4   12

_____ _____ _____
  14   3   7

_____ _____ _____
    13   8   2

_____ . _____ ___:___
  10   6   9 11

Choosing to Cooperate

Letting God Work

Sometimes cooperation means stepping back and allowing God to work. Peter and other disciples learned this truth firsthand. God did many wonderful things to help the church. In the illustrations below, the middle of each incident is given. See if you know what happened before and after the illustration.

Acts 3:1-10

What happened first?

_____

What happened afterward?

_____

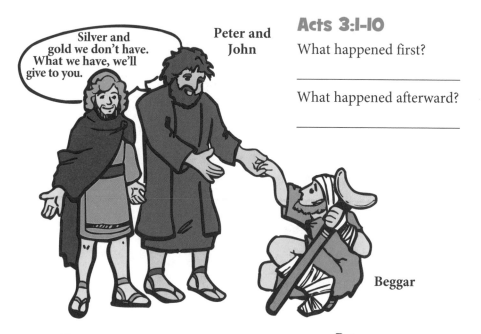

Acts 12:1-17

What happened first?

_____

What happened afterward?

_____

Prayer

God, I will cooperate with you even if I don't understand what you have in mind. I can trust you. Amen.

Everything Is in God's Hands

I have learned to be content whatever the circumstances.

– Philippians 4:11

What About the Future?

Vanessa picked at her food. "I'm scared, Dad. "Carla Evers' dad died. He had a heart attack on his job. What if…?" She stared at her father.

"What if something happened to me?" Dad finished.

Vanessa nodded. She was too afraid to even voice the possibility.

"God doesn't want you to be worried about that, Munch," Dad said. "Instead of worrying about what could happen, talk to God. He'll never leave you. I can't make that same forever promise. Instead, what I've done is make sure you're taken care of now. That's why we have insurance. That's why your mom set up a college fund for you before she died. And, remember, Aunt Edna and Uncle Henry are your godparents. If something happens to me, you would live with them."

Vanessa was now confused. "If we're to trust God, why do we need to plan for the future?"

"God is in control," her father explained. "But he doesn't expect us to sit around and wait for him to do everything. We make plans and submit them to God, knowing he has the final say."

Your Turn

1. What plans have you made for the future?
2. How do you show God that you know he's the boss of your present and your future?

_____

_____

Prayer

Lord, there's nothing about my present, past, and future you don't know. I trust you with my life and choices. Amen.

Everything Is in God's Hands

I have learned to be content whatever the circumstances.

– Philippians 4:11

Beyond Today

Justine's Journal, Tuesday

Dad asked me about the future for the millionth time. What is it with parents? I keep telling him I don't know. Today I said I just want to make enough money babysitting to buy skates.

"Well, that's something," he said. "But what about college? It's expensive."

"*I'm* supposed to pay for college?"

"We'll help you all we can, but we're not wealthy. I want you to learn to make short-term and long-term plans. Now you want skates, but what about tomorrow or next year? You might even consider saving for the car you'll want one day."

My dad gets really strange ideas. Here I am, twelve years old. Never had a driving lesson. And my dad thinks I should save for a car! The future? I hardly think about it. Except for high school. Sometimes I think about that. I also wonder what could happen to the planet. Sometimes I do worry, I guess. Dad says I should pray about it. "Prayer is one way to plan for the future," he said.

Maybe all of Dad's ideas aren't weird.

Your Turn

1. What worries you about the future?
2. What would you like to pray about right now concerning the future?

_____

_____

Prayer

Lord Jesus, you are my future. Guide me in the way you want me to go. Amen.

Everything Is in God's Hands

I have learned to be content whatever the circumstances.

– Philippians 4:11

Career Day

Larissa Meadowlark was pleased and embarrassed that her mother, a research chemist, was speaking at Career Day. "You can't say anything about God," Larissa warned.

Mrs. Meadowlark's eyebrows rose. "You mean I can't pass out Bibles?"

"Moooom!"

"I'm teasing, Larissa! I know the school's policy. That's too bad. It's difficult to help kids prepare for the future without including God."

"God doesn't seem important to my classmates," admitted Larissa. "My friend Kei said God makes us choose certain professions. She said we don't get a choice."

"God didn't make us robots," corrected Mom. "He gave us talents and abilities that help us prepare for the future, including careers. You love science, so we sent you to space camp last summer."

"That was fun."

Mom nodded. "Well, in ten years or so, do you think you'll become a ballet dancer?"

"Hardly!" Larissa laughed. "I've never taken ballet. I don't even like it."

"God is in control of our lives," her mother affirmed. "But he's not an ogre or a tyrant. He makes good plans for our lives."

Your Turn

1. What plans do you have for the future?
2. What do you think God wants you to do?

_____

_____

Prayer

Lord, let me know your plans for me. Amen.

Everything Is in God's Hands

I have learned to be content whatever the circumstances.

– Philippians 4:11

I Wish...

Madeline Ryan sighed as she looked in the mirror. *Wish I could see a difference.* She'd tried everything to get rid of her freckles—the strongest sunscreen, special soap, even lemon juice. Her freckles remained as bright as ever. *I'll work on my hair,* Madeline decided. She combed gobs of gel through it.

Her parents didn't say a word when Madeline entered the kitchen. They just looked at each other and raised their eyebrows.

Her brother didn't keep quiet. "Yikes! What did you do?"

"I hate my curly hair," Madeline replied.

Mom said, "Maddy, your hair is part of what makes you special."

Madeline complained, "How can people like me when I have freckles on my face and this red bush on my head? I wish I looked like Jen. She has straight black hair and no freckles."

Mom continued. "God made each of us special, and we should be content. And how you act is more important. When you're kind and helpful, people will want to be your friend."

"I guess I'll comb some of this stuff out of my hair," Madeline said.

Your Turn

1. Do you try to change your looks or personality to fit in?
2. What can you do to enjoy who you are?

_____

_____

Prayer

Dear God, you made me. Help me be content with things I can't change. Amen.

Everything Is in God's Hands

I have learned to be content whatever the circumstances.

– Philippians 4:11

A Raise

Genevieve looked glumly at her money. Her father had docked her allowance $2 a week until she'd paid back what she owed. That meant only $2.50 for eleven weeks! She marched into her father's office. "Dad, I need a raise in allowance."

Dad glanced up from the computer. "A raise, huh? Why?"

"Everything costs more. And some of my friends get $10 a week."

Dad looked thoughtful. "Would you be willing to do more chores?"

"More?" Genevieve. "I already have to take out the garbage, set the table, and load the dishwasher."

"If I want a raise, I have to do extra work," her father said. "God's Word says if we don't work, we shouldn't eat. Will you do more work?"

"Like what?" asked Genevieve.

"Oh, chop wood. Wash windows. Shovel snow." Dad laughed. "Yes, I'm exaggerating. But I can give you five more jobs, each worth another 50 cents a week."

Genevieve said, "How about I work for $6 a week?"

"How about $2.50?" Dad smiled.

"Five dollars sounds good, Dad!"

Your Turn

1. Did Genevieve deserved an allowance raise because her friends received more?
2. Why do you think her father wanted her to do more chores for more money?

Prayer

Dear God, money seems so important to people. Help me worship you instead of money. Amen.

Everything Is in God's Hands

Plans for the Future

When you consider your plans for the future, think about God's wisdom found in Scripture. Find these references in the puzzle, then look up each one. Note: Colons aren't included. For example, "Hebrews 13:6" will read "HEBREWS 136." Philippians is abbreviated "Phil" (PHIL 419).

1 John 3:18	Joshua 24:15	Philippians 4:19
1 John 4:4	Luke 1:37	Psalm 119:105
1 Peter 5:7	Matthew 11:28	Psalm 23:6
Hebrews 13:6	Matthew 22:37	Psalm 32:8
John 14:6	Matthew 28:20	Revelation 22:20
John 3:16	Philippians 1:6	

O	M	A	T	T	H	E	W	2	2	3	7	U
P	S	A	L	M	3	2	8	R	O	J	I	M
U	N	I	T	A	J	R	U	X	Z	Y	6	5
N	H	O	J	T	O	E	N	O	P	O	3	1
S	H	O	U	T	H	V	B	H	1	3	2	4
P	A	I	M	H	N	E	I	B	D	4	M	2
S	H	O	N	E	1	L	W	Z	C	9	L	A
A	E	I	K	W	4	A	U	2	B	8	A	U
L	B	7	L	1	6	T	6	K	8	4	S	H
M	R	5	9	1	N	I	1	1	E	2	P	S
1	E	R	5	2	6	O	3	J	O	1	0	O
1	W	E	A	8	A	N	N	O	P	H	3	J
9	S	T	H	A	H	2	H	H	B	L	U	7
1	1	E	O	O	V	2	O	N	T	H	I	E
0	3	P	J	P	Z	2	J	4	M	U	N	E
5	6	1	H	O	S	0	N	4	C	A	N	E

Prayer

Dear Lord, I'm so grateful that everything in my past, my present, and my future is in loving your hands. Amen.

Everything Is in God's Hands

Future Fears

Sometimes the future seems like a big, scary unknown because life is full of changes. One thing *never* changes. Break the code to discover the secret.

A	B	C	D	E	F	G
1910	2000	1954	1879	2010	864	1311

H	I	J	K	L	M
1785	1776	411	30	70	1902

N	O	P	Q	R	S	T
1999	1620	1948	1515	1865	702	2005

U	V	W	X	Y	Z
432	1011	1947	1500	1832	1212

411 2010 702 432 702   1954 1785 1865 1776 702 2005

____ ____ ____ ____ ____   ____ ____ ____ ____ ____ ____

1776 702   2005 1785 2010   702 1910 1902 2010

____ ____   ____ ____ ____   ____ ____ ____ ____

1832 2010 702 2005 2010 1865 1879 1910 1832

____ ____ ____ ____ ____ ____ ____ ____ ____

1910 1999 1879   2005 1620 1879 1910 1832   1910 1999 1879

____ ____ ____   ____ ____ ____ ____ ____   ____ ____ ____

864 1620 1865 2010 1011 2010 1865

____ ____ ____ ____ ____ ____ ____ .   **Hebrews 13:8**

Prayer

Lord, life means change. I know I can count on you to never change. I love that. Amen.

Loving God Daily

Create in me a pure heart, O God,
and renew a steadfast spirit within me.

– Psalm 51:10

Great Expectations

"That is totally out-of-the-question impossible!" declared Kelly. "I'd have to be Jesus himself to do this! Listen to this, Dad. Deuteronomy 8:1 says, 'Be careful to follow every command I am giving you today.' Right. Like I said—impossible."

Dad nodded. "You're right. We're mere humans and sinners, so we aren't capable of obeying all God's commandments all the time. That's why Jesus died for us—to forgive us when we fail and disobey. We do need to be consistent in striving to obey God and in asking Jesus for forgiveness when we fail or disobey."

" 'Consistent.' I don't understand exactly what that means," said Kelly.

"Consistent is being steady in your beliefs and character. Your actions go along with what you believe. What you do tomorrow is in agreement with what you did today. Consistency means people generally know what to expect of you and how you will react."

"Like I consistently get up late and have to rush for school."

Dad laughed. "Yes! You are consistent in your time-challenged morning behavior."

Your Turn

1. Think of one consistent behavior you have. Is it good or not-so-good?
2. Do you think it makes a difference to others if you're consistent?

Prayer

Dear God, thank you for your consistent behavior. Help me follow your example. Amen.

Loving God Daily

Create in me a pure heart, O God,
and renew a steadfast spirit within me.

– Psalm 51:10

Like the Cherubim

Celine pointed to the picture of the seraphim in her Bible dictionary. "We were talking about these in Sunday school," she told her mother. "Do you think they look like this for real, Mama?"

Mama shook her head. "Honey, no one knows exactly what those beings look like. The artist just had to draw something. What made you look that up anyway?"

Celine tugged on one of her braids. "We were talking about the story in Isaiah 6, where Isaiah saw God in the temple. I was just wondering what seraphim look like. Why do you think they covered their eyes and feet with their wings?" She pointed to the drawings.

"Maybe to remind us that God is holy—too holy to gaze upon. His glory is too radiant. When we worship God, we think about who God is. He's above sin. His holiness inspires our worship."

Celine put her hands over her eyes.

"What are you doing?" her mother asked.

"I'm imagining myself like the seraphim in front of God."

"Now that's the way to worship!" Mama said.

Your Turn

1. God is holy. What does that mean to you?
2. How does knowing that God is holy help you in your worship?

_____

_____

_____

Prayer

Lord God, you are holy. Thank you for loving me. Amen.

Loving God Daily

Create in me a pure heart, O God,
and renew a steadfast spirit within me.

– Psalm 51:10

Attitude Counts

"Well, I'm glad that's over with," Leslie said with a grin. Her friend Jalise didn't immediately agree, which was odd. They usually complained about church as they waited for their parents. "Hel-lo? Did you hear me?"

"I heard you," Jalise answered softly.

"What's with you?"

Jalise blushed. "I…um…I liked the youth service today."

Leslie stared at her. "Are you kidding?"

"No. I—I just like coming to church these days. It's like my dad said: 'Attitude is everything.' I prayed and asked God to help me want to worship him."

Leslie wanted to call Jalise a traitor, but that seemed a bit too strong and, well, disrespectful to God. As they waited in silence, Leslie thought about something her mother once said: "People who love God are glad to worship him." Leslie flipped a blond strand behind her ear as she cast a glance at Jalise. Her friend did look happy. Three weeks ago she'd acted like she had to be dragged to church, but now…

Humph, Leslie thought, frowning. *I can't help it if I don't want to go to church sometimes.*

Your Turn

1. Why is a person's attitude important in worship?
2. What do you think it takes to have a worshipful attitude?

_____

_____

Prayer

Lord, help me to have a worshipful attitude and a desire to grow in you. Amen.

Loving God Daily

*Create in me a pure heart, O God,
and renew a steadfast spirit within me.*

– Psalm 51:10

Chameleon Kid

Upset by how her friend Vanika was acting, Brooke went to her older sister for advice. "I never know how Vanika is going to act or what she's going to say. When she's with the church group, she seems honest and sincere. But when she's around the kids at school, she makes fun of God and going to church. Why does she act that way?"

"Vanika is a real 'chameleon kid,'" Diane answered. "A chameleon is a lizard that changes color according to its surroundings. It might be green or yellow one minute, and the next minute it might be brown or black. Temperature, light, and feelings control the changes. Sometimes people are like chameleons. They say what people want to hear or go along with the crowd to fit in."

"I think I have some chameleon in me too," Brooke admitted.

Diane nodded her head. "It's a matter of degree. We're all a little lizardly at times. Fortunately for us, God is never a chameleon. He always loves us no matter what we do. He is consistent."

Your Turn

1. What helps you to stand up for who you are and what you believe?
2. Why are you glad God is always consistent?

Prayer

Lord, thank you for never changing how you feel about me. Help me be consistent in who I am and what I do. Amen.

Loving God Daily

Create in me a pure heart, O God,
and renew a steadfast spirit within me.

– Psalm 51:10

Suppose

The fifth- and sixth-grade Sunday school class was playing its favorite game: "Suppose."

"Suppose your best friend wasn't a Christian and wanted you to do something wrong. Would you go along with your friend?" Mr. Connors asked.

"No way!" Matt said.

"Me neither," his cousin Michelle said softly.

"You would!" Matt hissed. "Remember what your friend Renae wanted you to do?"

Mr. Connors overheard them. "What was it?"

Michelle shot Matt a look. She didn't want to blab her life to everyone in the class. While she hesitated, Matt said, "Renae wanted her to ignore the new girl in their class and say nasty things about her."

"I didn't want to do it!" Michelle said. "But Renae said the girl didn't fit in because she dressed weird and talked with an accent."

Some of the other kids began talking at once. Mr. Connors called for quiet. "As we were saying earlier, God wants us to be loyal to him. If you had to choose between staying loyal to him and being loyal to a friend, which would you choose?"

Your Turn

1. How does being loyal to God apply to Michelle's situation?
2. How does being loyal to God affect your life every day?

Prayer

Lord, I want to be loyal to you in every way. I need your help. Amen.

Loving God Daily

Rainbow Cookies

Carefully following a recipe and directions makes the product turn out the same way consistently. That's what will happen with these rainbow cookies. May these cookies remind you and everyone who eats them that God is consistent and always keeps his promises. Ask your parents or an adult to make these with you.

What You Need

- Cookie dough (store-bought)
- Flour
- Food coloring
- Rolling pin
- Wax paper
- Cookie sheet

What to Do

1. Add a little flour to the dough so you can easily roll it out.

2. Divide the dough into five equal parts.

3. Add one or more different colors of food coloring to each part. For example, if you combine red and yellow, you get orange.

4. Roll each color of dough into strips ¼" thick. Cut the dough so each strip is about 4" long.

5. Stack the strips on top of each other by color, wrap them in wax paper, and put them in the refrigerator overnight.

6. The next day, arrange the colored slices on a cookie sheet and curve them into a rainbow shape.

7. Bake the cookies at 375 degrees for 6 to 8 minutes.

Prayer

Lord, please help me have a pure heart and a steady spirit. Amen.

Loving God Daily

Worship Your Way

Worship isn't just something adults do. You do it too. Why not create a psalm? Write your words of praise to God for his holiness, love, and mercy. Use words or pictures.

Prayer

Heavenly Father, there is no one more worthy of my worship than you. I will worship you only all the days of my life. Amen.

Faith in Action

Give thanks to the Lord, for he is good; his love endures forever.
– Psalm 107:1

Happy Thanksgiving?

For Thanksgiving, all the McPherson uncles, aunts, and cousins went to Grandpa and Grandma McPherson's. There was lots of delicious food and plenty of talking, singing, and teasing. After dinner everyone played games.

That's the way it was, thought Molly as she fought back tears. Grandpa McPherson had died two months ago, and Molly really missed him. How could she be happy and thankful at Thanksgiving when he wouldn't be there?

Molly and her family arrived and were greeted by tons of relatives. When it was time for dinner, Molly thought, *Grandpa always said the prayer.* Who will do it this year? Molly was surprised when Grandma stood up.

Softly, Grandma prayed, "Dear God, thank you for all the blessings you give us. Thank you for the people who are here and for the one we all miss, Grandpa. Thank you for all the love and fun he gave us. We are happy that Grandpa is spending this Thanksgiving in heaven with you, and someday we will too. Amen."

A smile spread across Molly's face as she thought of Grandpa's Thanksgiving.

Your Turn

1. For what are you most thankful?
2. Why is it important to thank God for his blessings?

_____

_____

Prayer

Lord, help me be thankful for all I have. Amen.

Faith in Action

Give thanks to the Lord, for he is good; his love endures forever.
– Psalm 107:1

The Swim Party

Jasmine and Gloria were doing their homework at Jasmine's house when Jasmine's brother, Kyle, stuck his head in the door. "Hey, Jas, a girl from your class called before you got home. Here's her name and number." He tossed a paper on the table.

Jasmine and Gloria looked at the scribbled name: Megan Miller.

"What do you think she wants?" asked Gloria.

"Guess we won't know unless I call," Jasmine said as she reached for the phone.

"I'm having a swim party for my birthday," Megan said. "It's on Saturday at two o'clock. Can you come?"

Jasmine could hardly believe what she was hearing. Megan and her four friends always did everything together. "I'll have to ask my mom," Jasmine stammered.

"Oh, one more thing," Megan went on. "I'm not inviting all the girls in our class. So don't tell Gloria about this, okay? Bye."

"What did she want?" Gloria asked.

What should I say? wondered Jasmine. *What am I going to do?*

Your Turn

1. If you were Jasmine, what would you do? What would you say to Gloria?
2. Does being loyal mean you limit who you do things with?

_____

_____

Prayer

Lord, thank you for the friends you've given me. Help me be loving and loyal. Amen.

Faith in Action

Give thanks to the Lord, for he is good; his love endures forever.
– Psalm 107:1

The "Hot" Book

Boy! did I luck out, thought Ashley. *No homework! I can read all night.* Soon she was settled into a corner of the couch with a bag of chips and the hottest book in sixth grade. Ashley was so absorbed that she didn't hear her mother come into the room.

Mom said, "Hi, Ashley. What are you reading?"

Ashley was so startled that she jumped in surprise. "Wow, Mom, you scared me!" She held up the book. "All the girls in my class are reading this book. Chloe loaned me hers for a few days."

Her mother took the book and read the description of the story on the back cover. "I read a review of this book, Ashley. I really don't think it's something you should read. It's about witches."

"But Mom!" Ashley protested. "Everybody is reading it! I know it's not real—it's just a made-up story."

"Even if it is fiction, it might make you comfortable with thoughts and ideas that aren't biblical. When that happens, you're not being loyal to God or to your beliefs as a Christian."

Your Turn

1. Why is loyalty to God important?
2. Can you stay true to God and dabble in activities he might not approve of?

Prayer

Dear God, give me discernment so I will know your views on activities. Amen.

Faith in Action

Give thanks to the Lord, for he is good; his love endures forever.
– Psalm 107:1

A Theory of Repentance

Gena looked at her sister's paper. "What's that?"

Lola explained, "It's a Pythagorean equation."

Gena stared at it. "A2 + B2 = C2? Weird." She flopped on a chair at the table. "Mom's really mad at me."

Lola glanced up. "You know why."

Gena shrugged. "I said I was sorry I lied."

"Yes, but you you keep lying." said Lola. She wrote a word on a piece of paper and passed it to Gena. "Repentance," Gena read. "What does that mean?"

"It means being truly sorry and changing what you do. Here's another equation." Lola wrote something else on the paper for Gena.

"Thought + will = action," Gena read. "So?"

"That adds up to repentance. You think, 'I don't want to lie to Mom.' Then you decide, 'I won't lie to Mom anymore.' Then you don't lie!"

Gena looked at her older sister. "You think you're so smart. I think so too!"

Your Turn

1. When you're sorry about something, how do your actions show it?
2. Look at Lola's equation for repentance. How will you put that into action?

_____

_____

Prayer

Dear Jesus, help me be sorry when I sin. Remind me about repentance. Amen.

Faith in Action

Give thanks to the Lord, for he is gsood; his love endures forever.

– Psalm 107:1

Really Sorry

"Why doesn't Uncle Jerry believe in Jesus?" Trina asked as she watched her mother prepare dinner.

"Well," said her mother as she wiped her hands on a dish towel, "I think Uncle Jerry believes in God, but he doesn't want to follow God."

"Why not?"

"It's hard to explain. I don't think Uncle Jerry is really sorry for the bad things he's done. We've all done wrong things. God wants us to be sorry about those things and turn to him."

"Maybe he's sorry and just doesn't know how to say he's sorry." Trina loved her uncle. She couldn't imagine that he'd done anything wrong, but all people do. She knew he didn't go to church or read the Bible.

"God knows when we're really sorry or when we're just faking it," her mom said. "He wants us to be sorry for our sins and to want to do the right thing. Then he helps us."

"Maybe Uncle Jerry can ask God to help him be sorry."

"That's a good idea."

Your Turn

1. What do you think about Trina's suggestion?
2. Do you need to talk to God and ask for forgiveness?

_____

_____

_____

Prayer

Lord, I'm sorry for my sins. Please forgive me and help me stop. Amen.

Faith in Action

Love in Action

Christians show their love to God through their actions. Moving left to right, circle the word that doesn't belong in each heart. Then write the circled words, in order, on the lines. You will discover an important way to show love.

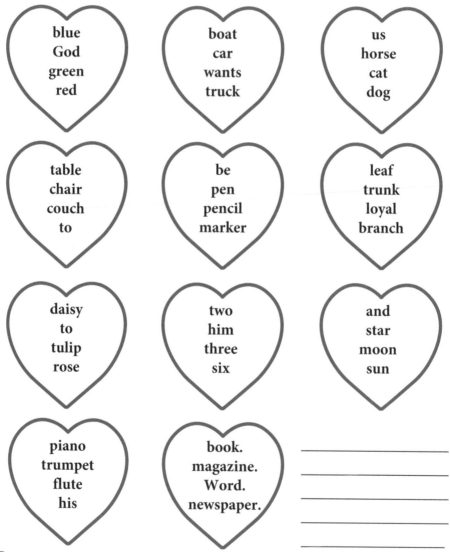

blue
God
green
red

boat
car
wants
truck

us
horse
cat
dog

table
chair
couch
to

be
pen
pencil
marker

leaf
trunk
loyal
branch

daisy
to
tulip
rose

two
him
three
six

and
star
moon
sun

piano
trumpet
flute
his

book.
magazine.
Word.
newspaper.

_____
_____
_____
_____
_____

Prayer

Lord God, I want to be loyal to you and your Word. Amen.

Faith in Action

A Change of Heart

Many people in the Bible were sorry for their sins and turned to God. Find the names in the puzzle. When you find "Paul," you'll also find a three-word message diagonally that includes the "A." Write the message on the lines. If you don't recognize a name, look the person up!

David

Job

Judah

Lost son

Lydia

Matthew

Paul

Peter

Sinners

Woman [at the] well

Zacchaeus

```
L Y D I A Q U E R T Z
L H I I H S A Z A C C
E L O H W U Z R I G H
W P J N A E Y L O H E
N E P O D A V I D Y M
A T H S B H B K O A T
M E L T X C A U V L L
O R E S T C C D J O Y
W O L O P A U L U K T
B X Q L N Z M V C J O
M H Y T S R E N N I S
Q M O L K P J B C E T
M O O N J U N E T U N
```

These people repented.

_____

_____

_____

Prayer

Lord, when I do or say something wrong, please let me know right away. Amen.

Following Jesus

Give praise to the Lord, proclaim his name!

– Isaiah 12:4

Gratitude Attitude

Katie went to sleep imagining herself twirling her baton as she marched ahead of the band in the Fair parade the next day. She practically flew out of bed when the alarm rang.

"Good morning! Come help us with the animals," said Dad. Katie muttered, "I'll be out in a minute."

One minute stretched into thirty. Katie dawdled over breakfast and thought of the parade. Her daydream was interrupted when the back door banged and her sister stomped into the kitchen, with Dad right behind her.

"Well, Princess, at least you're finally up!" Susie said.

"What's your problem?" Katie asked.

"Susie did all of the barn work alone this morning," Dad said.

"I guess I lost track of time thinking about the parade," Katie admitted.

"Have you thanked Susie for doing your work?" Dad asked.

Katie said, "Thanks, Susie. May I buy you a corn dog and soda at the fair?"

Susie smiled. "That will be great!"

"Good. You both have a gratitude attitude!" Dad said.

Your Turn

1. If someone does something nice for you, why is important to say thank you?
2. Is there someone you can thank today—your parents or your friends? Don't forget God!

Prayer

Lord, help me to have an attitude of gratitude and share my appreciation. Amen.

Following Jesus

Give praise to the Lord, proclaim his name!
– Isaiah 12:4

The Way of the Faithful

Every Saturday at 9 a.m., Molly or her friend Lisa walked Mrs. Herman's dog. Mrs. Herman was her 86-year-old next-door neighbor. Today was Molly's turn. When Molly looked outside, she groaned. All night long snow had fallen. With the cold wind blowing, the ground also had a covering of ice.

Oh, great! Molly grumbled. I wish this was Lisa's day to walk Snapper. He was a large German shepherd who could get rambunctious.

The wind rushed to meet Molly as she stepped outside. It was so cold, it felt like her braces were in deep-freeze mode. Then she noticed that the walk had been shoveled. In fact, the snow had been cleared all the way to the end of the block—her usual route with Snapper.

"I knew you'd come," Mrs. Herman said as Molly walked into the house. "I had the neighbor boys shovel a path for you. They also put salt down so you wouldn't slip."

"Thank you, Mrs. Herman!" Molly said. As she walked Snapper, Molly also thanked God for taking care of her.

Your Turn

1. How was Molly faithful?
2. How did God take care of her?

Prayer

Thank you, Lord, for watching over me and leading me. Amen.

157

Following Jesus

Give praise to the Lord, proclaim his name!

– Isaiah 12:4

Is That All?

What a mess! It looked like Tornado Christmas had touched down right in the family room. Paper, ribbons, bows and empty boxes littered the floor. Marcy's little brother, Joey, was having a great time running his new fire engine through paper tunnels and around box buildings. Marcy's mom was smiling as she looked through a book she'd received. Mr. Wilkens was eagerly trying out a new kitchen tool.

Marcy checked the far corner under the tree once more. She sighed.

"Is something bothering you?" asked her mom. "Don't you like your gifts?"

"Oh, Mom, these are really cool gifts. B-b-but..." Marcy stuttered.

"But you didn't get the new boots you wanted," Mom finished. "I'm sorry you're disappointed. Your old boots are still good. We don't always get what we want. But Jesus gives us what we needed most: love, forgiveness, and salvation. Those are amazing gifts."

Marcy gave her mom a hug. "I think I'll put on my still-good boots and go build a snowman," she said.

Your Turn

1. What makes you feel discontented sometimes?
2. How did Marcy go from disappointment to joy?

_____

_____

_____

Prayer

God, help me be content and thankful with what I have. Amen.

Following Jesus

Give praise to the Lord, proclaim his name!
– Isaiah 12:4

Faithful or Forgetful?

"And just where do you think you're going, Joelle?"

Joelle's hand was already on the doorknob. "I was going next door to Jill's to see her kittens," she replied to her stepmother.

"You haven't taken Spotty out for his walk yet. I don't think you've fed him this morning." She pointed to the terrier lying on her mat near the stove.

Joelle sighed, causing her light-brown bangs to flutter. "Oh, Jane, can't I do that when I get back?" She knew the request was hopeless when she saw the firm look on her stepmother's face.

"Joelle, you promised you'd take care of the dog if we got her for you."

"Okay, okay." Joelle sighed again as she moved to feed Spotty. She bent toward the dog. "I'm sorry I forgot about you, girl."

Spotty licked the back of her hand as if saying, "I forgive you."

Joelle smiled. "Jane's right. You're faithful even when I'm not."

Your Turn

1. What are some differences between being faithful or forgetful?
2. What chores are you forgetful about? What helps you to be more faithful in doing them?

_____

_____

_____

_____

Prayer

Father God, I need your help to be faithful. Amen.

Following Jesus

Give praise to the Lord, proclaim his name!

– **Isaiah 12:4**

A Faithful Friend?

"Ugh." Sherise Miller tossed the pamphlet she'd just been handed into the garbage. "I'm sick of those."

Laura glanced at the one she'd received. It was one her Sunday-school class had once given out. She glanced at Sherise, wondering if she should say something.

"Don't you just hate it when people give out those things?" Sherise asked. "My mother says that people shouldn't try to force you to believe in God. That's why we don't go to church."

Laura didn't say anything. Then she remembered a promise she'd made in church that Sunday to be faithful to God even when others weren't.

"Want to sleep over Saturday night?" Sherise asked. "You can go out to breakfast with us on Sunday morning."

Laura hesitated. Her family went to church on Sundays, so she knew her mother would say no to the sleepover idea. She didn't know what to tell Sherise.

Your Turn

1. If Laura doesn't say anything about God to Sherise, is Laura denying her faith?
2. How do you show faithfulness to God? Why is faithfulness important??

_____

_____

_____

Prayer

Lord Jesus, help me be faithful to you no matter what. Amen.

Following Jesus

Thanks, God

God gives us many blessings every day. Fill in the journal page with words that show how God has blessed you.

Dear Journal,

When I looked out my window this morning,

I enjoyed seeing _____.

I got dressed and put on _____

and _____. I'm glad to live with

_____. When I was hungry,

I ate _____. I worked on

_____ and played with

_____.

I also enjoyed these other blessings from God:

_____

_____

_____

_____

_____

_____

_____

Prayer

Lord, writing a blessings journal every day reminds me to be thankful for all you do for me. Thank you! Amen.

Following Jesus

The Greatest Gift

Think of the most awesome gift you ever received. How did you feel when you got it? Do you still have it? Do you still like it? God gave you a gift that is far greater than anything you have received.

Decode the message on the present by crossing out: C, G, J, K, P, Q, X, Z. Write the remaining letters in order on the lines, and then separate them into words.

_____

_____

_____

_____

Prayer

Heavenly Father, every day I'm thankful for your great gift to me. I praise your holy name. Amen.

Knowing What to Do

We must obey God rather than human beings!
– Acts 5:29

A True Score

Shawna and Kelsey lived on neighboring farms. They usually spent the hour-long bus ride to school chatting, but this morning's ride was different. Kelsey could tell Shawna was upset as soon as she slid into the seat next to her.

"Are you sick?" Kelsey asked.

"Don't I wish! Then I could miss the science test today," Shawna said.

"Yeah, I know." Kelsey sighed. "I've been studying for days. I feel like my brain is ready to burst."

Shawna looked like she could cry. "My brain is empty. Not one scientific fact in it. I kept putting off studying. I was going to cram it all in last night. But I forgot my book at school. Then I couldn't sleep. Now I'm tired and ignorant!"

Kelsey thought for a minute. "I'll write really big. When you don't know an answer, you can look at my paper. No one will know."

Kelsey's very smart, thought Shawna. *She'll probably know all the answers. It would be easy.* But Shawna shook her head. "I can't do that. It would be cheating. Cheating is dishonest."

Kelsey said,"Then let's use this hour. I'll teach you all I can!"

Your Turn

1. Has your disobedience ever caused trouble for you or someone else? What happened?
2. Has your obedience ever prevented trouble? What happened?

_____

_____

Prayer

Lord, help me always be honest, even if it causes trouble. Amen.

Knowing What to Do

We must obey God rather than human beings!
– Acts 5:29

Spiritual Glue

Each student was given a Bible word to explain at the next class. Karina's word was "prayer." *I know all about that,* she thought. After church, she went to her aunt's house. Soon Karina and Aunt Linda were chatting while they glued paws, legs, and body parts to create rabbits, chicks, and ducks for the craft fair.

"What's new with you, Karina?" Aunt Linda asked.

"Not much. Wait! There is something new in Bible study." Karina explained her word assignment. "I've been praying forever though. What else is there to know?"

Aunt Linda told Karina to look at the finished wooden creatures. "What's the most important part of these animals?"

"Patterns and cutting them out exactly," Karina decided.

"That's important," her aunt agreed. "But the most important part is the glue. Without glue, they'd be a pile of pieces. Prayer is spiritual glue. It holds your Christian life together. Prayer is having heart-to-heart talks with God about anything and everything."

Karina picked up a rabbit. "May I take this to use in class?"

"Sure, hop to it!" Aunt Linda said with a laugh.

Your Turn

1. When do you pray?
2. How does prayer affect your relationship with Jesus?

Prayer

God, I'm glad I can always talk to you through prayer. Thanks for listening. Amen.

Knowing What to Do

We must obey God rather than human beings!
– Acts 5:29

Listening and Doing

"Are you listening to me, Amber?" Mother said.

"Yes," she said. She shoved a dirty sock under her bed as her mom stood in the doorway of her bedroom.

"Excellent," Mom said. "I suggest you not only listen, but also act. I want this room cleaned and the dirty clothes sloshing in the washer by the time I get back…or else!"

Amber nodded as she surveyed the disaster area. She knew that tone. Her mom wasn't just suggesting she get busy–she expected her to do it. Amber knew what "or else" meant: grounded for a week. No TV or phone privileges. This wasn't the first time her mom had asked her to clean her room.

As Amber started picking up stuff, she noticed a devotional book from her mom. Today's entry was "Obeying God." *Obey, obey, obey. Everyone wants me to obey.* Then she noticed another word: love. Amber knew her mother loved her, even though she expected her to work. *Maybe God is like that too,* she thought as she gathered dirty clothes from the floor, chairs, and closet.

Your Turn

1. How are you obeying God when you obey your parents?
2. What do you find hard and/or easy about obeying?

_____

_____

_____

Prayer

Lord, help me willingly obey you and my parents. Amen.

Knowing What to Do

We must obey God rather than human beings!
– Acts 5:29

Too Scary!

"It's too scary. I just can't do it!" exclaimed Kendall.

"Are you talking about the new roller coaster at Fun World?" asked her mother. "I know you kids have been thinking about it all week."

"No, I was thinking about how scared I would be to just walk up to a complete stranger and start preaching about Jesus."

Mrs. Baker looked surprised. "Why do you need to do that?"

Kendall answered, "My Sunday-school teacher, Miss Markson, said millions of people don't know about Jesus. Christians are supposed to obey God. Jesus said to preach the good news about him to everyone in the entire world."

"Kendall, there are lots of ways to obey Jesus' command to spread the Good News. You can invite someone to church or Sunday school. You can pray. You can give money for missions. You can share your faith by starting with people you know."

"Whew!" Kendall said. "I think I'll ask Uncle Tom to go to church with us next week. And I can ask Aleesha to go to Sunday school with me."

Your Turn

1. Do you ever feel like Kendall when you think about what God wants you to do? What do you do about it?
2. Do you find it difficult to be obedient to God? Why or why not?

_____

_____

Prayer

Jesus, I want to let people know how amazing you are. Give me the courage and the words I need. Amen.

Knowing What to Do

We must obey God rather than human beings!
– Acts 5:29

What Can I Say?

Diana was very quiet on the way home from Sunday school. She slumped in the seat and stared out the window.

Finally, her mom said, "Diana, you seem really upset. Do you want to talk about it?"

Diana sigh. "It's the same old thing. Our lesson today was about worship and going to church. All I could think of was Dad and how he never goes to church. I love Dad, and I want him to go to church with us. It's great when he goes on special occasions, such as Christmas and Easter, but I want him to go all the time."

"Maybe you should talk to your father about it," her mom said.

Diana shook her head. "I do talk to him. I ask him to come with us. He always says he's busy or tired. Sometimes he says he'll think about it. What else can I do?"

"Your heavenly Father always listens. Why not ask for his help in talking to Dad."

"Can we pray right now?" asked Diana.

Her mom answered by pulling off the road and turning off the engine.

Your Turn

1. Look up Psalm 50:15 and write it out.
2. How can you put Psalm 50:15 into practice in your life?

_____

_____

Prayer

Heavenly Father, thanks for listening to my prayers and helping me. Amen.

Knowing What to Do

Following and Obeying

The Bible is full of people who followed and obeyed God. Sometimes their obedience caused them many problems—even torture and death. Find the names of these people in the word search. If you don't know who they are, look them up!

Abraham	Esther	Job	Noah
Asa	Gideon	John	Paul
Daniel	Isaac	Joseph	Peter
David	Isaiah	Mary	Ruth
Dorcas	Jeremiah	Moses	Samuel

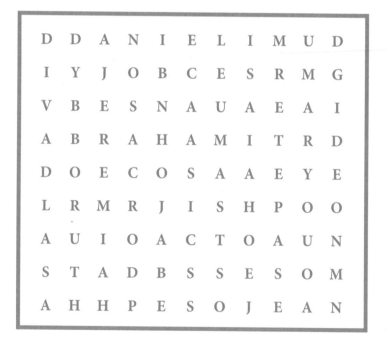

```
D  D  A  N  I  E  L  I  M  U  D
I  Y  J  O  B  C  E  S  R  M  G
V  B  E  S  N  A  U  A  E  A  I
A  B  R  A  H  A  M  I  T  R  D
D  O  E  C  O  S  A  A  E  Y  E
L  R  M  R  J  I  S  H  P  O  O
A  U  I  O  A  C  T  O  A  U  N
S  T  A  D  B  S  S  E  S  O  M
A  H  H  P  E  S  O  J  E  A  N
```

Prayer

Just like the men and women in the Bible, I want to learn to obey you every single day. Amen.

Knowing What to Do

Prayer Pretzels

The first pretzels were made as a tasty treat for kids who learned their prayers. The pretzels were shaped to look like the crossed arms of someone praying. The three holes came to represent God, Jesus, and the Holy Spirit. Ask your parents or another adult to help you make your own pretzels.

What You Need

- 4 cups flour
- 4 tablespoons sugar
- 1 teaspoon salt
- 1 package yeast
- 1½ cups warm water
- 1 egg, beaten
- Vegetable oil

Enjoy!

What to Do

1. Combine the yeast and water. Let stand for 5 to 10 minutes.
2. Add the egg, flour, salt and sugar.
3. Knead the dough on a lightly-floured surface until a smooth ball forms.
4. Ask an adult to preheat the oven to 425 degrees.
5. Roll the dough into 24 balls for small pretzels, 16 balls for larger pretzels.
6. Flatten each ball into thin strips about 10 inches long.
7. Shape the strips into pretzels by crossing the ends to make a loop, then flipping the ends back across the loop. Sprinkle with salt.
8. Place on lightly-greased baking sheets.
9. Ask an adult to bake the pretzels 15 to 20 minutes. Yummy!

Prayer

Lord, please remind me to pray about everything because I know you care. Amen.

Using Your Talents and Resources

God has given each of you a gift from his great variety of spiritual gifts. Use them well to serve one another.

– 1 Peter 4:10 NLT

A Good Steward (Part 1)

"Grandma gave me $20 for my birthday!" Cate said as she burst into the family room. There was a big grin on her freckled face as she proudly displayed the crisp bill. "Now I have enough to get those inline skates!"

Her father glanced up from the newspaper. "What's wrong with your old pair?" he asked, pulling off his reading glasses.

"Daaaad! Everybody has the new Rollmatic 2000s."

"Don't they cost more than $160? There's nothing wrong with your old skates. You haven't even had them a year. Do you remember when we talked about being good stewards?"

Cate looked at the floor. "Yes, but I didn't know what that meant."

"It means taking good care of what God gives you. That includes being careful about how you spend money. It also means using what you have to help others. If you spend all your money on skates, are you being a good steward?"

Cate wanted to say yes, but decided to say nothing.

"I just want you to consider your options. What could you do instead of buying expensive skates?"

Your Turn

1. Why did her father think Cate she rethink her money plan?
2. What other things could Cate do with her money?

Prayer

Teach me, Lord, to be a good steward over everything you give me. Amen.

Using Your Talents and Resources

God has given each of you a gift from his great variety of spiritual gifts. Use them well to serve one another.

– 1 Peter 4:10 NLT

A Good Steward (Part 2)

"Where are you off to?"asked Jake.

Cate smiled at her best friend. "I'm going to tutor Mrs. Frankel's nephew in math." Mrs. Frankel was Cate's neighbor. Her nephew Mark had just come to live with her.

Jake's mouth dropped open as he gazed at her over his glasses. "Tutor? You? I thought you hated doing that."

Cate felt a little reluctant to tell Jake that she was trying to be a good steward. She knew he'd scoff.

"So, what's the deal, Cate? You like him or something?"

Cate blushed to the roots of her carrot-colored hair. "No! I'm just trying to do something to help someone."

"You like him." Jake sounded confident.

"I don't!" Cate asserted.

"So, why are you doing this?" Jake persisted.

She didn't know where to begin. She'd always been good at math. It came easily to her. Her mother reminded her of that one day, and that's why she'd decided to do more tutoring. "It's a long story, Jake. If you're home, maybe I'll tell you about it when I get back."

Your Turn

1. How did Cate plan to be a good steward?
2. Have you ever been hesitant to share plans because they involved God?

Prayer

I want to do my part to help others, Lord. Please show me what to do. Amen.

Using Your Talents and Resources

God has given each of you a gift from his great variety of spiritual gifts. Use them well to serve one another.

– 1 Peter 4:10 NLT

Turn Off the News

Brianna walked into the family room just as her dad turned on the evening news. "Could we please watch something else?" she asked. "Maybe there's something better on channel 15." Her dad didn't change the channel, so Brianna turned to leave.

"Wait a minute," said her dad. "You don't have to leave just because you can't watch what you want."

"Dad, I'm not upset because you didn't change channels. It's just that watching the news makes me upset. All the terrible things that happen."

"I have a suggestion. Not seeing or hearing about bad news won't make it go away. Why don't we watch the news together and talk about it when it's over? If you understand what's going on and why, you might find some way to change things. Also, you can pray about specific situations."

"That sounds like a good idea, Dad. It will be interesting to discuss what's going on in the world with you." She sat down next to her dad, ready to try a new experience.

Your Turn

1. How do you react to distressing news stories you hear or read about?
2. How will discussing the news with her Dad help Brianna?

Prayer

Loving God, please help and comfort people who are having trouble. Amen.

Using Your Talents and Resources

God has given each of you a gift from his great variety of spiritual gifts. Use them well to serve one another.

– 1 Peter 4:10 NLT

Trust Exercise

"Okay, let's try a trust exercise," The youth pastor announced.

"Now what?" Sharon whispered to her friend Lacey. "Last week he had us fall backwards into each other's arms."

Lacey nodded. Nobody had wanted to do that at first. The nervous feeling was confirmed when Jason failed to catch Patricia. Everyone had gasped when she'd crashed to the floor.

"Okay, I want everyone to think of one thing that worries you a lot."

Sharon instantly thought of her upcoming science quiz. She had to pass it or get an F for the year.

"Got something? Good. Now give it totally to God. Trusting God is the opposite of worrying. When you give something to him, you let go of it."

Sharon glanced at Lacey. That's easy to say, Sharon thought.

"That's easy to say, right?" the youth pastor said, as if he'd read Sharon's mind. "We worry because we're leaning on our own understanding about a problem or situation. That's not what God wants us to do."

Sharon frowned. How would giving it to God help her pass?

Your Turn

1. What does it mean to you to trust the Lord?
2. What worries you? Make a list and then talk to Jesus about them.

Prayer

Lord, I get so worried about what's happening around me and around the world. Please help me trust you to let me know what to do. Amen.

Using Your Talents and Resources

God has given each of you a gift from his great variety of spiritual gifts. Use them well to serve one another.

– 1 Peter 4:10 NLT

Too Trusting?

"I told you. I told you not to trust her."

Jenna hated hearing "I told you so." Her older sister, Brianna, was good at saying that. Jenna was almost sorry she'd told Brianna about Sarah. At sixteen, Brianna acted like a know-it-all at times.

Still, Jenna could hardly believe what Sarah had done. She'd stolen Jenna's idea for the School Spirit Poster Contest. Jenna had shown Sarah what she planned to enter in the contest when it was finished. The next thing she knew, Sarah had copied the poster and entered it herself.

"I thought I could trust her," Jenna said." After all, she was my friend." Tears filled her green eyes.

Brianna snorted. "Some friend! What did she ever do to earn your trust?"

Jenna thought about that. She couldn't think of anything. She hadn't known Sarah that long.

"It doesn't pay to be too trusting. Well, in most cases. There's only one person you can always trust, no matter what."

Jenna thought she knew the answer, but decided to confirm it. "Who?"

"Jesus!"

Your Turn

1. How did Sarah betray Jenna's trust?
2. Has a friend ever done that to you? How did you feel?

Prayer

Jesus, I put my trust totally in you. Amen.

Using Your Talents and Resources

What Can You Do?

How will you use your talents to help others? Come up with a plan of action!

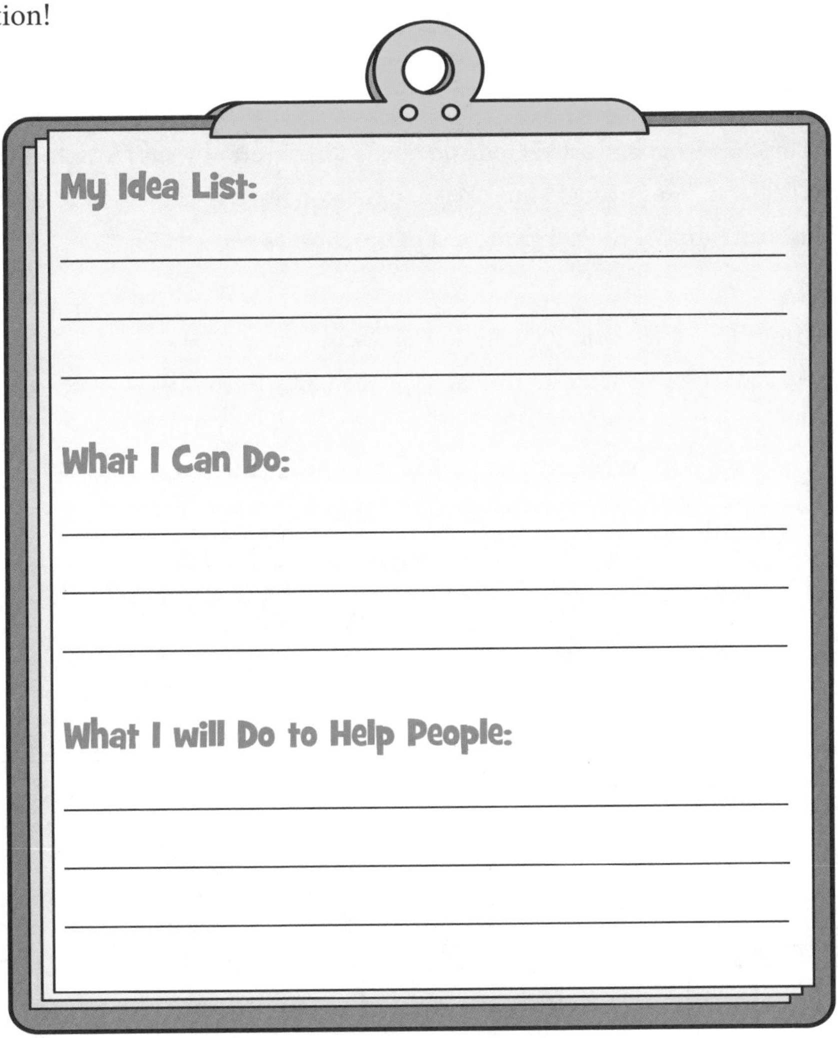

My Idea List:

_____

_____

_____

What I Can Do:

_____

_____

_____

What I will Do to Help People:

_____

_____

_____

Prayer

Heavenly Father, you have blessed me with certain abilities and resources. Show me how to share them. Amen.

Using Your Talents and Resources

Trust—New Testament Style

Many people in the New Testament showed their trust in God. Solve the crossword clues to find out some of their names.

Across

4. Jesus helped this _____ woman to trust him as the Messiah (John 4).

7. This businesswoman trusted God and opened her heart to Jesus (Acts 16:14).

9. This helper of Jesus trusted him enough to walk on water (Matthew 14:28-29).

10. This man introduced Paul to the rest of the apostles (Acts 9:27).

Down

1. This apostle met Jesus on the road to Damascus (Acts 9:1-9).

2. He trusted God to care for him even in prison (Acts 16:16-40).

3. She believed Jesus could help her brother Lazarus (John 11:24-27).

5. He said Jesus was the Messiah and brought his brother to him (John 1:40).

6. He wanted to call "fire down from heaven" (Luke 9:51-54).

8. She believed God's word that she would have a son (Luke 1:26-38).

When Life Isn't Easy

Offer your bodies as a living sacrifice, holy and pleasing to God.

– Romans 12:1

I Don't Accept!

"You just don't want to be my friend!" Faith yelled into the phone before shutting it down.

She realized her Uncle Ned stood in the kitchen doorway staring at her. "It's Jenny," she explained, almost spitting the name out. Her brown eyes flashed angrily. "Her excuse this time for not wanting to come to my sleepover is that her family is having company."

"Why do you keep inviting her?" Uncle Ned asked.

Faith shrugged. She didn't want to admit how much she wanted Jenny to be her friend.

"You know, you sounded just like your grandma did when you said you couldn't accept your friend's excuse. Do you remember she had trouble accepting that Jesus died for her sins? Some people are not as accepting as others."

"What does that mean?"

Uncle Ned walked into the kitchen. "Well, it takes longer for them to adjust to a new situation. They make excuses like your friend Jenny did."

"Ex-friend. Why can't they just change?"

"Change takes time and patience. Gentle persuasion and perseverance go further than irritation."

Your Turn

1. What do you have trouble accepting?
2. How can you change your approach to it?

Prayer

Lord, I joyfully accept your love and forgiveness. Help me accept others the way you accept me. Amen.

When Life Isn't Easy

Offer your bodies as a living sacrifice, holy and pleasing to God.
– Romans 12:1

True Friends

Caitlyn felt her cheeks grow hot, She knew they were as red as a stoplight. *How could I be so stupid?* she thought. *I wish I could just disappear into thin air.* Instead, she had to walk across the auditorium stage and sit down.

Caitlyn had been the school spelling champ for two years. But today she had misspelled "handkerchief," so she was out of the spelling bee.

At lunch, Caitlyn sat in the corner by herself. She kept her head down as she nibbled at her sandwich.

Abigail scooted in next to her. "Why are you sitting way over here? Come, eat with the rest of us."

Caitlyn mumbled, "I'm too embarrassed. I studied for weeks and then I bombed out on an easy word. Everyone probably thinks I'm stupid."

"Don't be S-I-L-L-Y. We know you can out-spell us any day. Besides, we're your F-R-I-E-N-D-S, and friends like you all the time, even when you are upset or E-M-B-A-uh E-M-B A…um, embarrassed," Abigail said.

Caitlyn laughed as she joined her friends. "Thanks, guys. You are true friends."

Your Turn

1. How can you be a friend who never strands or abandons someone?

_____

_____

_____

Prayer

Lord, I want to stick with my friends. I can do that with your help. Amen.

When Life Isn't Easy

Offer your bodies as a living sacrifice, holy and pleasing to God.

– Romans 12:1

Karen's Cousin

Karen paused outside the hospital room. What do you say to a 12-year-old who is dying of cancer? When she walked into the room, Melissa sat up in bed and waved to her.

Karen was surprised to see the big smile on her cousin's thin, pale face. *I'd be miserable if I were her,* Karen thought.

"I'm glad you came," Melissa said. "Where's your mom?"

"She stopped to talk to the nurse. So, how are you feeling?"

Melissa shrugged. "Okay. Hey, want to watch some TV with me?"

Karen nodded. How could Melissa seem so normal?

"Why are you so quiet?" Melissa asked. "Actually, everybody's been that way ever since the doctor said I'm going to die."

Karen was relieved that Melissa said the "D" word herself. It was less awkward. "I think God is really mean to let this happen to you," Karen said.

"I'm not mad at God anymore," Melissa said. "I was at first, but now I know this isn't God's fault."

Karen held back her tears as she hugged her cousin.

Your Turn

1. Why was Melissa so calm about dying?
2. Look up Job 1:21 and write it out. What does this verse mean?

_____

_____

_____

Prayer

Lord, I trust you even when life is hard. Amen.

When Life Isn't Easy

Offer your bodies as a living sacrifice, holy and pleasing to God.

– Romans 12:1

The Perfect Day

"Yahoo!" whooped Toneika as she clicked off the phone. Her brother almost got trampled as she danced around the kitchen.

"Have you gone completely ballistic?" Todd asked.

Out of breath, Toneika flopped into a chair. "Uncle Stu said I could invite six friends for a day at his ranch. He'll take us trail riding, and we can have a campfire dinner. It will be a perfect day—just horses and friends."

"Hard to tell who's more important to you—horses or friends."

Toneika ignored her brother. She absolutely loved everything about horses. She'd been riding since she was four.

"Who you gonna invite?" Todd asked.

Toneika hesitated. "Well, Sara, Tiffany, Michelle, and Paige would be fun."

"How about Liz? You can invite one more."

Toneika frowned. Liz was a terrible rider. She didn't ride much, so she was slow, cautious, and always asking for help.

Todd shook his head. "I guess horses are more important." He quickly left as Toneika glared at him.

What does he know? thought Toneika. Then she remembered all the times Liz helped her at things she couldn't do very well.

Your Turn

1. If you were Toneika, would you invite Liz? Why or why not?

_____

_____

Prayer

Lord, I want to always be a thoughtful, considerate friend. Amen.

When Life Isn't Easy

Offer your bodies as a living sacrifice, holy and pleasing to God.

– Romans 12:1

The Gift

Madison Gordon burst into the house, her face glowing with excitement. "Look what Mr. Wheeler just gave us, Dad!" she said as she placed a handful of cash on the table where her father sat reading the newspaper.

"Sixty dollars?" her father said, his eyebrows raised.

"He said he wanted to help us since…well, since you lost your job last week."

Her father frowned and then snapped the paper to another page. "Take the money back. We're not that bad off."

"But, Dad…"

"We don't need charity. We'll be fine." He pushed the money toward Madison.

Madison didn't understand why he wouldn't accept the money. Then she had an idea. "Hey, Dad, remember when you told me that God died for us and that his death was a free gift? We couldn't earn it. All we had to do was take it, right?"

Her father nodded.

Madison held out the money. "Why can't we look at this money like that?"

Her father sighed. "Okay, I get the message."

Your Turn

1. What was Madison's advice?
2. How has someone's advice helped you accept the truth about something?

Prayer

God, help me accept your will for my life. Amen.

When Life Isn't Easy

A Way to Accept

Here is a message that will help you be accepting and persevering when hard times come.

- EP + S +   - B

H +   - C - T

YOUR 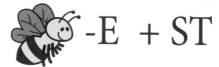 -E + ST

INTERESTS  -B

_____

_____

Prayer

Lord, please help me accept the things that come into my life. I belong to you and I believe you will work for my good. Amen.

When Life Isn't Easy

Jesus' Friends

Jesus is a friend to *all* people. The Bible tells us about some of Jesus' friends. Can you decipher their descriptions? To decode the words, remove the "ay" at the end of each word and then move the last remaining letter to the beginning of the word. For example, "undaysay choolsay" is "Sunday school."

Jesus was a friend of...

INNERSSAY _____

AXTAY OLLECTORSCAY _____

LINDBAY _____

AMELAY _____

OORPAY _____

EPERSLAY _____

HILDRENCAY _____

EGGARSBAY _____

Jesus is also a friend of _____ _____

(Write your name in code and then decode it.)

Prayer

Dear Lord, I want to be a friend to people like you are. Amen.

Helping People

We must help the weak…Jesus himself said:
"It is more blessed to give than to receive."

– Acts 20:35

A Pleasant Surprise

"Exciting news!" Mr. Simons announced. "We have the honor of visiting Manor View Nursing Home every other Sunday for the next two months. It will be fun singing for the residents and visiting with them."

Exciting, honor, fun? thought Aubrey. *Being with a lot of sick, old people?*

After the singing, Aubrey and Von approached a white-haired man who had tapped his foot to the music. Mr. Simons came and said, "Aubrey and Von, meet Paul Banks. "Paul, Von and Aubrey."

Paul was tall and portly. He held a cane with a dragon's head. He shook hands with Aubrey and Von. "I'm glad you came. I was a teacher, and I miss seeing young people."

Soon Aubrey was having a great time listening to Paul's stories about teaching school before computer technology. Von enjoyed the stories of farm life. Paul encouraged both kids to enjoy learning and to try new things.

When it was time to leave, Aubrey said, "I can't wait to come back next time. I'll bring pictures of my family and dog."

"This was fun," Von announced.

Your Turn

1. How was Aubrey and Von helpful to Paul?
2. How was Paul helpful to Aubrey and Von?

Prayer

Dear God, everyone has interesting stories. Give me a discerning heart and wisdom for listening. Amen.

Helping People

We must help the weak...Jesus himself said:
"It is more blessed to give than to receive."

– Acts 20:35

A Dirty Job

"Whew! What stinks?" gasped Erika.

"Smells like something died!" said her sister, Julia, as she held her nose.

They'd just gotten off the school bus. The closer they got to home, the worse the smell became. When they rounded the corner, they found the "stinker." A huge pile of mulch and compost had been dumped on their mom's garden. Their mother was trundling a wheelbarrow of the stuff to a corner flowerbed.

"Hi, girls!" she said. "Isn't it a beautiful spring day?"

"Maybe if you put a clothespin on your nose," said Julia.

Their mother laughed. She looked at the pile. "Three cubic yards of compost is a lot! It's going to take me forever to get this spread."

While the twins were having a snack, they discussed Mother's Day, which was Sunday. After considering several gift ideas, they settled on one.

In the garden, Erika said, "Mom, we're going to give you an early Mother's Day present. We'll borrow two wheelbarrows, and help you move this smelly pile."

"It's a dirty job but somebody's got to do it," chimed in Julia. "Any gas masks?"

Your Turn

1. What made the girls' gift really special?
2. Are you willing to use your time and energy to help someone?

Prayer

Lord, show me how to be helpful to those around me and then do it. Amen.

Helping People

We must help the weak…Jesus himself said:
"It is more blessed to give than to receive."

– Acts 20:35

Way to Go!

Maren had watched her three older brothers play baseball from the time she was a toddler. As soon as she was old enough, Maren played on Little League teams. She loved everything about baseball. Her first baseman's trapper mitt was her prized possession. She dreamed of playing professional baseball.

Maren played for the Springfield White Sox. The team wasn't bad, but they weren't good either. That didn't matter. Maren always did her best when she was playing first base and batting.

Maren was also the team's cheerleader. She encouraged the pitcher from first base: "Way to go, girl! Two down and one to go. You can do it."

When she was sitting in the dugout, Maren talked up each batter. "Slow and steady!" "Keep your eye on the ball." "Hit that baby."

One day after a game, Coach Wilson said to Maren, "I think your mouth gets as much of a workout as the rest of your body."

Oh, thought Maren. *I'm talking too much. Guess I'd better tone down.*

The coach continued. "You're an encouragement. Keep it up!"

Your Turn

1. How do you feel when someone says kind or encouraging words to you?
2. How can you encourage people—including yourself?

_____

_____

Prayer

Lord Jesus, help me to say helpful, kind, and encouraging words to those around me. Amen.

Helping People

We must help the weak…Jesus himself said:
"It is more blessed to give than to receive."

– Acts 20:35

"Let Me Carry Them!"

"Why do you keep trying to carry my backpack?" Steve asked as he paused in the middle of the sidewalk in front of the middle school.

Mindy Gerard almost giggled when she saw the annoyed look on her friend's sunburned face. "I'm trying to carry your burdens," she said as she yanked the bag's strap from his shoulder. He almost fell over.

"My what?" The look on Steve's face changed to puzzlement.

"Your burdens," Mindy patiently explained. "That means I'm supposed to care about you, ya dope. Now, let me carry your backpack to the bus stop."

Steve turned to look at the bus stop. "Wow. A whole ten feet from here. Gee, thanks."

He turned back to Mindy. "So, when I asked you to help me figure out my algebra homework yesterday, how come you didn't want to help if you're so concerned?"

Mindy laughed. "I'd rather carry your backpack."

"Oh," laughed Steve. "You are a 'selective' burden carrier?"

Your Turn

1. Look up and write out Galatians 6:2. How does it apply to you?
2. Do you choose how to help or do you let the person you're helping choose?

_____

_____

_____

Prayer

Lord, show me how to best help people. Amen.

Helping People

We must help the weak...Jesus himself said:
"It is more blessed to give than to receive."

– Acts 20:35

Wesley Street Church

Heather Billek couldn't help being curious after hearing her mother say, "How terrible!" several times.

"What's terrible?" she asked after her mother turned off the phone.

"Wesley Street Church had a fire in its Sunday-school wing yesterday."

Heather grabbed an apple from a nearby bowl. "I thought we didn't like that church."

Mrs. Billek threw her a puzzled look. "Just because we don't worship together doesn't mean we don't care about each other."

Heather remembered a conversation they'd had the previous year. Her church and Wesley Street Church used to be one church. Because of a big argument, some of the members had left to form Wesley Street Church.

"I still don't understand why we're not all worshipping as one church," Heather said.

"Well, people don't always get along together. But even when we disagree, we will help each other—especially if something bad happens. We can still care for each other even though we have different views."

Your Turn

1. Do you have to like someone to care about that person?
   Why or why not?
2. Who do you have a difficult time with? What will you do about it?

Prayer

God, I don't always get along with people 24/7. Please break open my heart so your love pours through it. Amen.

Helping People

Dori and Emily

Dori the Discourager looks for faults and failings in people. Emily the Encourager looks on the positive side and tries to be helpful in what she says. How would Emily respond in these situations?

Dori: I've told you 10 times how to do these math problems. Why can't you learn it?

Emily: _____

_____

Dori: What is that supposed to be a painting of? I can't recognize anything on it.

Emily: _____

_____

Dori: You need batting practice. You left two girls on base when you struck out.

Emily: _____

_____

Dori: Your clothes are okay, I guess. Where did you say you got them?

Emily: _____

_____

Prayer

Lord, please help me be an encourager. Amen.

Helping People

God's Helper

You can be God's helper by helping people who are sad, lonely, or in negative situations. Look at each picture and write down how you can help and what you can say to remind these people that God loves them and is with them.

_____

_____

_____

_____

_____

_____

Prayer

God, please help me be active in helping people and praying for them. Amen.

Letting God's Heart Show

Let us draw near to God with a sincere heart and with the full assurance that faith brings.

– Hebrews 10:22

Prayer Isn't Magic

"God, please help me get an 'A' on my algebra quiz. If you do, I promise I won't tease my sister for a week. In Jesus' name and your will be done. Amen." She was satisfied about her prayer until she received her grade. "A 'C-'!" she complained later to her aunt. Chelsea ran a hand through her hair in frustration. "I needed an 'A' to get a 'C' for the year, so that's what I prayed for."

"You said you prayed about this? What did you pray?"

Chelsea grabbed a bag of fruit snacks. "That I'd get an 'A.' I even said, 'Your will be done,' like the Lord's Prayer says."

Her aunt shook her head. "Did you study for the quiz?"

"Well…a little."

"Chelsea, prayer isn't a magic formula. God will help you, but he seldom does all the work for you. You have to put in the necessary time and energy for what you're praying for. Remember Colossians 3:23? 'Whatever you do, work at it with all your heart, as working for the Lord.' Did you do that?"

Your Turn

1. Was Chelsea's heart in the right place when she prayed?
2. What happens when your prayer doesn't match your willingness to work toward the goal?

Prayer

Lord God, sometimes I may need to be reminded that I need to do my part when I ask you for something. Amen.

Letting God's Heart Show

Let us draw near to God with a sincere heart and with the full assurance that faith brings.

– Hebrews 10:22

A Big Phony?

"You're looking lovely today, Mom."

Brooke almost gagged when she heard her twin brother, Brett, compliment their mother in the hallway.

"Why thank you, Brett." Mrs. Gleason squeezed his shoulder as she went by.

"You phony!" Brooke hissed as Brett grinned. She felt tempted to grab a handful of his hair. "I know why you're being all nice to Mom. You're trying to butter her up so she'll let you go to the movies on Friday even though you're on punishment." Brooke rolled her eyes. She was tempted to tell her mother what a phony Brett was, but she didn't want to be a snitch, even though Brett deserved it.

Later that day, Brooke was about to enter the family room when she overheard her mother talking to Brett. "Brett, your father and I told you that you can't go to the movies. You're on punishment."

"Aw, Mom…"

"Honey, I've lived on this earth a lot longer than you have. Don't you think I know when you're being sincere and when you're up to something? Next time, try a little sincerity. You might get further."

Your Turn

1. Was Brett sincere or insincere?
2. Are you sincere all the time, most of the time, some of the time, or just a few times? Explain.

Prayer

Lord Jesus, help me be sincere and honest in my thoughts, words, and actions. Amen.

Letting God's Heart Show

*Let us draw near to God with a sincere heart and with
the full assurance that faith brings.*

– Hebrews 10:22

A Sincere Way to Love

Caroline came home in a snit.
If she saw Shannon once more, she'd have a fit.
    Shannon made her life a tale of woe.
    From morning 'til recess she bugged her so.
    Shannon was in her sixth-grade class.
    She once tripped Caroline as she tried to pass.
On Sunday, Caroline heard some bad news.
It threatened to change all of her views.
"You must love your enemies," her teacher said.
Those words filled Caroline with dread.
    When the teacher said, "Love must be sincere,"
    Caroline thought, *Okay, stop right here.*
    I cannot love Shannon. She makes me sick.
    To her I only can say sincerely, "Ick."
"I'll show you the way to truly love,"
her teacher said. "This love comes from God above.
"He is the key to hope so dear.
He'll love through you—never fear."
    Now Caroline's heart felt truly glad.
    God does all the work. That ain't so bad!

Your Turn

1. God does all the loving, but what must Caroline do?

_____

_____

Prayer

Lord, I want to open my heart to your love for everyone. Amen.

Letting God's Heart Show

Let us draw near to God with a sincere heart and with the full assurance that faith brings.

– Hebrews 10:22

Share-o-Lot?

"Cassie, may I have some?"

Cassandra shook her head. *Every time I get a candy bar, Kayla wants some.* Cassie happened to have her favorite candy bar in the world: Chock-o-Lot. She didn't want to share it with anyone.

Kayla, the beads in her braids softly clicking, skipped over to Cassandra's friend. "Stephanie, may I have some of yours?"

"Sure. Here you go." Stephanie broke off half of her candy bar.

Kayla ran off to play with her friend Samantha. She returned to the porch ten minutes later with her hands behind her back. "I've got something for you," she said to Stephanie. "Guess which hand."

Stephanie tapped Kayla's left arm.

Kayla nodded and brought both hands forward. The left one held a cupcake covered with M&Ms. "Samantha's mom just made these. She said I could give one away."

Stephanie said thank you, and Kayla skipped off.

As Cassandra sighed in annoyance, Stephanie grinned and bit into the cupcake.

Your Turn

1. Besides half her candy bar, what did Stephanie give Kayla?
2. When it comes to sharing something you enjoy, what is your usual attitude?

_____

_____

Prayer

Lord, sometimes I don't want to share. Remind me that all I have comes from you, and you want me to share. Amen.

Letting God's Heart Show

*Let us draw near to God with a sincere heart and with
the full assurance that faith brings.*

– Hebrews 10:22

A Generous Return

Randi Patterson glanced at the two quarters in her hand. They were
all she had to give in Sunday school. They were all the money she had
period. *It's not much, but at least I have something to give,* she thought
as she tossed them into the offering basket at the door. *Now I don't have
any money for Temira's party. Oh, well.*

Temira's birthday party was held right after church at a pizza parlor.
Invited kids lined up at a booth to buy tokens to play the arcade games.
Randi hung around the table, talking to Temira's parents.

"Need some money for tokens?" Temira's father suddenly asked. He
handed Randi two dollars without waiting for an answer.

Randi thanked him and ran off to play Skee Ball first. She was
thrilled when, after sinking her second ball, a blue light flashed and bells
sounded. Dozens of prize tickets came out of a small box at the end of
the Skee Ball lane. Randi jumped up and down with excitement.

Your Turn

1. What did Randi give? Who did she give it to?
2. Does giving money to God mean you'll receive money, prizes, and
   other earthly rewards?

_____

_____

_____

Prayer

Lord, help me give from my heart with no expectation of reward. Amen.

Letting God's Heart Show

A Sincere Need

To be sincere, you'll need this. With a bright crayon or marker, color the shapes with the letters found in the word "sincere."

Prayer

Dear Lord, please teach me to have a sincere and loving heart. Amen.

Letting God's Heart Show

The Pledge

Cross out the X's, Q's, J's, and Z's to find a pledge you can make to increase your sincerity.

QBJEZ   JDEXQVJOTZEQD   TZOJ

____   _____   ____

XOZNEQ   ZANJOXTQHEJR   JIQXN

____   _____   ____

JLOQVXE   ZHOXNOQRJ

____.   _____

JOZNQE   AXNOJTQHZERJ

____   _____

XAZBOQVJE   ZYOJURQSEJLXVEZSQ

____   _____.

Prayer

Show me, Father, how to be sincerely devoted to you and everything you created. Amen.

Honesty and Respect

Show proper respect to everyone, love the family of believers, fear God, honor the emperor.

– 1 Peter 2:17

The Mistake

One Saturday, Kari, Jasmine, and Brigit met at the mall for an afternoon of shopping. After having a snack, they headed toward their favorite stores. Kari found two CDs she wanted, and Jasmine bought a fuzzy sweatshirt.

"Brigit, what are you going to buy? You haven't spent a cent," said Kari.

"Let's go to Teen Town," Kari suggested. "I need some new jeans and maybe a sweater. They have some really fun clothes."

After much looking and trying on, Brigit found the perfect jeans. She also found a sweater, but she didn't have quite enough money.

The girls decided to end their shopping with ice cream sundaes. Brigit opened her wallet. "Something's wrong! I have too much money." She spread it out on the table. "I should have six dollars, but I have eleven. The cashier at Teen Town must have given me too much change. I need to take it back. Wait for me."

"Are you crazy?" asked Kari. "It was her mistake. Now you can buy that sweater."

Brigit shook her head as she got up. "That wouldn't be honest."

Your Turn

1. Is being honest that important? After all, many people aren't.
2. Is telling "white lies" or "not sweating the little lies" acceptable sometimes? Explain.

Prayer

Lord, help me be honest in every situation. Amen.

Honesty and Respect

*Show proper respect to everyone, love the family of believers,
fear God, honor the emperor.*

– 1 Peter 2:17

The Music Story

Ellery did some quick thinking when she saw her mother's car in the driveway. What could she say to convince her she had a good reason for being late instead of stopping at a friend's to listen to music when she was supposed to go straight home? *I'll say I had some music things to do after school,* she decided. That was sort of true since she'd taken five minutes to help Ms. Bentley straighten the music room.

Ellery slithered into the house, but her mother heard.

"Why were you so late?"

Ellery busied herself putting away her school things as she rattled off her explanation in one breath.

Her mother said, "Ellery, I've known you since you were born. So, why don't you start over and tell me the whole truth this time?"

Ellery twisted her hair and blew out a big breath before blurting out the entire reason for being late.

Mother gave Ellery a long, serious look. "Ellery, you know lying is wrong. When you only tell part of the story, that's the same as lying. Next time be completely honest."

Your Turn

1. When are you usually tempted to keep back part of the truth?
2. Do you agree that not telling the whole truth is the same as lying?

_____

_____

Prayer

Lord, help me follow your rules so I'm not tempted to lie. Amen.

Honesty and Respect

Show proper respect to everyone, love the family of believers,
fear God, honor the emperor.

– 1 Peter 2:17

A Gentle Answer

"Look at me!" said five-year-old Moira as she twirled into Vanessa's bedroom.

"Why do you have those clothes on?" Vanessa asked as she surveyed her little sister's outfit. Moira was wearing a pink shirt with purple flowers and a blue-and-yellow plaid skirt. Red tights covered her legs, and on her feet were white sandals. Shiny beads were the finishing touch.

Moira looked in the mirror. "Aunt Sue and Uncle Ron are coming for dinner. I like them, and I wanted to look pretty. What do you think?"

Words like "yuk" and "terrible" came to Vanessa's mind. Any of them fit. Moira could be pesky and annoying. But the happy look on Moira's face stopped Vanessa's negative words. "You sure picked out a colorful outfit," she said honestly. "Aunt Sue and Uncle Ron will love it." That was honest too, because their aunt and uncle always loved seeing them. They thought Moira was funny, so they would appreciate this bizarre outfit.

"Oh, goody! I can't wait to see them. Thanks, Nessa." Moira whooshed out of the room singing her favorite song.

Your Turn

1. Why do you think Vanessa didn't tell Moira exactly what she thought?
2. How can you always give an honest, yet gentle, answer?

Prayer

Father, I want to be honest, but I don't want to hurt people. Help me know the difference. Amen.

Honesty and Respect

Show proper respect to everyone, love the family of believers,
fear God, honor the emperor.

– 1 Peter 2:17

Worthy of Respect

The soccer game between the Hartsville Hornets and the Midland Marvels was about to commence. "I wish we'd just start," Renee said to April. "I hate waiting around."

"We're going to be waiting a little longer," April responded, pointing to the band and color guard who performed the flag ceremony. Everyone stood for the national anthem.

More delay! Renee thought impatiently. *Might as well tighten my shoelaces.*

It was a rough-and-tumble game, but the Hornets won. The girls whooped it up as they settled on the bench after the game.

Coach George said, "You played a great game! I'm proud of you. Unfortunately, I'm not proud of something I observed."

The girls had puzzled looks on their faces. What was coach talking about?

"Most of you were doing something else during the flag ceremony. The proper behavior is to place your hand over your heart, look at the flag, and join in singing the national anthem. When you respect our country's flag, you show respect to your country, its leaders, and the people who fought to give you the freedoms you enjoy—including playing soccer."

Your Turn

1. How do you show respect for your flag?
2. Why does God expect us to respect our country and its leaders?

Prayer

Lord, thank you for the freedoms I enjoy. Help me respect my country and its leaders. Amen.

Honesty and Respect

Show proper respect to everyone, love the family of believers,
fear God, honor the emperor.

– **1 Peter 2:17**

"R" Is for Respect

The fifth-grade Sunday-school class was waiting for Mrs. Tober. They weren't waiting quietly. Boys were clowning around, and everyone was talking. Tami grinned. "Hey, let's play the name game." In this game, players took turns thinking of descriptive words for a person using each letter in his or her name. Sometimes it was fun; sometimes it was kind of mean.

Three other girls joined Tami and Ramona. "Let's do Tober," Tami suggested.

Ramona suggested "timid" and "tiny" for the letter "T." Tami said "O" for "out-of-style," which caused a lot of laughing. "Boring" seemed to go well with the letter "B," and "easy" was paired with "E" because it was easy to get away with things in class.

Tami poked Victoria. "Your turn. You have 'R.' Make it good!"

"How about 'respect'?" Victoria said. "Mrs. Tober shows respect to God and teaches us God's Word, so we should respect her. Respecting people is the right thing to do even when we don't like everything about them."

The girls were still quiet when Mrs. Tober walked in.

Your Turn
1. Do you show respect to adults? Why or why not?
2. How does showing respect for adults help you?

Prayer
Lord, remind me to be respectful in my words and actions. Amen.

Honesty and Respect

Expressing Your Respect

You probably have many adults, other than family, with whom you come in contact. They may be schoolteachers, coaches, Sunday-school teachers, and club leaders. How can you show respect and appreciation for what they do? Use one (or several) of these suggestions to brighten the day of an adult.

Write a Note
Tell what you like about your leader and the class.

Send a Card
If you're not sure what to say, find a card that says "thank you" for you. Then write a short note and sign it.

Draw a Picture
If you can express yourself better by drawing than writing, go for it! Draw something you did together or something the person likes (cars, flowers, animals, etc.).

Tell Them
Tell the leaders "thank you" personally after a class or meeting.

Group Project
Get some of the other kids to work together on a group project. Create a poster with pictures and notes or a card signed by everyone. Give it to the leader on a special occasion, such as a birthday.

Prayer
Dear Lord, help me be respectful to the adults in my life and not a burden. Amen.

Honesty and Respect

Researching the Flag

Your country's flag is so familiar that you may hardly notice it. But it is the symbol of your country, and there is a reason for each color and item on the flag. Do a little research to find out more, and then find information on the Christian flag. It's quite interesting!

What do the symbols on your country's flag represent?

_____

What do the colors stand for?

_____

When was the first flag of your country made? What did it look like?

_____

What are some ways people show respect to your country's flag?

_____

What do the symbols on the Christian flag represent?

_____

Name one interesting thing you discovered about the Christian flag.

_____

Prayer

Heavenly Father, help me respect my country and my country's leaders. Amen.

Mercy and Real Love

The wisdom that comes from heaven
is first of all pure; then...full of mercy.

– James 3:17

Dina's Dilemma

Dina smiled, amazed at what had happened. She'd owed a dollar in library fines. After searching her pockets, she realized she'd forgotten her money. She really needed to check out some books that day to write a report for school.

A teenaged boy at the circulation desk had pulled a dollar out of his own pocket and entered the payment to clear the fine. "You can pay me back when you come in next time," he said.

As Dina left the library, she saw her uncle, a traffic policeman, standing next to a parked car, getting ready to write a ticket.

"Wait!" she heard someone yell from the window of the library. "I'll be out in a second." It was the boy who had given her a dollar to pay her fine.

"Please don't give him a ticket!" Dina pleaded. She explained the situation.

Her uncle sighed but agreed to wait. When the teenager ran out with change in his hand, Dina's uncle said, "You owe this young lady some thanks."

The boy looked at Dina and smiled.

Your Turn

1. How did the library employee receive mercy in return for his merciful act?
2. Have you ever received mercy instead of punishment? How did you feel?

Prayer

Lord Jesus, thank you for showing mercy to me. Amen.

Mercy and Real Love

*The wisdom that comes from heaven
is first of all pure; then…full of mercy.*

– James 3:17

Right Where I Want You

Anna smiled grimly. She had Devon right where she wanted her! When they were in the fourth grade, Devon used to make fun of the way that Anna played volleyball. Over the summer, Anna had taken volleyball lessons at the gym. Now she was one of the best players in the fifth grade. That's how she wound up being chosen to be the captain of one of the volleyball teams. "You can pick who you want on your team," the gym teacher said.

Anna watched Devon squirm. Anna knew that Lisa, the other team captain, would not be in a hurry to choose Devon because Devon used to make fun of her too. Devon would probably be the last one chosen. *That will embarrass her for sure,* Anna thought. Suddenly Matthew 5:7 popped into her mind. "Blessed are the merciful, for they will be shown mercy." She tried to ignore it as she opened her mouth to choose Staci, but she couldn't do it.

With a sigh, Anna said, "Devon."

Devon's smile of gratitude was huge as she ran to join the team.

Your Turn

1. How did Anna show mercy toward Devon?
2. Why do you think God wants us to show mercy toward others?

_____

_____

_____

Prayer

God, I don't always feel like being merciful. Please help me be merciful even when I don't feel like it. Amen.

Mercy and Real Love

*The wisdom that comes from heaven
is first of all pure; then…full of mercy.*

– James 3:17

Wanted: Tara Purcell

Tara knew she was in trouble. She didn't have to guess when she saw the expression on her mother's face. *So what if I'm a little late coming home from Steph's house?* she reasoned. She glanced at her mother's face again. *Okay, a lot late. Two hours late. I'm going to be grounded for sure. Or at least I'll get "the talk."*

Mom folded her arms. "I know we taught you how to tell time."

Tara almost laughed. "I'm sorry I'm late, Mom. I know I was supposed to be home at 3:30. I lost track of time."

Mom pursed her lips. "Hmm. What should I do with you now?"

"Give me a kiss?" Tara said and grinned.

Mom abruptly caught her daughter in a hug. "I'm feeling merciful today. I will give you that kiss." She kissed Tara's forehead.

Tara was shocked in a good way.

"Next time, come home when I tell you or call. I don't make rules just to hear myself talk. I want you to be safe, Tara."

Your Turn

1. What did Tara receive instead of what she deserved?
2. Do you show your friends mercy?

_____

_____

_____

Prayer

Father God, thanks to Jesus, I won't receive the punishment I deserve for my sins. Thank you for your mercy. Amen.

Mercy and Real Love

*The wisdom that comes from heaven
is first of all pure; then...full of mercy.*

– James 3:17

Mrs. Rice

Deborah walked into the house mad. She shouted to her mother, "Mrs. Rice made us move again!"

"Sweetie, you know she doesn't like you and your friends hanging out in front of her house," Mom said.

Deborah tossed her head. "Mom, the bus bench is public property."

"Yes, but it's in front of her house," Mom said. "And you do attract kids."

Deborah had many friends. ""I can't help that, Mom! It's not fair!"

"Deb, do you remember? Mrs. Rice's daughter who died would be in sixth grade, like you are now. Maybe seeing you all reminds her of what she lost.

So, WWJD?" Mom asked with a grin.

Deborah stood still, thinking.

"What would Jesus do? Okay. I guess Jesus would probably find a new place to hang out." She paused. "Maybe I could make Mrs. Rice some cookies."

"I think she'd like that," said her mom.

Your Turn

1. How was Deborah encouraged to be more thoughtful?
2. How would you respond to Mrs. Rice? Why?

Prayer

Lord, help me look beneath the surface to find the true reasons people are upset. Amen.

Mercy and Real Love

*The wisdom that comes from heaven
is first of all pure; then...full of mercy.*
– James 3:17

An Unselfish Example

Martina Jane Edwards—Student Leader of the Year! Marti could almost hear the principal calling out her name in assembly. In her mind's eye, she pictured herself strolling to the stage and accepting a big plaque. And why not? All the teachers had complimented Marti on parent conference day. "Martina is so helpful," she remembered hearing her fifth-grade teacher, Mr. Webb, say to her mother.

"Marti! I need some help cleaning the garage," her brother, Doug, called from her bedroom doorway, interrupting her daydream. "Will you help me?"

"I'm busy!" Marti said as she relaxed on her bed. "Ask Caitlin!"

Yes, Marti thought as she returned to her daydream. *My teachers are right to think I'm helpful.*

"Marti, will you help me with my art project?" her brother, Raymond, called from his room.

"I'm busy!" Marti yelled. She dropped back into her daydream. I *can't wait for that assembly. I'm sure my helpful attitude will get me that award.*

Your Turn

1. What is Marti missing in her self-evaluation?
2. How would your friends and family describe your helping attitude?

Prayer

Lord, teach me to help others with a smile even when I think it's inconvenient. Amen.

Mercy and Real Love

A Time of Mercy

Use the first space to write about a time when someone was merciful to you. Use the second space to describe how you can be merciful to someone this week. If you can't think of a way, write a prayer asking God how you can make life easier for someone.

Prayer

Lord, help me recognize those times when someone shows me mercy. Help me offer mercy to others. Amen.

Mercy and Real Love

A Word from Our Sponsor

A prophet named Zechariah had an important message from God for the people of Israel—and people today. Use the sign language code to decipher the message.

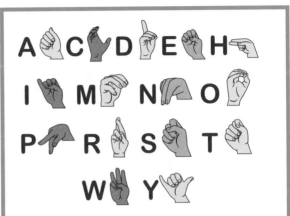

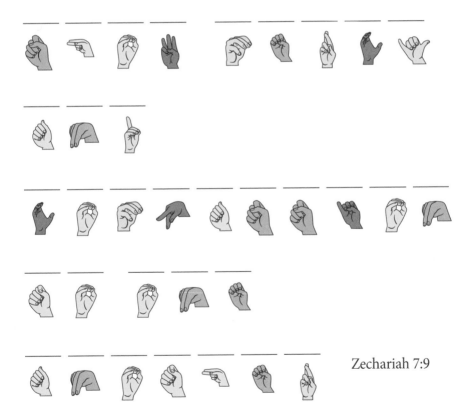

Zechariah 7:9

Prayer

Father God, please teach me to be wise and merciful. Amen.

211

Contributing to Harmony

*Carry each other's burdens, and in this way
you will fulfill the law of Christ.*

– Galatians 6:2

The TV Blowup

Lilly raced to the family room, grabbed the remote, and turned on the TV. Denzel followed her and groaned when he saw the show Lilly chose.

"Yuck! Who wants to watch this dumb show?" Denzel wailed. He flopped on the floor, making horrible gagging sounds. "It's my turn to choose," he argued. "I want to see the basketball game."

Lilly said, "No way! I'm watching this. And I have the remote."

"Dad!" yelled Denzel. "Lilly's hogging the TV!"

Dad didn't look happy when he came in. He turned off the TV and motioned for Lilly to give him the remote. The remote went into his pocket. He folded his arms over his chest. "Watching TV is not a competitive sport with a winner. It should be a team sport with cooperation. Taking turns makes everyone happier—the people involved and God. God wants us to live peacefully with each other."

Dad continued. "TV watching is off limits for three days. During that time, we'll work out a cooperative plan for taking turns in choosing programs."

Lilly and Denzel moaned but agreed.

Your Turn

1. What do you and your family members fight about?
2. How can you cooperate to make things more peaceful?

_____

_____

_____

Prayer

God of peace, help me live in harmony with my family. Amen.

Contributing to Harmony

Carry each other's burdens, and in this way
you will fulfill the law of Christ.

– Galatians 6:2

Quinn's Request

"So, will you take out the garbage for me?" Quinn asked his younger sister, Rachel. "It needs to be taken out before Dad gets home. Pedro and his dad are in the driveway waiting for me."

Rachel considered Quinn's request for a second. They were almost late for karate practice. But she was sick of doing favors for him. What was she, the maid?

"No," she said, just as she heard a car horn blow.

"Please?" Quinn begged. "I'll wash the dishes for you tomorrow night."

"Won't work this time," Rachel stated.

Quinn looked disgusted. "Great. Dad's going to kill me." He ran out the door.

Rachel grinned as she slipped on the earphones. Her favorite music group sang about Jesus' kindness, and how he'd willingly come to do God's will.

As she listened, she couldn't help but think about the way she'd treated Quinn. Sure, he was a pest, always wanting favors. But in God's view, that was not a valid excuse to not help. She got up and took out the garbage. She smiled thinking how surprised Quinn would be.

Your Turn

1. What unselfish act inspired Rachel? What two things gave her joy?
2. What do Jesus' sacrifices inspire you to do?

Prayer

Jesus, thank you for your kindness and sacrifice. Amen.

Contributing to Harmony

*Carry each other's burdens, and in this way
you will fulfill the law of Christ.*

– **Galatians 6:2**

Read It Again

Laura was talking to Jennifer on the phone when her mother and sister came in the door. Three-year-old Sophie was fussing. "I want my kitty book!" she wailed. "I don't want to take off my coat! I just want my book!"

As she took off her toddler's coat, Mom looked at Laura. "Please get off the phone. I need you to entertain Sophie while I fix dinner."

"Jenn, I have to say goodbye. My whiny sister is driving Mom nuts. I'm on baby patrol."

"Why do I have to entertain Sophie?" Laura complained. "She can play by herself." Then Laura noticed that Mom looked really tired. Sophie was still sniffling, but at least her coat was off. Laura looked at Sophie, who stood with her little arms folded over her chest, just waiting to see what was going to happen.

"Oh, all right, Sophie," Laura said. "Go get your kitty book."

"Yea!" squealed Sophie as she raced to the bookshelf. Mom smiled at Laura and gave her a thumbs-up.

Maybe I'll only have to read about Katie Kitty four times today, thought Laura.

Your Turn

1. Why is it important for family members to work together?
2. What are some ways you can help your family by being available?

Prayer

Heavenly Father, thank you for putting me in my family. Amen.

Contributing to Harmony

*Carry each other's burdens, and in this way
you will fulfill the law of Christ.*

– Galatians 6:2

The Talent Fair

The kids were getting ready for the annual Talent Fair. Ms. Stone announced to the fifth-graders, "Our class has been asked to make posters advertising the Talent Fair. They'll be put up around school and in the stores downtown. We have two weeks." She divided the class into groups of three, with each group responsible for two posters. Alexandria, Beth, and Allen were in one group.

Ms. Stone gave them the information and materials they needed. She stressed that they really needed to get busy and not waste time.

"I've made posters before," Beth said importantly. "I know what to do."

"Well, who died and made you boss?" Allen snarled as he grabbed a piece of poster board and some markers.

Alexandria leaned back in her chair. "I don't care who's boss. I can't draw."

Ms. Stone had been watching and listening. She came over. "This is called a talent fair because everyone does something he or she is good at. Everyone also cooperates to make it successful. This includes making posters too. Think about that for a minute."

Your Turn

1. How can the group cooperate to make the posters?
2. Do people consider you cooperative person?

_____

_____

Prayer

Lord, show me ways to cooperate and get things done. Amen.

Contributing to Harmony

Carry each other's burdens, and in this way you will fulfill the law of Christ.

– Galatians 6:2

The Note

"Get away from her!" That was all Danielle could think to say after seeing the note taped to her friend's backpack. It read, "Chubbo."

Danielle had caught two seventh-graders—Jason and his friend Eddie—in the act of leaving the note. They liked to tease kids in the sixth grade. They'd locked on to Michaela that week. They made loud comments about her weight. Danielle snatched the note off the backpack, thankful Michaela hadn't noticed. She was still drinking water at the drinking fountain. Danielle hated seeing hurt looks on her friend's face.

Just as she started to ball up the note, a hand touched her shoulder. Danielle jumped and whirled around.

"I'll take that," the vice principal, Mr. Hathaway, said.

"But I didn't…"

"Don't worry. I know the culprits. They've been causing trouble all week." He took the note and went back inside the school.

Danielle nodded. The look on Mr. Hathaway's face told her that Jason and Eddie were going to answer for their meanness. She was glad they were going to get called out for their behavior.

Your Turn

1. What would you have done if you'd seen the boys teasing Michaela?
2. Have you stood up for or defended a friend? What happened?

_____

_____

Prayer

Lord, help me be kind and defend those who are teased and picked on. Amen.

Contributing to Harmony

Kindness Ingredients

Good cooks create great recipes. There is a recipe for kindness too.
Break the code to find out the necessary ingredients.

A	C	D	E	F	G	H	I	J	K	L
✡	⚜	♣	✤	✦	✧	★	☆	✪	✫	✬

M	N	O	P	R	S	T	U	V	W	Y
✝	✯	✩	✬	✽	✳	✶	✴	✴	✹	✺

Add to your faith _____

and to goodness, _____ ;

and to knowledge, _____ _____;

and to self-control, _____;

and to perseverance, _____;

and to godliness, _____ _____;

and to mutual affection, _____.   2 Peter 1:5-7

Prayer

Dear Lord, thank you for giving me goals for being kind. Amen.

217

Contributing to Harmony

Godly Appeal

Discover some great advice by figuring out the clues and writing the answers on the appropriate numbered blanks.

_____ _____ _____ _____ ... _____ _____
　1　　　　　5　　　　　4　　　　12　　　　　　11　　　　　3

_____ _____ _____ _____ _____
　7　　　12　　　　　6　　　　　　8　　　　　　2

_____. _____ ___:___
　　10　　　　　　　13　　　　　　2　9

1. How you refer to yourself
2. First number
3. Everyone or everything
4. Opposite of "from"
5. "Ap" + what a bell does (rhymes with "real")
6. Think the same way (rhymes with "tree")
7. Remove the first and last letters of "soft"
8. Add a "w" to the front of "it" and an "h" to the end
9. Number of disciples – 2
10. Add an "a" to the front of "not" and "her" to the end
11. Doing this and [rule] (rhymes with "cat")
12. Opposite of "me"
13. Seventh book of the New Testament

Prayer

Heavenly Father, I want to be more kind and cooperative. Show me the way. Amen.

Becoming Fair and Just

Doing what is right and just and fair.

– Proverbs 1:3

It's Not Fair!

"What's wrong?"

What's right? Molly wanted to say in answer to her father's question. She'd been glad to see he was home early when she'd come home after school. She sniffed the air. And he was making lasagna. That was the only thing right about today.

"I wanted to be on the sixth-grade party-planning committee, but Mrs. Douglas picked Allison. She always picks her for everything because her dad owns everything in town. It's not fair!" Molly paused for breath. "And what's worse, Allison's been assigned to my math study group. We're supposed to help each other. Well, I'm not going to help her."

Her father didn't say anything for a few seconds. "Need a hug, Mol?"

Molly nodded, fighting back angry tears. "Daddy, I don't want to help Allison!"

Daddy smoothed his daughter's hair. "I know it's not fair, but I also know you'll do the right thing."

"And what's that?"

"What Jesus wants you to do."

Your Turn

1. What do you think Molly will do?
2. What would you do in this situation?

_____

_____

Prayer

Jesus, life isn't fair, but you never said it would be. Help me follow your ways all the time. Amen.

Becoming Fair and Just

Doing what is right and just and fair.

– Proverbs 1:3

Kris' Choice

Kris went to school early to run on the track. When she went around the corner of the gym, she saw Kyle Farnsworth and a few other kids tagging the bleachers with spray paint. She stopped in her tracks. *Should I go to the track and ignore them? Should I find a janitor? Should I wait to see if the art is nice or mean?*

Finally Kris retreated and went to the track a different way to avoid the situation. Later in the day, a school assembly was called. The principal talked about the graffiti. He said the people who did it were defacing public property, which was illegal. He also said some damage had been done and a few of the graphics were inappropriate. If students had information about this, they needed to come to his office after the meeting.

After being dismissed, the buzz was fierce. Some students thought the graffiti was from kids just having fun, and some thought the painters should be caught. Even though the principal had said the information would be confidential, Kris knew word usually got out about who had "sold out."

Your Turn

1. What would you do each step of the way if you were Kris?
2. What would you do if you were one of the graffiti people?

Prayer

Father God, making decisions about right and wrong, justice and fairness, can be scary. Please help me make wise decisions based on your Word. Amen.

Becoming Fair and Just

Doing what is right and just and fair.

– Proverbs 1:3

Equal Share?

"One for you." Megan handed her six-year-old sister a chocolate chip cookie. "And three for me."

Samantha stared at the one cookie. "Hey! You got more than I got."

"That's because I'm older than you. Mom told me to pass them out."

"But that's not fair!" Samantha's bottom lip quivered and her blue eyes filled with tears.

Megan shrugged. "When you get to fifth grade, you can have more."

"Mo-o-o-o-om! Megan only gave me one cookie!"

"You big tattletale!"

"I don't want to hear any fighting!" their mother called from her bedroom.

"Oh, here!" Megan threw a second cookie at her sister. "I was only teasing." She knew she hadn't been.

Samantha took the cookie and pointed to Megan's bracelet. What does 'WWJD' mean?"

Megan didn't want to admit it. "It stands for 'what would Jesus do.' "

"I don't think Jesus would've done what you did." Samantha stuck out her tongue and ran off.

Megan started to run after her, but stopped. Her sister was right.

Your Turn

1. Have you treated someone unfairly, either in a big way or a small way?
2. How can you develop an attitude of fairness and generosity?

Prayer

God, help me not to make excuses, especially when it comes to being fair. Amen.

Becoming Fair and Just

Doing what is right and just and fair.

– Proverbs 1:3

The Lie

Mr. Loy watched as his daughter came into the family bookstore. Her feet were dragging, and her head was down. "I can see you've had a bad day," he said.

"Worse than bad. Horrible. Terrible." Kim threw her backpack on the counter, almost knocking over a stack of books.

"Want to talk about it?" Dad asked.

Kim let out a big sigh and plopped onto a stool. She explained that her friend Natalie had told a lie about her. Natalie was trying to avoid getting in trouble for something she'd done. Although the principal had found out the truth, Kim had still been accused of something she hadn't done.

"It hurts when someone lies about you, especially a friend," her father sympathized.

Kim nodded. "Natalie told me she was sorry. I don't know if I can forgive her. I'm pretty mad."

"It can be hard, but Jesus said we are to forgive others as he forgives us. If you can't forgive Natalie on your own, ask Jesus to help you. Why don't we pray about it right now?"

Your Turn

1. Why would Kim have a hard time forgiving Natalie?
2. When you've found it difficult to forgive someone, what did you do?

_____

_____

Prayer

Lord, thank you for forgiving me. Help me to forgive like you do. Amen.

Becoming Fair and Just

Doing what is right and just and fair.

– Proverbs 1:3

Forgiving Joe

Nola had a brother named Joe.
He never listened when she said, "No!"
Joe got into Nola's room and all of her things,
Her books, her games and even her earrings.
One day everything was in a heap on her floor.
Nola screamed, "Get out!" and slammed the door.
"I'm sorry!" Joe wailed out in the hall.
Nola didn't think he meant it at all.
"Will you forgive me?" asked Joe.
"You're not really sorry. So, no."
Their mom heard everything they said.
She came in the door, shaking her head.
"I know you're angry with Joe for this mess
But you can't deny him your forgiveness.
Jesus forgives all your sins every day
He expects you to treat others in the same way.
Nola half-smiled at Joe and said, "Okay."
He grinned back and helped her put things away.

Your Turn

1. Did Nola have the "right" to not forgive Joe? Why or why not?
2. Have people ever said they wouldn't forgive you? What did you do then?

Prayer

Lord, sometimes I need to be reminded that you and some people forgive me a lot. Keep me humble. Amen.

Becoming Fair and Just

Who Deserves Fairness?

Does everyone deserve to be treated fairly? Look at the list of people. Decide who deserves fair treatment by putting a check mark by Yes or No for each person.

Kids younger than you?   __Yes __No

People you don't like?   __Yes __No

People in prison?   __Yes __No

People who treat you fairly? __Yes __No

Look up and write out Acts 10:34.

Does this verse change your view about who deserves fairness? Explain.

_____

_____

_____

_____

Prayer

Lord, I want to do what is right and just and fair. Amen.

Becoming Fair and Just

Forgiveness Formula

Fill in the blanks to find the true forgiveness formula.

1. Read Colossians 3:13. How are you to forgive?

_____

2. Read Mark 11:25. Who are you to forgive?

_____

3. Read Matthew 6:14. Why should you forgive someone?

_____

4. Read Luke 17:4. How many times should you forgive someone?

_____

I, _____,

have sin in my life.

God _____

me because of Jesus' death

and resurrection. Now I can

_____ others.

Prayer

Heavenly Father, I want to forgive because you want me to forgive.
Amen.

Some Truths About Love

[Jesus taught,] "Whatever you did for one of the least of these brothers and sisters of mine, you did for me."

– Matthew 25:40

Valentine Party

"This will be the coolest party ever!" Keisha said excitedly.

"You said it, girl," Selena agreed as she high-fived her friend. "We'd better get busy or this party will never happen!"

Both girls were sitting at a dining room table heaped with colored paper, lace doilies, stickers, markers, scissors, and glue. They sang along with their favorite music as they worked.

"Whoa! What's happening?" asked Selena's oldest sister when she came in.

"Mom said I could have a Valentine party, so we're making invitations. Then we need to decide on food, games, and music," explained Selena.

"Sounds like fun," said Tia.

"Except for one thing," complained Keisha. "We have to invite all the girls in our sixth-grade homeroom. There are some we'd rather forget about."

Selena chimed in. "Becky and Andrea just don't fit in. They're weird."

Tia was quiet before she said, "Those girls need to be the first ones you invite. They need your friendship more than anyone else. Remember, Jesus said when you're friends with someone who has no friends, you are being his friend."

Your Turn

1. Who seems unlovable to you?
2. Name two ways you can show love to that person.

Prayer

Lord, loving people can be uncomfortable. Help me see them as you do. Amen.

Some Truths About Love

[Jesus taught,] "Whatever you did for one of the least of these brothers and sisters of mine, you did for me."

– Matthew 25:40

Love Yourself

Heather sat in front of the mirror brushing her hair. "I give up! Nothing helps—every day is a bad hair day. Guess it goes with my big nose and bony legs."

Her twin sister, Paige, asked, "Why are you so hard on yourself?"

"I want to look like Annie or be graceful like Samantha."

"That makes you ugly? Just because you don't look or act like people you think are super cool?" asked Paige. "I look like you. Would you call me ugly?"

Heather shrugged.

"You know you wouldn't," said Paige. "Would you call Ms. Bailey ugly?" Ms. Bailey was their piano teacher. The twins thought of her as an older sister.

"Of course not!" Heather exclaimed.

"So if you don't treat others that way, why treat yourself that way?" asked Paige. "You can't love others well if you don't love yourself."

Heather was ready to shoot back a smart remark, but she couldn't think of one. She brushed her hair again. This time she piled it on top of her head. The result made her laugh out loud, and Paige joined in.

Your Turn

1. Why is it important to love yourself?
2. How will loving yourself help you love your neighbor?

_____

_____

Prayer

Father, help me to love myself as you do. Amen.

Some Truths About Love

[Jesus taught,] "Whatever you did for one of the least of these brothers and sisters of mine, you did for me."

– Matthew 25:40

Babysitting Blues

Sierra only had to listen to her mother's phone conversation for a few minutes to get a huge knot in her stomach. She shook her head vigorously and waved her arms in the air, but Mrs. Morris just said, "I'll ask her, Ruth. I'm sure she'd be happy to watch your kids for a few hours. Bye."

When her mother clicked off the phone, Sierra said, "No! I don't want to watch the Bradley kids. The twins are always fighting. James thinks he's too old to have to listen to me."

"Mrs. Bradley has an important business luncheon on Saturday and can't find anyone to stay with the kids," Mom said. "I told her you would let her know tonight."

"Mo-o-o-om!" Sierra wailed. "Nobody wants to sit for her. Sometimes I think no one in that house likes each other."

"I know they aren't very loving neighbors sometimes," said Mom. "That's why God helps us love those we have a hard time loving."

Sierra almost smiled as she said, "Okay. I'll load up on love and wear them down with kindness on Saturday."

Your Turn

1. How do you usually respond to people difficult to love?
2. What do you think God wants you to do?

_____

_____

_____

Prayer

Jesus, help me love and be patient with difficult people. Amen.

Some Truths About Love

[Jesus taught,] "Whatever you did for one of the least of these brothers and sisters of mine, you did for me."

– Matthew 25:40

Christina's Diary

Today at school, Weird Clarence told me that he forgave me. Just like that. Well, after he heard me telling Tai and Shelly how uncool I think he dresses sometimes. I didn't know he was around the corner! I felt terrible. But everybody thinks that—that's why he has the nickname Weird Clarence.

Even after hearing me say that, he loaned me money at lunchtime to buy milk because I lost the money Mom gave me.

Shelly said, "I think Clarence likes you." But I don't think that. Neither does Tai. I think Clarence is just…nice. I've heard other kids say that, even the ones who call him weird. He once told me that he's a Christian. Mom says she doesn't believe in God, but I think there is one. Clarence's kindness when everyone teases him proves that.

Maybe I should stop calling him Weird Clarence…

Your Turn

1. How did Clarence show kindness to Christina?
2. What does Christina think about God, based on Clarence's example?

Prayer

God, I want to have the same love in my heart that Jesus has. Amen.

Some Truths About Love

[Jesus taught,] "Whatever you did for one of the least of these brothers and sisters of mine, you did for me."

– Matthew 25:40

Unselfish Erin

Erin wasn't selfish, not one bit—
Just ask her brother, "the little twit."
(That's what Erin called him, when she was mad.
She was often angry with her brother Brad.)
    Unlike Brad, she was always good.
    She did everything right, best as she could.
    She shared her toys, (at least the ones she didn't like).
    She even gave away her least favorite bike!
When Brad asked to watch his favorite show
On TV that night, Erin didn't say "no."
Instead she made a deal: he had to agree
To do a chore for her...or two or three.
    And it was her night to pick the show,
    As she reminded him, just so he'd know.
    No, Erin wasn't selfish, not one bit—
    Just ask her brother, "the little twit."

Your Turn

1. Look up and write out 1 Corinthians 13:4-5.
2. Based on those verses, what advice do you have for Erin?

_____

_____

_____

Prayer

Lord, when I'm tempted to be selfish, remind me to be kind and generous. Amen.

Some Truths About Love

Free Advice

Here is some advice for Erin and you regarding selfishness. Start with the letter at the arrow. Skip every other letter in two trips around the circle. Print the letters on the lines at the bottom. (As you go around the circle the second time, ignore the first letter "T" you started with.)

_____

_____

Prayer

Dear Lord, please show me ways I can think of others instead of me. Amen.

Some Truths About Love

Loving for the Heart and Tummy

Let your family know you love them. Surprise them with these loving treats.

What You Need

- ½" x 3" strips of paper
- Pencil
- Graham crackers
- Bible
- Store-bought frosting

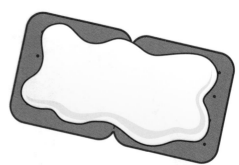

What to Do

1. Write a "loving" message on the strips of paper, such as "God loves you," and "You are special."

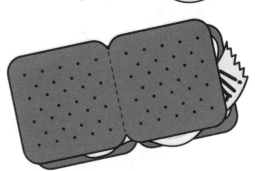

2. Spread a thin layer of frosting on a graham cracker.

3. Lay on a paper strip, with part of it sticking out the side.

4. Add a cracker top and gently squeeze them together.

5. Serve the treats at dinner. Have each person read his or her message to everyone.

Prayer

Dear Lord, thank you for encouraging me to show my love. Amen.

Peace and Joy

The kingdom of God is…
of righteousness, peace and joy in the Holy Spirit.

– Romans 14:17

The Report (Part 1)

As Julia Tompkins walked the four blocks to school, that sinking feeling returned. She'd felt it for days. Today was oral report day—the most dreaded of all days. In front of the class, she had to talk about a book she'd read. Julia thought she'd rather wrestle an alligator than give a speech.

She passed a shaky hand through her short, dark hair. As she walked, the thought came to her to pray. "Whenever you're feeling scared, pray," her Sunday-school teacher had said. Julia shrugged. *Can't hurt. God, I'm scared to do this. Will you help me?*

As she neared the school, Julia realized the sinking feeling was gone. Inside she felt calm. The calm lasted until just before she had to give her report. After another quick prayer, the nervousness disappeared and peace filled her spirit. Her voice shook a little as she talked about the book, but she made it through the ordeal just fine. *Thank you, God!*

Your Turn

1. How did Julia feel about giving the oral report?
2. Think of a time you needed peace. What did you do?

_____

_____

_____

Prayer

Lord, I need courage in my life. Thank you for sending the Holy Spirit to fill me with your peace. Amen.

Peace and Joy

*The kingdom of God is…
of righteousness, peace and joy in the Holy Spirit.*
– Romans 14:17

The Report (Part 2)

Julia smiled as she let herself into the apartment after school. She grabbed a package of cheese and crackers and went into the living room. She sat down and smiled at her grandfather. He was in his favorite spot—the recliner.

"How did your book report go?" Grandpa asked. "I see you survived. You didn't think you would."

Julia's smile widened. "It went okay."

Grandpa looked pleased. "You seem pretty calm. I know you were nervous about giving a speech."

"I prayed as I walked to school. I was nervous but then I felt peaceful." Julia grinned. "I'm sure I would've felt even more peaceful if I hadn't had to get up in front of people at all!"

Her grandfather chuckled before saying, "Being peaceful doesn't mean avoiding what you have to do. When you ask, God gives you peace and strength to do what you need to accomplish."

Your Turn

1. Do you think God giving you peace means you don't have to experience difficulties? Why or why not?
2. Look up and write out John 14:27. Why not memorize it this week?

_____

_____

_____

Prayer

Lord, you promise in the Bible to give strength to your people and to bless us with peace. I'm counting on you for that. Amen.

Peace and Joy

The kingdom of God is...
of righteousness, peace and joy in the Holy Spirit.
– Romans 14:17

Rancorous Roni

"Hey, Roni, what's the opposite of 'rancorous'?"

Veronica came out of her reverie and stared at Tom, her older brother. She'd been making a mental list of people who made her mad. If only she could get even with Bailey for what she said during lunch!

"Why are you asking me?" Veronica asked. "I don't know what 'rancorous' means."

Tom grinned. "I do. It means bitter or hostile. That sounds like you, all right."

Veronica slammed her math book shut, wishing she'd studied in her room instead of joining her brother at the kitchen table. "You just made my list!"

"What list? Oh, your 'I'm mad at' list." Tom looked thoughtful. "You're always mad at somebody these days. That's all you ever say—'I'm so mad!' "

His imitation of her was pretty good, and Veronica laughed despite how irritating he was.

"Instead of always getting mad at somebody, why don't you do something positive that will increase friendships?" Tom asked. "Aren't you tired of being angry all the time?"

"Why don't you mind your own business?" Veronica hissed.

Your Turn

1. What happens to us when we hold a grudge?
2. Instead of holding a grudge, what can you do to make friends?

Prayer

Lord, help me to pursue peaceful relationships and not hold grudges. Amen.

Peace and Joy

*The kingdom of God is...
of righteousness, peace and joy in the Holy Spirit.*
– Romans 14:17

The Visit

Grace wasn't sure what she'd expected when she went to visit her cousins. She hadn't anticipated all the smiles and laughter. Her cousins' dad was still out of work, so Grace decided she'd expected doom and gloom. Yet her three cousins, her uncle, and her aunt greeted her with hugs and plenty of joy.

During a break in the action, Grace followed her aunt into the kitchen. "Do you guys have good news?" she asked Aunt Phyllis. "Did Uncle Simon find a job?"

"No, not yet," Aunt Phyllis replied. "Why do you ask?"

"Oh, I thought…" Grace didn't want to say what she thought.

"You thought you'd find us sitting around with long faces," her aunt finished for her. She smiled. "God has helped us so far. We've been able to pay our bills and get by. I can't say it's been easy, but God is still good. The joy he gives us is something no one can take away."

Grace stared at her, amazed. "Wow! I thought I came to cheer you up—and you've cheered me!"

Your Turn

1. When times are hard, how can you choose to radiate God's joy?
2. When someone is struggling you can pray. What would you ask God for?

_____

_____

_____

Prayer

Lord, I praise you for the joy you fill me with. Amen.

Peace and Joy

The kingdom of God is...
of righteousness, peace and joy in the Holy Spirit.

– Romans 14:17

Elizabeth's Praise

Hearing the teacher say, "As we close in prayer, all who wish to can share a sentence of praise," Rachel closed her eyes. She wasn't one to "share a sentence of praise" out loud. *What do I have to be thankful about?* she thought. Her parents had cancelled the family's summer trip to the beach. "Money's tight," they'd said.

The classroom was silent. Rachel opened one eye and gave the other kids in Sunday school a quick glance. She noticed other eyes were open as well.

A soft voice said, "God, thanks for always being with us."

Rachel was surprised to hear Elizabeth. If anyone had a right to be miserable, she did. Her father was often sick, and her mother had died two years ago.

After several people prayed, the teacher said, "Amen." Looking up, Rachel was again surprised by Elizabeth. She was smiling. *But then Elizabeth always smiles. What's with that?* Rachel thought of a memory verse they'd learned. *Where was it from? Philippians 4:4. How did it go?* "Rejoice in the Lord always." *Humph,* Rachel decided. *I don't feel like rejoicing.*

Your Turn

1. Should you wait until you feel like rejoicing to praise God?
2. When hard times come, do you usually respond like Rachel or like Elizabeth?

Prayer

God, I rejoice in knowing you. Amen.

Peace and Joy

Cross Out

Use the clues to know which words to cross out in the chart below. The leftover words provide good advice when hard times come. After crossing out the extra words, read the advice by going up and down, starting in the left column.

Cross Out Words

Seasons of the year

Girl names

Numbers

Names of Bible people

Barbara	of	three	Abraham
seven	Spring	Nadia	thoughts,
Instead	Peter	sad	Summer
Winter	thinking	Fall	rejoice

Prayer

Lord, when I am feeling sad, remind me to rejoice in you. Amen.

Peace and Joy

Before and After

Many people in the Bible faced scary problems. Read the Scriptures and write about how you think each person felt and how God helped.

Hannah

How did Hannah feel? (1 Samuel 1:10-11)

_____

How did God help? (1 Samuel 1:17)

_____

How do you think Hannah felt then? (1 Samuel 1:18)

_____

Jehoshaphat

How did Jehoshaphat feel? (2 Chronicles 20:2-3)

_____

How did God help? (2 Chronicles 20:15)

_____

How do you think Jehoshaphat felt then?
(2 Chronicles 20:18)

_____

Hezekiah

How did Hezekiah feel? (2 Kings 20:1-3, Isaiah 38:14)

_____

How did God help? (2 Kings 20:4-5)

_____

How do you think Hezekiah felt then?
(Isaiah 38:15, 20)

_____

Prayer

Lord, only you give true and lasting peace. Help me turn to you for everything. Amen.

Confident and Ready

[God said,] "Never will I leave you; never will I forsake you."
So we say with confidence, "The Lord is my helper; I will not be afraid."
– Hebrews 13:5-6

The Blank Key

Leanne pointed toward the TV where a door appeared on the screen. "I wouldn't go into that room without the 'Blank Key,' " she said. "You'll get clobbered instantly by the fear creatures. The Blank Key is a great weapon that opens any door in the game."

Abby worked the game controls and said, "Thanks, Le."

"Why are you two hogging the TV?" Abby's older brother asked. He stood in the doorway to the family room. Both girls jumped.

Abby tossed a sofa pillow at him. "Go away!" She turned back to Leanne. "This key is awesome. I wish I had something like it in real life. I wouldn't be afraid of anything."

Jason flopped on the couch behind the girls sprawled on the floor. "You've got something better than some old key. God goes with you everywhere you go. Because of him, you don't have to fear anything."

Leanne and Abby exchanged a look.

"I've played this game before. That key won't work against the slithering monsters on the next level."

Leanne and Abby groaned.

"Good thing God can do anything and never changes!" Jason said.

Your Turn

1. What is the real key to finding courage and overcoming fear?

_____

_____

Prayer

God, I'm thankful you are always with me. Knowing that helps me be courageous. Amen.

Confident and Ready

[God said,] "Never will I leave you; never will I forsake you."
So we say with confidence, "The Lord is my helper; I will not be afraid."

– Hebrews 13:5-6

First Day of School

New neighborhood. New school. In the summer, Tina had been excited about the move to Carroll Park. But now that the first day of school was just two days away, nervousness was setting in. As she stared at her reflection in the mirror, Tina couldn't help worrying about the first day of sixth grade. *What if no one likes me at this school? What if I don't make any friends?*

"You were awfully quiet at dinner tonight, my niña," her mother said from the doorway.

"What if no one likes me at this school?" Tina blurted. She turned a worried face to her mother.

"Is that what's been bothering you, my little one?" Mom moved into the room. "How can they not like you? You're kind and thoughtful and fun. And don't forget you can ask God to give you the courage to face all the new kids and situations."

"Thanks, Mom!" Tina said. She hadn't prayed. In fact, she hadn't considered God at all. The thought of God's presence and help made her feel a lot better.

Your Turn

1. Will Mom's advice help Tina at school?
2. Look up and write out Joshua 1:9. Memorize it to use the next time you get anxious or afraid.

_____

_____

Prayer

Thank you, Lord, for the courage you give me. Amen.

Confident and Ready

*[God said,] "Never will I leave you; never will I forsake you.
So we say with confidence, "The Lord is my helper; I will not be afraid."*
– Hebrews 13:5-6

Just Say No?

Allison waited while Jenna ran to catch up with her in the school hallway.

"Are you coming to my sleepover?" Jenna asked as they walked toward the school bus. "We're going to tell ghost stories and call the psychic hotline. My mom has given us permission already. My older sister's going to do the call for us. Won't that be fun?"

Allison nodded, even though she didn't think the last idea sounded like fun or a good idea. Last Sunday, the youth pastor at church had talked against using psychic hotlines. "It's playing with the occult," he'd said.

Allison sighed. She wanted to be Jenna's friend. Jenna was nice, and her family had a stable with two horses. Allison loved horses. Being invited to the sleepover was wonderful. But…

"Let me talk to my mom and get back to you, Allison said. "I'd love to spend time with you." Allison knew her mom would help her figure out what to say and do without offending her friend.

Your Turn

1. Look up and write out 1 Corinthians 16:13. How will this verse help Allison?
2. What would you do if you were in a similar situation?

_____

_____

Prayer

Lord, thank you for giving me parents who know you and want to help me. Amen.

Confident and Ready

[God said,] "Never will I leave you; never will I forsake you."
So we say with confidence, "The Lord is my helper; I will not be afraid."
– Hebrews 13:5-6

Joining the Group

"I thought you wanted to join. Are you a 'fraidy cat?" Jolene stood in her bedroom, hands on her hips. She and the other girls were staring at Donna.

Donna thought about the group's rule: Each girl had to take a selfie in her underwear and send it to the group. It didn't have to be suggestive.

"We've all done it," Ruth said. "We're all girls, and it's just between us. It shows we trust each other."

Donna didn't like it, but was there any harm? She'd be covered like she was wearing a swimsuit. She wanted to be part of the group. They did a lot of fun things. But… She wavered before applying her personal screening question: Will Jesus be pleased? The answer was obvious.

Peggy pushed her toward the bathroom. "You can go in there if you're too modest."

"I can't do this," Donna said quietly. "I love Jesus, and this isn't something he'd want me to do."

On her way home, Donna whispered, "Thank you, Jesus, for giving me the confidence in you to say no."

Your Turn

1. Is your confidence in God strong enough to see you through difficult decisions?
2. What would you do in Donna's situation?

_____

_____

Prayer

Lord, give me confidence to always go to you and rely on you for wisdom. Amen.

Confident and Ready

[God said,] "Never will I leave you; never will I forsake you."
So we say with confidence, "The Lord is my helper; I will not be afraid."
– Hebrews 13:5-6

Science Project

"I don't believe it! What a traitor! I can't believe she did that!" Valerie stomped around the kitchen punctuating her words by shaking her fists.

"Did somebody sell your secret diary to the newspaper?" her brother Joe asked.

Valerie gave him an angry stare. "Don't be such a jerk!"

"All right. Cool it," Mom ordered. "Valerie, what are you so hot about?"

"The science fair is in two days. There are four kids in our group, and each of us picked which part of the project to do. Russell just called and said Sandra told him she didn't have anything done. For two weeks she's been saying she's working on it and didn't need help. We trusted her to do what she said. Now she ditches us. We're scrambling to do her part."

"I'm sorry Sandra didn't live up to her part of the project," Mom said. "Why don't you call Russell and Tiffany and have them come here after supper? Maybe I can help fill in the missing pieces."

"Thanks! I hope you remember your science teaching days!" Valerie said.

Your Turn

1. What happens when you lose confidence in someone?
2. How does it help you to know you can always count on God?

Prayer

Lord, I'm confident you will always do what you promise. Help me follow your lead. Amen.

Confident and Ready

The Courage to Trust

Courage comes from trusting God. To figure a good truth to know, put the letters below each column in the boxes above that column. The letters may not be listed in the order they appear in the text. Mark off letters you use because a letter may only be used once. The black boxes are ends of words.

```
G  A  N  D  R  T  D  D  M  U  S  P  H  P  I  E  D  R  M  Y
T  H  E  A  A  O  E  T  H  Y  L  S  S  Y  E  N  T  H  E  M
   H  H     L  N  R     R  I  S  T  S  I  M  S           I  N
   T  E        H           E        M        L
```

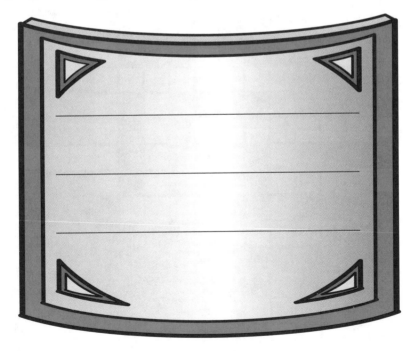

Prayer

Lord, thank you for being my strength and shield. Amen.

245

Confident and Ready

Loads of Confidence

Many Bible people had loads of confidence in God. They knew he would be with them and help them no matter what. Fit these names into the grid.

Abednego	James	Noah
Abraham	John	Paul
Daniel	Joseph	Peter
David	Mary	Shadrach
Elijah	Meshach	Silas
Esther	Moses	

Developing Self-Control

God has not given us a spirit of fear and timidity,
but of power, love, and self-discipline.

– 2 Timothy 1:7 NLT

Fear of Failure

Laura paged through the chapter in her social studies textbook and lowered her head on top of it. "I'm going to fail next week's test! I just know it!" she wailed.

Iris, who was in Laura's fifth-grade study group, poked her with the eraser end of a pencil. "You've got a whole week to study, so what are you whining about?"

Laura raised her head, but her face was hidden behind a curtain of light-brown hair. "I haven't been studying at all." She paused. "I'll bet you're already prepared for the test."

Iris looked smug. "I've been studying for two weeks."

Laura threw her friend a look. "I don't see how you do it. You never seem afraid you'll fail."

"That's because I try to be prepared. I wasn't always like this. My dad taught me. Besides, God doesn't want us to waste time worrying over what might not happen."

Laura still didn't feel prepared.

Your Turn

1. What can Laura learn from Iris to help her be prepared?
2. Using this week's Scripture, what advice would you give Laura?

_____

_____

_____

Prayer

Lord, help me not waste time on fear. Amen.

Developing Self-Control

God has not given us a spirit of fear and timidity,
but of power, love, and self-discipline.

– 2 Timothy 1:7 NLT

All at Once or Patiently Waiting?

Sarah's mom brought them to the mall and told them to meet her at the entrance in an hour. She headed down the mall. Sarah quickly pointed her friend Margie in the opposite direction.

"I can't wait to spend my allowance!" Sarah said.

"Not me. I'm saving my money," said Margie.

"I can't save money. Spending is too much fun. My dad says I'm a spendaholic." Sarah looked proud of her father's description.

"I used to be, but I started telling myself, 'Just wait. You don't have to spend everything all at once.' "

Sarah paused by a pretzel shop. "Want to get a pretzel?"

Margie shook her head. "Aren't we going to stop at McDonald's after the movie? I'll wait until then."

Sarah stared at Margie. "Are you for real?"

Margie smiled. "I'm learning to be patient. I like to wait until I find exactly what I want." She paused. "Whenever I want to spend, I tell myself, 'No. Just wait a bit and then decide.' So I do."

Sarah shook her head. She couldn't imagine waiting for anything.

Your Turn

1. Look up and write down the main definition of "self-discipline." Now write it down in your own words.
2. Self-discipline involves being patient and in control. Are you more like Sarah or Margie?

Prayer

Lord, I want to be more self-disciplined. Please give me patience and wisdom. Amen.

Developing Self-Control

God has not given us a spirit of fear and timidity,
but of power, love, and self-discipline.

– 2 Timothy 1:7 NLT

Good Enough?

Kathy was picking at her dinner, taking a few bites and pushing the rest around the plate. Her food-pushing was accompanied by a lot of sighing.

"What's with all the dramatics? You sound like a sick cow," complained her older brother, Mike.

"Enough already," warned their father. Kathy and Mike were known to get into some pretty heated arguments. "You do seem to have something on your mind, Kathy," he added.

Kathy nodded. "Coach Woods wants me to be the starting forward in tomorrow's basketball game against Hillcrest. They're a tough team, and I don't know if I'm good enough to start against them. What if I mess up?"

Her father reached over and patted her shoulder. "God gave you quickness and strength. He also gave you a good brain. You know how to play. Just be confident and believe you can do it."

"I'll remember how I sometimes outscored my big brother shooting hoops in the driveway," Kathy said with a teasing grin.

"You asked for it, kid!" responded Mike. "Meet you in the driveway in fifteen minutes!"

Your Turn

1. Have you felt like Kathy did? What did you do that helped you?
2. What gives you confidence in your ability to do something?

Prayer

God, I know I can always be confident of your love and care. Thanks. Amen.

Developing Self-Control

God has not given us a spirit of fear and timidity,
but of power, love, and self-discipline.

– **2 Timothy 1:7 NLT**

A Self-Disciplined Mouth

Karen Farmer shook her head as she watched her aunt say good-bye to the last customer in the small bookstore. She was surprised to hear her aunt's pleasant, "Thanks! Come again!"

"That was the rudest man I've ever met!" Karen declared as soon as the door closed. "You were really nice to him, Aunt Becky." She paused. "In fact, you're always smiling and being courteous. I've never seen you yell at anybody or get really mad. Do you ever, like, lose it?"

Aunt Becky laughed. "I get mad at people. I even yell sometimes. Your Uncle James will tell you that I used to have a really bad temper. God helps me do better now. People like that man who just left used to really set me off. Nowadays, I bite my tongue to keep from saying something mean back."

Karen laughed. "I wish I could be like you."

"Don't wish that!" said Aunt Becky. "I still have a long way to go. Instead, ask God to help you be more like Jesus!"

Your Turn

1. Are you tempted to say unkind words? What do you do during those moments?
2. How can knowing you belong to God help keep your words kind and uplifting?

Prayer

God, help me to behave in such a way that everyone will know I'm your child. Amen.

Developing Self-Control

God has not given us a spirit of fear and timidity,
but of power, love, and self-discipline.

– 2 Timothy 1:7 NLT

Give a Shout!

As soon as Cinnamon Philip's last whoop died, she noticed her mother standing in the doorway leading down to the basement. She gave her mother a wide smile, showing pink braces.

"What on earth is all that racket down here?" Mom asked. "I heard you hollering clear outside."

Cinnamon pointed to the TV. "They won! My favorite soccer team won the championship! Yeeeeeeesssss! " She ran to the stairs to give her mother a high-five.

Mom Philip smiled. "Never let it be said that my daughter has no lungs."

"I can't help it if I'm happy." Cinnamon gave another shout of joy.

Mom folded her arms. "Hmm. You tell me all the time you're happy being a Christian, yet I don't hear you celebrating like this at church."

"Mooooommm!" Cinnamon groaned. After a second's pause, she yelled, "Yea, God!" She grinned at her mother. "There!"

Your Turn

1. When do you excited about God?
2. Find and write out Psalm 66:1, 8. What are ways you celebrate God? What are ways you haven't yet tried?

_____

_____

_____

Prayer

Oh, God, I lift my voice and sing your praises. Amen.

Developing Self-Control

Get Ready, Get Set...

Athletes work hard and discipline themselves to reach their goals. Self-control means you set goals and work consistently to achieve them. Answer these questions and then meditate on them as you do your daily exercise or activities. What do you need to do to...

Prayer

Lord, please help me to be disciplined and enthusiastic when it comes to your ways and your commands. Amen.

Developing Self-Control

A Verse to Live By

Solve the puzzle by substituting the letters for the numbers.

KEY

A	B	C	D	E	F	G	H	I	J
2	9	14	22	11	23	8	1	16	12

K	L	M	N	O	P	Q	R	S	T
4	13	7	3	7	21	6	24	10	15

U	V	W	X	Y	Z
18	26	19	25	20	5

9 11 　　12 17 20 23 18 13 　　16 3 　　1 17 21 11

_____ 　_____ 　_____ 　_____,

21 2 15 16 11 3 15 　　16 3 　　2 23 23 13 16 14 15 16 17 3

_____ 　_____ 　_____,

23 2 16 15 1 23 18 13 　　16 3 　　21 24 2 20 11 24

_____ 　_____ 　_____.

24 17 7 2 3 10

_____ 12:12

Prayer

Lord, when I live in the Spirit of faith and power in you, I am joyful.
Thank you! Amen.

253

Discovering Discernment

I will instruct you and teach you in the way you should go.

– **Psalm 32:8**

Teachable Tess

The Dickersons always talked about what they learned in Sunday school at Sunday lunch. Questions were encouraged, and some lively discussions took place.

"By the way, Tess," Mom said, "your teacher talked to me this morning."

"Ha!" snickered Jimmy. "Probably said you flirt with all the guys!"

His twin brother, Jared, said, "No, I think she talks too much. Yackety, yackety!"

Tess had no idea what the teacher might have said. She sort of wished everyone else would forget the conversation, but she was curious.

"Mr. Wilkens said he really likes having you in his class, Tess," her mom continued. "He told me you listen to the lesson and ask questions about what you don't understand. Your questions often spark questions from the other kids. This encourages searching the Bible. Mr. Wilkens said you are very teachable."

"'Teachable Tess,'" her dad said. "That has a nice ring to it."

Jimmy and Jared looked at each other and rolled their eyes. "And what would your Sunday-school teacher say about you guys?" their dad asked.

Neither one answered as they dug into desserts.

Your Turn

1. Why is being teachable such a valuable attitude?
2. Are you teachable? How can you improve?

Prayer

Lord, I have many things to learn. I'm eager to learn about you. Amen.

Discovering Discernment

I will instruct you and teach you in the way you should go.

– Psalm 32:8

Different Ideas

All night the wind whistled around the house and sleet pinged the windows. Megan snuggled under the covers but couldn't sleep. It wasn't just the icy storm. She kept thinking about what had happened in school.

The next morning, everything was covered with ice—it looked like a fairyland.

"No school today," Megan's mom announced. "It's too dangerous for the buses to be out. What are you going to do with your free day?"

Megan just shrugged her shoulders and stared at her oatmeal.

"What's bothering you, Megs?" her dad asked. "Would you rather go to school?"

"School is confusing," Megan said. "I'm having trouble sorting out all the different ideas. In biology, the teacher talks about evolution and how the world and people came about over millions of years."

Dad patted her on the shoulder. "I know you're very smart and learn easily, but not everything you're going to be taught is true. Remember what you learn in church, Sunday school, and Bible study. Trust the people who know God and his Word."

Your Turn

1. Have you been taught something different than what you believe? What did you do?
2. When you are confused about what to believe, who do you talk to?

_____

_____

Prayer

Jesus, you are my master teacher. I want soak up your wisdom. Amen.

Discovering Discernment

I will instruct you and teach you in the way you should go.

– Psalm 32:8

Atten-tion!

As usual, the youth church noise had reached a high pitch. Jeff Wallace, one of the youth pastors, waved two fingers in the air. That was the sign for quiet.

"Atten-tion!" he usually said that when he wanted them to focus. "Our topic today is on that very subject: paying attention. That means you, Eva."

Eva Miller suddenly stopped whispering to her friend Natalie. They both grinned.

"God wants us to pay attention to what he put in the Bible. He wants us to listen with our ears as well as our hearts. Why do you suppose that's important? Eva, what do you think?"

Once more, Eva had been caught talking to her friend. "Because we're supposed to?"

"Yes, but paying attention also helps us stick close to God."

After the meeting, Eva went up to the youth pastor. "I'm sorry I wasn't paying attention."

Pastor Jeff smiled. "Well, at least you knew to repent and confess. You must have been paying some attention along the way."

Your Turn

1. What makes it hard for you to pay attention?
2. Look up and write out Hebrews 2:1. What helps you to keep from "drifting away"?

Prayer

Lord, open my eyes and ears to your truths. Amen.

Discovering Discernment

I will instruct you and teach you in the way you should go.

– Psalm 32:8

The Rumor

Terry Davis clicked on the icon labeled "Kids Only" chat room. Some of her friends planned to log on at 6:30. She glanced at the clock: 6:27. *They'll be on soon, might as well log on.* She joined a discussion about her favorite author.

She typed: I've read all of Martin's books. I can't wait for her new one!

Someone with the screen name "EekCat" replied: She's not really a Christian.

Terry: How do you know?

EekCat: Someone in another chat room told me.

Terry's heart gave a sick lurch. *That can't be true…can it?*

Terry's friend Renee entered the discussion room.

Ren123: That is totally bogus. There was a notice in the chat room about that rumor. It's totally false. Be careful with your facts.

EekCat dropped out of the conversation.

Terry's parents had warned her about not believing everything she read. "Some people don't tell the truth," her dad had said.

That is the truth, Terry thought as she asked Renee what she was going to wear to Sydney's birthday party.

Your Turn

1. What did EekCat want Terry to believe?
2. Why do you think her parents told her not to believe everything she read?

Prayer

Lord, show me how to discern your truth and stand up for you. Keep me safe. Amen.

Discovering Discernment

I will instruct you and teach you in the way you should go.

– Psalm 32:8

Are You Listening?

"Cybil, are you listening to me?"

Cybil half-heard her three-year-old brother talking. Tyler talked nonstop sometimes. Most of her attention was reserved for the program blasting from the TV. Abruptly the TV went black.

"Mom! Cable's out!" Cybil yelled.

Her mother poked her head through the doorway. "Not really. I turned it off."

"Mo-o-o-om! I was watching something!"

"You weren't paying attention to your brother."

"Mom!"

"Don't 'Mom' me. You were the one who told me you wanted to be less selfish. You said you made a decision in church to pay more attention to the needs of others."

Cybil remembered. She almost regretted having told her mom.

"Uh, okay. Tyler, what did you want?" Cybil realized Tyler had left the room. "Where'd he go?"

"To his room," Mom replied.

Cybil sighed as she got up from the sofa. She was a little sorry she'd tuned out her brother.

Your Turn

1. What message was Cybil sending to her little brother?
2. Is there someone you're tuning out? What will you do to tune in?

Prayer

Jesus, I want to pay attention to the people I love. I also want to be considerate and listen to everyone I meet. Amen.

Discovering Discernment

God, the Teacher

God wants to teach you something very important. Follow the directions to find out what he wants you to know.

- Color all the squares that have an "＊" or "+" in them
- Color every square that has one of these letters: "F," "L," "W"
- Color each square that has an "X" or "Z"
- Color each empty square.

Z		＊			L	X		+		W		F
I	+			＊			X		W		T	Z
+		＊	F		I	＊		S		L		W
	＊	Z		B		X		+	Y		X	
	G	+		W	R		L	A		C	＊	E
	W		+		Y	F	O		＊	U		Z
H	＊	L		A		+	V			E	L	+
+		B	＊		E		F	+	E		N	W
S	＊		L		A	Z	V		+	E		D
+		＊		F		L		W	Z		+	X

You've discovered a great truth about you!

Prayer

Lord, No matter how much I learn, the most important lessons for me are to love you, listen to you, and obey you. Amen.

Discovering Discernment

Your Attention, Please!

Pay attention to the scene for three minutes. Now use paper or something to cover the image. (No peeking!) Turn the book upside down. See how many questions you can answer without looking at the picture.

4. Was the jump rope on the bed or near it?

3. Name at least two items on her desk.

2. What stuffed animal sat on her desk?

1. What was the girl reading?

Prayer

Lord, when I pray and read your Word, open my heart and mind to you. Amen.

Gaining Wisdom

The Holy Scriptures...make you wise for salvation through faith in Christ Jesus.

– 2 Timothy 3:15

Crazy Quilt

Great-aunt Gertrude was staying with Lily's family. Auntie had arthritic knees and couldn't walk without a cane. She always had a cheery smile and liked being busy. Lily's father set up a quilting frame in front of a sunny window so Auntie could be with everyone while she quilted.

Lily liked to watch her sew the colorful pieces together with tiny, even stitches. She also liked listening to Auntie's stories about growing up. Each day the quilt was a little larger and more colorful, but Lily couldn't see any pattern. Auntie said, "Lily, this is a 'crazy quilt.' The pieces are leftover scraps of cloth I fit together. I never know how it's going to turn out until I'm all finished. This quilt is like life. I've had lots of experiences—sad and happy. They all fit together because of something I learned at your age."

Lily asked, "What was that?"

"God's Word will help me be wise. It tells me God loves me and is with me through every crazy bit of life," Auntie said as she stitched in another colorful piece.

Your Turn

1. If a friend needed advice, would you recommend God and his Word?
2. What would you say?

Prayer

Lord Jesus, thank you for your Word. Amen.

Gaining Wisdom

The Holy Scriptures…make you wise for salvation through faith in Christ Jesus.

– 2 Timothy 3:15

The Haircut

Maria sneaked in the side door and tiptoed to her bedroom. After she closed the door, she faced the mirror. She hardly recognized herself! *Why did I do this?* she wondered as she tugged at her very short black hair. It looks like I'm wearing a fuzzy black cap.

All Maria's friends had cute, short hairstyles. Maria wanted to look cool too.

"Hey, Maria, nice buzz!" hooted José when she came to dinner. Self-consciously, Maria touched her head.

Maria's mom looked shocked. "What happened to your beautiful hair?"

"I wanted to look cool like the other girls. I took my birthday money and got a haircut. But I don't look cool at all. I look ugly," she wailed.

"Well, not ugly, but you certainly look different," Mom said. "You are a very smart girl, but you didn't make a very wise decision. A wise person asks for advice. Why didn't you talk to me first? Now you will have to live with your decision. Fortunately, hair grows back."

Your Turn

1. Have you ever made a decision you regretted later? What happened?
2. Why is it wise to ask for advice before important decisions?

Prayer

God, I need wisdom to your wisdom. Please help me. Amen.

Gaining Wisdom

*The Holy Scriptures…make you wise for salvation
through faith in Christ Jesus.*

– 2 Timothy 3:15

What to Do?

Abby was working on a poster for art class. At least that's what she'd intended to do. But actually she was staring off into space with a frown creasing her forehead. That's how her dad found her when he came home from work.

"Hi, Princess," he said. "Something wrong?"

"I just don't know what to do," Abby answered.

Dad moved around the table and looked at Abby's poster. "Looks good to me," he said. "You're a good artist. All you need to do is finish it."

Abby shook her head. "I wasn't talking about the poster. I just don't know the right thing to do sometimes when things come up at school. Like when some girls make fun of another girl or something. It's hard to figure out."

"You can always ask God to help you know what to do. Knowing to ask God for help is the beginning of wisdom," Dad said. "Hmm, do you want my help with this poster? Would that be a wise decision?"

"Hmm, maybe not," said Abby with a grin.

Your Turn

1. When you're not sure what to do about a problem, where do you go for advice?
2. Is having wisdom mean the same as being smart? Why or why not?

_____

_____

Prayer

Lord, help me remember to ask for your help when I'm not sure what to do. Amen.

Gaining Wisdom

The Holy Scriptures...make you wise for salvation
through faith in Christ Jesus.

– 2 Timothy 3:15

Nola's Responsibility

"Why can't you keep up!" Nola demanded.

Garrick had fallen again. Why was he so clumsy? He couldn't seem to walk fast without tripping over something.

Nola tapped her foot while she waited with arms folded. She was so sick of being responsible for her five-year-old brother! She couldn't even go to the park two blocks from their house without having him tag along.

A small crowd and two police cars near a tall, yellow house caused her to pause. She knew the family who lived in the house. One of them was a girl in her class. "What's going on?" she asked a boy she knew. He was in a different fifth-grade class.

"Stacey's little sister is missing," he said. "They thought she was out in the backyard playing, but…"

Nola quickly looked down at her brother. He tugged on her hand.

"Can we go now?" he asked.

Nola nodded. Her little brother was a pain sometimes, but she didn't want anything to happen to him. She held his hand a little tighter and slowed down.

Your Turn

1. What did Nola learn after hearing about Stacey's sister?
2. What are your responsibilities? How do you feel about them?

Prayer

Jesus, thank you for the responsibilities I have. Teach me to faithfully carry them out. Amen.

Gaining Wisdom

The Holy Scriptures…make you wise for salvation through faith in Christ Jesus.

– 2 Timothy 3:15

What's So Great About Responsibility?

"You've got chores? Your parents treat you like a slave!' Sharon exclaimed.

Daisy wished she could agree. She was almost sorry she'd said anything. "My parents want me to learn to be responsible, I guess." Daisy glanced with envy at Sharon's laughing face as they rode the school bus. Sharon didn't have to do chores. Her parents gave her lots of spending money. Daisy wished her life was like that.

As soon as they walked into class, Mrs. Nygren whispered to Daisy, "I want to talk to you after class."

Daisy nodded, but her stomach flip-flopped. *Now what?*

After school, Mrs. Nygren said, "Daisy, I know you're a hardworking, responsible student. That's why I want to recommend you to be on the sixth-grade student council. Each teacher can nominate a student. I'd like to nominate you."

Daisy grinned. *Maybe responsibility isn't so bad!*

Your Turn

1. Why did Daisy want to be like Sharon?
2. Did Mrs. Nygren make a good choice in nominating Daisy? Why or why not?

_____

_____

_____

Prayer

Lord, show me how to value responsibility and always do my best. Amen

Gaining Wisdom

The Way to Wisdom

The letters and numbers below the empty boxes fit in the column directly above them, but not necessarily in the order listed. Decide which letter goes in which box and write it in. Cross off each letter as it is used.

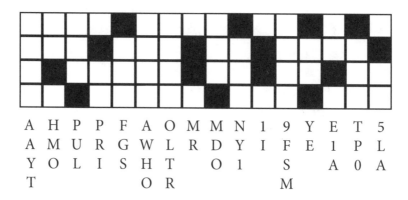

```
A H P P F A O M M N 1 9 Y E T 5
A M U R G W L R D Y I F E 1 P L
Y O L I S H T   O 1   S   A 0 A
T         O R       M
```

Prayer

Dear Lord, I know your Word lights the way I should go. Thank you for your help. Amen.

Gaining Wisdom

A Walk to the Park

Nola is responsible for taking Garrick to the park. But there are distractions along the way. Will you help Nola take Garrick to the park and then back home a different way?

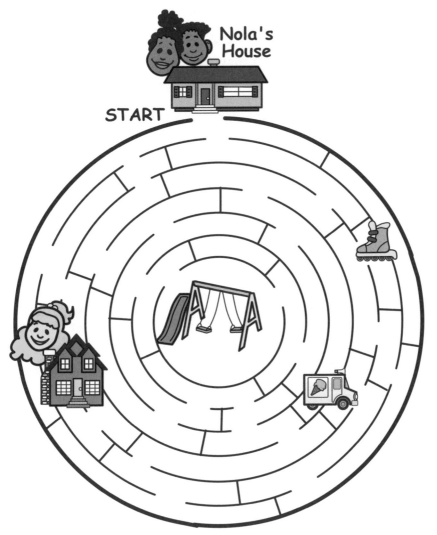

Prayer

Father, help me accept the responsibilities that are given to me. I want to please you always. Amen.

A Humble Spirit

Humble yourselves before the Lord, and he will lift you up.

– James 4:10

Put God First

The kids in Kendra's fifth-grade Sunday-school class were filled with questions. Kendra had started it all with her question about humility: Why was it important to have?

"Why do we have to ask God for stuff? Why can't he just give us stuff automatically?" Curtis asked.

"Asking him reminds us that he's God and we should obey him," Peter, the college guy who led the class, answered. "We're supposed to put him first. Doing that keeps us humble."

Some of the kids sighed loudly when Peter said the word "humble."

Peter smiled. "That's why we bow our heads when we pray. Some people in the Bible got on their knees and put their faces on the floor. It's a sign of respect." Peter suddenly dropped to his knees and placed his forehead against the floor.

Some of the kids giggled. After a second or two, he got up. "Want to try it?" he asked.

No one moved.

Peter laughed. "Well, there are other ways of being humble before God. If you're willing to do what he says, you're willing to put him first."

Your Turn

1. Why do you think you need to be humble?
2. How do you put God first?

Prayer

When it comes to you, God, help me have a "You first" attitude. Amen.

A Humble Spirit

Humble yourselves before the Lord, and he will lift you up.
– James 4:10

Mr. Plotz

"Hi, Mr. Plotz," Sara called to an older man placing books on a bookshelf.

"Hi, Sara." He waved and went back to shelving books.

"Why do you speak to him?" Sara's friend Benita asked.

"He's nice and always helpful," said Sara.

Benita grabbed her arm. "Come on, there's some space over here." They joined the crowd gathered for a book signing by their favorite new author. The kids were abuzz with excitement as they waited for the author to show up.

One of the bookstore employees came to the microphone. He gave a brief background on the author and said, "Here he is!"

Applause broke out. Sara turned and was stunned to see Mr. Plotz walk forward.

"Hi! I'm sure I caught some of you by surprise," Mr. Plotz said. "My pen name is E. Arthur Smith. God has blessed me, and I found a publisher interested in my books. I continue working here because I like helping people. Besides, it keeps me humble. I'm glad you like my books!"

Sara glanced at Benita and almost laughed at the amazed look on her face.

Your Turn

1. How do you expect someone famous to act?
2. Why does working in the bookstore keep Mr. Plotz humble?

Prayer

Help me be humble, God, as Jesus is. Amen.

A Humble Spirit

Humble yourselves before the Lord, and he will lift you up.

– James 4:10

The Contest

"Second place!" Stella grumbled as she looked at the ribbon attached to her drawing. "I know my poster deserved better than this!" She jerked her thumb at the poster next to hers. A large, first-place ribbon dangled from it.

"Well, I'm happy with fifth place," her best friend, Iris, said. "I didn't think I'd get a ribbon at all. There are so many cool posters in the contest."

"Most of them are ugly," Stella said. "I worked hard on this school spirit poster. I know I deserve better than second place."

"Ssshhh. Ms. Watson will hear you."

Ms. Watson was one of the teachers judging the contest. She suddenly headed their way. "Oh, girls, there's been a mix-up," she said. "Someone placed the ribbons on the wrong posters. I'm really sorry about this."

Stella threw Iris an I-told-you-so look.

Ms. Watson swapped the first-place ribbon with Iris' fifth-place ribbon. "There! That's correct."

"Congratulations," Ms. Watson said. "Sorry about the mix-up."

Stunned, Stella stood there in silence.

Your Turn

1. Who was humble?
2. When it comes to what you do best, are you like Stella or like Iris?

_____

_____

Prayer

Lord, you gave me my abilities. Thank you. Amen.

A Humble Spirit

Humble yourselves before the Lord, and he will lift you up.

– James 4:10

Makeover List

Madeline and her friend, Quinn, were watching the New Year's Day parade on TV. The girls were giggling and talking about their New Year's Eve sleepover.

Between munching on nachos, pretzels, and chips, they oohed and aahed over the gorgeous floats. During a quiet moment, Madeline heard the TV announcers talking about their New Year's resolutions. "What's a resolution?" she asked Quinn.

Quinn shrugged and kept munching.

Madeline's mom heard the question. "A resolution is when you decide you're going to do something or change something about yourself. On New Year's Day, lots of people resolve to do things better, like get in shape."

Quinn and Madeline decided to make some New Year's resolutions. Soon they were writing like crazy. After a few minutes, Madeline tossed down her paper. "I'd like to change things about myself, but I don't know if I can it."

"You probably can't do them all by yourself," agreed her mom. "God can do anything, and he will help you keep your resolutions if they are reasonable."

"Hope I don't keep him too busy," laughed Madeline.

Your Turn

1. What would you like to change in the way you act or the things you do?
2. How can God help you keep your resolutions?

Prayer

Dear God, help me change the things in my life that hold me back from living for you. Amen.

271

A Humble Spirit

Humble yourselves before the Lord, and he will lift you up.
– James 4:10

The To-Do List

The refrigerator door in the Gomez household served as the family bulletin board. There were reminders of appointments and meetings, notices from school, and pictures and artwork. The items were constantly changing—except for Mama's to-do list.

"Why do you always have that list on the fridge?" Rosa asked her mother.

"Well, it helps keep me focused on what I need to do. It gives me a purpose in my everyday life," her mama explained.

"Do you always get everything done?"

Mama Gomez laughed. "Not usually. Then I add them to next week's list, or I decide they weren't as important as I thought. But the first thing on the list is always the same."

Rosa read "Work for God" across the top of Mama's "What does that mean?" she asked.

"Praying and studying the Bible helps me know what God wants me to do. That gives purpose to my life and work."

"Hmm, I think I could use a to-do list," decided Rosa.

Your Turn

1. Do you make to-do lists for each day or week? Why not try it?
2. What three or four things would you put on your life's to-do list?

_____

_____

_____

Prayer

Lord, help me focus on you and your purpose for my life. Amen.

A Humble Spirit

David's Plea

David usually put God first in all he did. To find a beautiful description of loving God, complete the puzzle Put the letters below each column in their proper places in the same column in the puzzle. The letters may not be listed in the exact order in which they'll be used. Mark off used letters to help you keep track; a letter may only be used once. Black boxes indicate the end of a word.

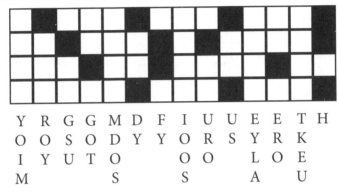

Prayer

Father God, my soul thirsts for you. Fill me with your presence. Amen.

A Humble Spirit

Some New Resolutions!

You can make resolutions anytime. Think about you and your life. What could be improved? What should you stop doing? Answer these questions to get started, and then fill in the chart.

What are some things about your life, actions, and attitudes you'd like to change?

_____

Pick one of your answers and make a plan—a resolution—about how to accomplish it. Fill in the grid. Put a check mark in the boxes showing how you're doing. (You can mark for morning, afternoon, and evening if you'd like.) Keep track for a month to see your progress.

	Prayed	Always	Usually	Seldom
Week 1				
Week 2				
Week 3				
Week 4				

Prayer

Lord God, I know that all things are possible when I turn to you for help. Amen.

Purposes, Plans, Promises

The LORD is our lawgiver.

– Isaiah 33:22

Oops!

Jessie slipped through the classroom door and down the hall, looking over her shoulder to make sure no one had seen her. Her class had a substitute teacher, so hopefully no one would notice she was gone.

"Oops!" Jessie rounded the corner and ran directly into Mrs. Gibson, her teacher. "Oh! I thought you were going to be absent today, Mrs. Gibson!"

"Just for half a day, for a doctor's appointment," answered Mrs. Gibson. "Jessie, do you have a hall pass?"

Jessie fidgeted. "Um, I needed to do an errand for the substitute," she began, but the discernment and care in Mrs. Gibson's eyes stopped her lie.

Jessie hung her head. "I left," she confessed. "I didn't want to be there."

"I'm glad you told the truth, Jessie," said Mrs. Gibson. "I care about you. That's why our class has the hall pass rule—so I can know you're safe."

"I never thought about rules actually helping us," Jessie admitted.

"You bet they do!" said Mrs. Gibson. "Now, let's both go to class."

Your Turn

1. Why did Mrs. Gibson make the hall pass rule for her students?
2. Why do you think God gave us the Ten Commandments?

_____

_____

Prayer

Thank you, Lord, for giving me your guidance. I know you love me! Amen.

Purpose, Plans, Promises

The LORD is our lawgiver.

– Isaiah 33:22

Samantha's Big Meeting

"You look terrific, Samantha!" said Claire, Samantha's younger sister, as she eyed Samantha's new dress enviously.

"Thanks," Samantha replied, smoothing the skirt. "Mom and I found the dress on sale last week."

"Wow. Did Mom say you could wear lipstick too?" Claire peered at her older sister's face. "And blush?"

Samantha grinned. "Yes. She said this was a special occasion, and that it was important for me to look my best. I'm meeting with the high-school principal to talk about tutoring some children in the elementary school."

"It's your first job interview!" said Claire. "That's really important. What else did you do to get ready?"

Samantha reached for a folder. "I put together a list of past experiences," she said. "Like helping with Vacation Bible School." Samantha bit her bottom lip. "Can you tell I'm a little nervous? I don't know what to expect."

"You'll do great—you've done so many good things to prepare," said Claire. "And I'll be praying for you."

"Thanks, little sis!" Samantha gave Claire a hug.

Your Turn

1. Name a time when you had a big meeting, audition, test, or tryout. How did you feel beforehand?
2. What did you do to get ready? How did it turn out?

Prayer

Dear God, thank you for giving me the desire to try new things. I'll do my best with your help. Amen.

Purpose, Plans, Promises

The LORD is our lawgiver.

– Isaiah 33:22

Anna Helps Out

Anna's father was at the computer. When she heard him sigh in frustration. She asked, "Do you need help, Dad?"

"I can't figure out how to transfer these pictures to a desktop folder," Anna's dad replied. "I've been working at it for an hour. I'm totally stuck."

"May I give it a try?" asked Anna.

Her dad looked doubtful. "You can give it a shot if you'd like."

Anna slipped into the seat. "I learned how to do something like this at Kerry's house last week," she said, moving the mouse across the screen.

"Well, look at that!" said Anna's dad, as the photos appeared in the right file. "You were just the person I needed. Where were you an hour ago?"

Anna and her father laughed and grinned at each other.

Your Turn

1. Has God given you a special task or ability?
2. How can you get ready to help?

_____

_____

_____

_____

Prayer

Lord, I want to be ready when you have a task for me. I'm listening and ready to learn and do. Amen.

Purpose, Plans, Promises

The LORD is our lawgiver.

– Isaiah 33:22

Sydney's Big News

Sydney stared at the papers in front of her, and then looked over at her parents. "I'm adopted?" she asked in shock and disbelief.

Her dad reached over to Sydney and grasped her hand. "Yes, Sydney. We wanted you so badly. We asked God to give us our own baby, and he gave us the most wonderful girl we could ever ask for—you!"

Sydney was confused. "What exactly do these papers mean?" she asked, flipping through the packet.

Her mom put her arm around Sydney. "It's a special agreement," she explained. "When the judge had us sign these, we promised that no matter what happened, we would be your parents and love you. And you would be our daughter forever. Does that make sense?"

Sydney nodded slowly. She felt calmer. Her parents really wanted her!

"We made a commitment, Syd," her dad went on. "It looks like you're stuck with us."

Sydney looked at her dad. There were tears in his eyes.

"I wouldn't have it any other way," she said, reaching up to put her arms around his neck.

Your Turn

1. Sydney's parents signed an agreement regarding Sydney. What did they promise to do?
2. God made a similar agreement about his family. He promised to be our God forever.

Prayer

God, thank you for loving me so much that you adopted me into your family! Amen.

Purpose, Plans, Promises

The LORD is our lawgiver.

– Isaiah 33:22

Someone Like You

"What's this?" Emma asked her mom, pointing to the notebook on the kitchen counter.

"It's our new House Manual," her mom answered. "We're going to use it to record rules and agreements for our family."

Emma thought for a moment. "Why do we need a record of our rules? When we forget to do something, you just remind us."

"Precisely the point," said her mom. "Let me ask you a question, Emma. Do you have a hard time understanding our family rules?"

"Only once in a while, when we have a new rule," Emma answered. "But then I ask you or Dad to explain why it's important. Most of the time things make sense."

"Then why do you forget to follow the rules?" her mom asked.

"I guess I don't think about them very often," Emma admitted.

"So when you and your brothers help us write them down, you'll be more likely to remember them," her mother answered, pointing to the kitchen sink. "Like loading your dishes in the dishwasher, perhaps?"

Emma grinned. "I think I see what you mean."

Your Turn

1. What makes it hard to remember house rules?
2. What helps you to remember and follow your house rules?

Prayer

Lord, thank you for loving me and giving me rules to follow to stay safe and help my family. Amen.

Purpose, Plans, Promises

Famous Promises

Promises can be "covenants" or agreements between two or more people.
Find out about three important promises.

Genesis 9:8-9, 11

Who? _____

What? _____

1 Samuel 18:3

Who? _____

What? _____

Hebrews 9:15

Who? _____

What? _____

Prayer

God, I know when I follow your commands I please you. Teach me your
ways. Amen.

Purpose, Plans, Promises

Moses' Big Meeting

God planned to meet with Moses to give him the Ten Commandments. He helped Moses get ready by giving him some special instructions. Read Exodus 19:10-19. Match the words from the list on the left to the list on the right to find out more about what Moses and the people did.

What the people needed to wash

What the people couldn't touch

What the people saw in the sky

What the people saw over the mountain

What the people heard

Trumpet blast

Clouds & smoke

The mountain

Thunder & lightning

Their clothes

Prayer

God, I want to read my Bible every day so you can teach me your perfect ways. Amen.

The 10 Commandments

Give to the LORD the glory he deserves!
– 1 Chronicles 16:29 NLT

What's the Point?

"I don't see what the big deal is," said Tina. "The Ten Commandments are just a bunch of rules."

"God wouldn't give us rules to follow unless there was a point to them," said Brianne.

Ms. Gray, their Sunday-school teacher, nodded. "And what do you think his point is?"

Brianne thought for a moment. "Maybe people weren't treating him right," she answered. "Maybe they needed to know what he expected."

"You've hit on an important idea," said Ms. Gray. "We have a relationship with God. In fact, the first four commandments give specific instructions about how God expects people to treat him."

"Do you mean like putting him first, honoring him, worshiping him, and using his name respectfully?" asked Brianne.

Ms. Gray nodded.

"I never thought about it that way before," said Tina. "Can we look at the first four commandments again?"

Your Turn

1. Which of the 10 Commandments tell us how to related to God?
2. What is a way you can show you treat God with respect?

_____

_____

_____

Prayer

Dear God, I want to have a close relationship with you. I will treat you with love and respect. Amen.

The 10 Commandments

Give to the LORD the glory he deserves!
– 1 Chronicles 16:29 NLT

Simple Rules

"What was that all about, Lacey?" asked Mom. "I could hear you yelling all the way in here."

"Matt is so embarrassing!" Lacey gritted her teeth. "He says the goofiest things in front of my friends. Why does he have to be my brother?"

"It's not just Matt who has been bothering you lately," her mom pointed out gently. "Remember the conversation we had about your friend Elizabeth?"

Lacey hung her head. "I know," she admitted. "I was jealous of her."

"Does it feel good to put down Matt and Elizabeth?" asked her mom.

"Not at all." Lacey groaned. "I'm having a hard time knowing how to get along with people. I wish there was a simple set of rules I could follow."

"I know where to find what you need." Mom grabbed her Bible. "The last six of the Ten Commandments teach us how to have good relationships."

"Give me that!" Lacey exclaimed. "Not that I meant to be disrespectful, of course!"

Laughing, Lacey and her mom turned the pages to find Exodus 20 together.

Your Turn

1. Name a time when you had a hard time getting along with someone. How did you respond?
2. If you could do it over, what, if anything, would you do differently?

Prayer

God, help me look to your Word for insights on good relationships. Amen.

The 10 Commandments

Give to the LORD the glory he deserves!
– 1 Chronicles 16:29 NLT

School Spirit Week

Kendra handed Rachel a list:

What to Do for Spirit Week
Monday: Wear blue and gold.
Tuesday: Wear crazy socks.
Wednesday: Put your key chains on the left zipper of your backpack.
Thursday: Wear a funny hat.
Friday: Wear your sports uniform or a school T-shirt.

"What's this?" Rachel asked.

"The guidelines the student council agreed on for Spirit Week," Kendra answered.

"But at the first meeting, the group decided to just ask people to wear blue and gold all week," Rachel said. "Lots of people don't play sports, don't own school T-shirts, don't have crazy socks, and don't have key chains. Including me."

"Guess you better get a school shirt," said Kendra. "The rules changed!"

Rachel shook her head. "Too many changes," she muttered to herself.

Your Turn

1. Changes happen in your world every day. Without naming who, record a change you've noticed in a friend recently.
2. God's rules never change. What are some advantages to rules that stay constant?

_____

_____

Prayer

Lord, thank you for your Word that never changes. You are my Rock. Amen.

The 10 Commandments

Give to the LORD the glory he deserves!
– 1 Chronicles 16:29 NLT

Grandpa's Microscope

"Now, Laurie, it's been a long time since I've used this," Grandpa warned. "It may need adjusting or be broken."

Laurie and her grandfather were up in the attic looking at his old microscope case. Together, they gently lifted the microscope out of its crinkly leather box.

Laurie took a soft cloth and wiped dust off the microscope's parts. "I understand, Grandpa," she said. "But let's try it anyway. If it works, maybe we can take a closer look at some of the things we collected this morning."

Grandpa placed a prepared slide beneath the eyepiece. For a few minutes, he fiddled with knobs. He took a deep breath. "Well, what do you know!" he whistled softly. "Take a look here, Laurie. It's a monarch butterfly wing."

Laurie leaned over the microscope and adjusted the fine focus knob. "Grandpa, there are so many details—it's gorgeous!" Laurie exclaimed. She looked up at her grandfather. "So the microscope still works."

"It sure does," Grandpa answered, nodding his head in wonder. "Even after all these years, I still get a thrill seeing God's handiwork so closely."

Your Turn

1. 1. What did the microscope enable Laurie and her grandpa to do?
2. 2. In what ways is the Bible similar a microscope?

Prayer

God, thank you that your Word gives me exciting glimpses into who you are. Amen.

The 10 Commandments

Give to the LORD the glory he deserves!
– 1 Chronicles 16:29 NLT

Jackie's Turn

"Your time's up!" Jackie yelled at her brother, Ryan. "It's my turn on the computer!"

"I'm not quite done with my history paper," Ryan answered. "Will you please give me another half hour?"

"No fair!" Jackie said. "You've been working for hours—ever since you got home from school."

"This is homework, Jackie, and it's due tomorrow," Ryan answered. "Plus, you're not exactly one to talk. What about all the time you spend on the computer instant messaging with your friends?"

Jackie scowled. It was true. She loved being online with her friends.

Their dad came into the room. "Jackie, did you finish folding your laundry and putting it away?"

She shook her head. "I was waiting for Ryan to finish at the computer."

"Are you becoming obsessed with the computer?" her dad asked. "You don't want to worship a box of plastic and wires."

Your Turn

1. An idol or god is something focused on to the exclusion of other important aspects of life. Do you think the computer might be an idol or god for Jackie?
2. Why do you think God wants you to worship him and nothing else?

Prayer

Lord, help me recognize when I'm beginning to worship someone or something other than you. Amen.

The 10 Commandments

Name the Six

Look up and read Exodus 20:12-17. Now, see if you can fill in the details without rereading the verses.

Exodus 20:12   Honor

Exodus 20:13   You shall not

Exodus 20:14   You shall not

Exodus 20:15   You shall not

Exodus 20:16   You shall not

Exodus 20:17   You shall not

Prayer

Father God, please help me to memorize your Ten Commandments so I can honor you and treat others well. Amen.

The 10 Commandments

False Gods vs. the Lord God

The items on the list are not evil. However, they can take on new meaning if they're given higher priority than they deserve. They can gradually become "gods." Understanding their appeal will help you keep them in proper perspective. Fill in the grid. Look at the false gods in the left column. In the middle column, write down why this false god can seem attractive. In the column on the right, write down why God is more significant than the false god.

False god	Why it is attractive	How the Lord God is more significant
money		
clothes		
popularity		
television		
good grades		
fame		

Prayer

Lord, it's easy to get caught up in the things of this world, but I want to always put you first. Amen.

Establishing Priorities

What is seen is temporary, but what is unseen is eternal.

– 2 Corinthians 4:18

Homesick

Madison reached for another tissue and wiped her eyes. It would be embarrassing if her cabin mates found her alone on her bunk crying. She'd been away from home overnight before, but this time, it was for a whole week. Camp was fun, but everything was different.

"Hey, Madison!" Counselor Celia, poked her head into the cabin. "May I come in?"

Madison rolled over in her bunk and sat up. "Sure."

"Tell me, Madison," Celia said, "what's your favorite thing about home?"

Madison looked at her in surprise. "I guess it's my family. I miss talking with my mom each day. When I'm in a new place, it feels like those things don't exist."

"Do you think your mom and your room are still there?" asked Celia gently.

"Of course," Madison answered.

Celia put her arm around Madison. "When things get hard or confusing for me, it helps me to remember what I know is true."

Your Turn

1. Why did Madison feel lost? What truths had she forgotten?
2. What truths about God can you remember to keep him first?

_____

_____

_____

Prayer

Lord, help me put you first in my life even when life is confusing. Amen.

Establishing Priorities

What is seen is temporary, but what is unseen is eternal.

– 2 Corinthians 4:18

Melissa's Calendar

On Sunday evening, Melissa looked at her calendar for the coming week. She groaned. She had something extra to do each day after school.

Monday: piano lesson

Tuesday: soccer practice

Wednesday: work on the science fair project at Allison's house

Thursday: student council meeting

Friday: McGraw family coming over for dinner

In addition to all of that, Melissa knew she'd have to practice piano and get her homework done each day. Plus, she'd promised her mom that she'd help clean the house on Thursday evening to be ready for their guests Friday.

"God, I'm so busy," Madison prayed. "All of these activities are important to me. What should I do?"

She sat down and made a simple schedule for the next five days. As she worked, Melissa saw that she had several hours free each night to complete her daily responsibilities. Quickly, she penciled in "time with God" next to "homework" and "piano practice."

Your Turn

1. Feeling too busy, Madison still prayed. How did it help her?
2. Why is spending time with God each day helpful?

Prayer

Lord, help me find time to spend with you today. Amen.

Establishing Priorities

What is seen is temporary, but what is unseen is eternal.

– 2 Corinthians 4:18

Brittany's Hard Day

It had been a hard day. Brittany looked at her science test paper once more: a dismal 76 percent. Then she thought about how Shannon, Stacey, and Angie had made fun of her at the bus stop. Brittany felt like she was going to explode. She really needed to be alone. When she got home, her sister, Megan, had the stereo blasting in the room they shared. Brittany wandered out into the kitchen. The phone rang. "Honey, will you get that?" her mom asked.

After delivering the phone to her mom, Brittany made a beeline for the living room. *Maybe there's some peace and quiet there,* she hoped. No, Evan, her little brother, had the television turned on to cartoons. "Hey, Britt," he said, "Want to watch?"

"No, thanks," Brittany murmured. She threw on a jacket and headed outside to her favorite tree in the backyard. The day was crisp. Brittany sat down and leaned against the tree's wide, strong trunk. *Lord, I love my family, but it's good to be alone once in a while. Thanks for this quiet place.*

Your Turn

1. Why did Brittany need to be alone?
2. Brittany had a special place to go to be alone with God. Do you?

_____

_____

_____

Prayer

Lord, help me make time with you a priority. Amen.

Establishing Priorities

What is seen is temporary, but what is unseen is eternal.

– 2 Corinthians 4:18

Kelly's Toucan

Hannah studied her bookcase. The shelves were crammed with dozens of stuffed animals: bears, giraffes, rabbits, flamingoes…even a bright-blue hippo. Hannah took good care of her animals, but today, she spent extra time organizing them. Her new friend Kelly was coming to spend the night.

When Kelly arrived, the girls arranged their sleeping bags in Hannah's room. "Wow, what a collection!" Kelly exclaimed, looking at Hannah's stuffed animals. "I only have one," she said, holding up a stuffed toucan.

Kelly grinned sheepishly. "Maybe it seems silly bringing him, but he's been a good friend. We've moved a lot, and my toucan has been everywhere with me."

"I've never taken my animals anywhere," Hannah confessed. "They just sit here on my shelf." Suddenly, that didn't seem quite right. She had an idea. "Let's find your toucan some friends!"

Your Turn

1. In what ways were Hannah's stuffed animals important to her?
2. Why was Kelly's toucan important to her?

_____

_____

_____

_____

Prayer

God, help me to love others deeply and share generously. Amen.

Establishing Priorities

What is seen is temporary, but what is unseen is eternal.

– 2 Corinthians 4:18

Molly's Favorite

Molly set the table while her mom prepared dinner.

"Now that you're in middle school, you have a different teacher for each class," her mom said. "Who's your favorite?"

Molly thought for a moment. Her language arts teacher, Ms. Walker, spent a lot of time on those pesky grammar rules, but she also suggested good books. She loved to read. Social studies was boring, but at least Ms. Morrison was kind. Mr. Roberts made science interesting. And even though algebra was her weakest subject, Mr. Atkins was patient with her.

"I'm not sure," Molly told her mother. "There's at least one thing I like about each of them." She sighed. "I wish I could take the best qualities of all my teachers and roll them into one. Then I'd have a perfect teacher!"

"Maybe you can," her mom answered. "God is one of your teachers. He is kind, patient, challenging, interesting, and a whole lot more!"

Molly grinned. "You forgot one other thing, Mom. He knows all the answers!"

Molly and her mother laughed together.

Your Turn

1. List your teachers and one thing you like about each one of them.
2. Why does God want you to respect your teachers?

_____

_____

_____

Prayer

God, thank you for my teachers. Help me to respect them, but put you first in my thoughts. In Jesus' name, amen.

Establishing Priorities

Look for the Hearts

It can be hard to see God's love. With practice, you'll get better and better. Can you find the six hearts hidden in this picture?

Prayer

Lord, I want to fix my eyes on you and your love for me even when I can't see you at work in my life. Amen.

Establishing Priorities

Looking and Loving Quiz

Do you value people more than appearances and possessions? Do you respond to people by how they look or how you can love? Find out with this unique and interesting quiz.

I. **Jenna's nail polish is chipped. You say...**
   A. "Don't you ever paint your nails?"
   B. "I like the color of your nail polish."

2. **Pastor Juan speaks with an accent. You...**
   A. Giggle with your sister about how funny he sounds.
   B. Try to listen to what he says and understand the message.

3. **The cashier at the grocery store has a large bandage on her cheek. You...**
   A. Whisper to your mom, "That makes her face look like a big marshmallow."
   B. Greet the cashier with a smile and thank her for being so helpful.

4. **Sara's gym shoes have holes in the heels and broken laces. You say...**
   A. "Don't you think it's time to get new gym shoes?"
   B. "Sara, you sure can run fast. I'm glad you're on our team."

5. **Jayme lives with her aunt and uncle. You say...**
   A. "Don't you wish you lived with your mom and dad?"
   B. "It was fun meeting your aunt and uncle. They're really nice."

Prayer

Dear God, teach me to see through your eyes. I want to love like you do. Amen.

The Ultimate God

Be holy because I, the LORD your God, am holy.

– Leviticus 19:2

The Social Studies Project

Madison walked home from school with Darcy. They planned to spend the afternoon at working on their social studies project.

"You've got our notes, right?" asked Darcy.

"Yes. Look, I've put them on cards and sorted them by topic," answered Madison.

Darcy rolled her eyes. "How can you be so organized?"

"Have you found some pictures online?" Madison asked. She knew Darcy was a computer whiz.

Darcy nodded. "It's really neat that we're working together," she said. "I like finding information, and you're good at organizing it."

The girls came through Darcy's front door. "Hi, Grandma!" shouted Darcy.

The house was silent. "She's probably talking with God," whispered Darcy.

Darcy's grandmother sat on a chair in the living room with her eyes shut.

The girls crept quietly to the kitchen for a snack.

"Why does she talk with God so much?" Madison asked.

"She says since God is so good and so holy, she spends time with him so he'll rub off on her." Darcy grinned. "She's probably also praying that you'll rub off on me and help me be organized!"

Your Turn

1. How do people "rub off" on each other when they spend time together?
2. What are some ways you'd like God to "rub off" on you?

Prayer

Lord, you are holy. Show me how I can grow to be more like you. Amen.

The Ultimate God

Be holy because I, the LORD your God, am holy.

– Leviticus 19:2

A Change of Focus

Ella dipped her hands into the barrel of chalk. She walked back to the sideline, nervously rubbing them together.

"Feeling okay, sport?" asked Mr. Fitzgerald, her gymnastics coach.

"I guess," said Ella. Ella was up next on the uneven bars, and right now her stomach was doing its own routine of flips and flops.

"Look, Ella," said Coach Fitz. "See all those people out there?"

Ella's eyes scanned the filled stadium. Scattered in the center of the arena, gymnasts from all over the state competed in different events.

"That's a lot of people," said Ella, her panic growing. "I'm not good enough to be here."

"No, Ella, you're wrong," said Coach Fitz firmly. "You're supposed to be here."

Ella felt better immediately. Coach Fitz didn't hand out compliments often. "But what if everyone does better than me?" she asked.

"Only God is greater than everybody here," said Coach Fitz. "Now, go out and nail that routine!"

The announcer called Ella's name. She bounded out to the bars and saluted the judges with a smile.

Your Turn

1. How was Ella making herself nervous?
2. How did Coach Fitz help her focus?

_____

_____

Prayer

God, help me be confident in my abilities because you gave them to me. Amen.

The Ultimate God

Be holy because I, the LORD your God, am holy.

– Leviticus 19:2

The Flute Competition

Kendra hurried into the band room and sat down. The first practice of the year was about to begin. Three girls entered the room, giggling and talking together. Each carried a flute case.

"Uh oh," said Kendra's friend Candace. "We've got some competition."

"What do you mean?" asked Kendra.

"Do you see that girl in the yellow shirt?" asked Candace, pointing to the group that had just entered. "She told me she's been playing for three years."

"Have you heard her play?" Kendra asked.

"Well, no," said Candace.

Kendra watched as the girl in the yellow shirt took out her Method Book 1 that Kendra and Candace had completed four months earlier. "Maybe she's good," Kendra said. "But don't be so sure. The real proof isn't in what she says; it's in what she does."

Your Turn

1. Whose point of view was more productive and positive?
2. What has God done that proves to you he is worthy of your love and praise?

_____

_____

_____

Prayer

God, you are worthy, and I praise you! Amen.

The Ultimate God

Be holy because I, the LORD your God, am holy.

– Leviticus 19:2

The Not-So-Perfect Day

Just an hour earlier, the sun had been shining on a picture-perfect summer day. Now, the wind whipped through the pine trees in the backyard, bending them until the treetops almost touched the ground.

"That storm sure came up fast," said Kasey's mother. "And it's getting worse. I didn't hear a tornado warning on the radio. Did you?"

"The electricity went out a few minutes ago," Kasey reminded her. Together, they looked through the windows. Rain pelted the window panes.

Kasey had never seen such fierce winds. A lawn chair flew by, followed by a large trash can and a toddler's bike.

"God is showing us his power today," said Kasey's mom. "Let's go to the basement so we'll be safe while we wait out the storm."

"Good idea!" Kasey agreed.

Your Turn

1. Describe a time when the weather surprised you.
2. Name different ways God shows his power through the weather.

_____

_____

_____

_____

Prayer

God, you show your power in the wind, rain, and storms. I'm awestruck. Amen.

The Ultimate God

Be holy because I, the LORD your God, am holy.
– Leviticus 19:2

What Money Can't Buy

Taylor moved carefully around the dining room table, gently setting down a dinner plate at each spot. The china was lovely.

"Try to finish quickly," Taylor's mom called to her from the kitchen. "The Jacobsons will be here in a few minutes."

In a hasty motion, Taylor set the plate down and it bumped a delicate cup. She heard an unmistakable crack. Taylor burst into tears.

"What is it, honey?" her mother asked, hurrying into the room.

"I broke a teacup," Taylor cried. "Mom, I'm so sorry. Your china is beautiful, and I've ruined a piece."

Taylor's mother looked at the broken pieces scattered on the white lace tablecloth. "Taylor, china can be replaced," she said gently. "In fact, I've broken several of these dishes myself."

Taylor looked at her in surprise.

"There are other things that are much more valuable," her mom went on. "Things that money can't buy."

"Like what?" Taylor asked.

"Like having a terrific daughter. Like being with friends tonight. Like having a God who loves us. Those kinds of things can never be replaced!" Mom hugged Taylor.

Your Turn

1. Name the most costly items you can imagine.
2. What are some things you value that money can't buy?

_____

_____

Prayer

Lord, thank you for your love. You are amazing beyond compare. Amen.

The Ultimate God

What It Means to Be Holy

Fill in the blanks to find out some of what makes Jesus the best example of holiness.

Jesus has a **H**___ ___ ___ ___ that is pure.

Jesus worships God **O** ___ ___ ___.

Jesus **L**___ ___ ___ ___ rightly.

Jesus sacrificed for **Y** ___ ___ and me.

Prayer

Lord, you alone are holy and worthy to be worshipped. Amen.

The Ultimate God

Worthy of Worship

God is awesome, and his Word gives us proof. To find a message that shows one reason God is worthy of our worship, cross out every S, Y, and Z. Write out the message below. The answer is in the back of the book.

FZYOR   XAXLYLX   THXEX   GZOXDS

OXYZF   TZHEX   NZATIXONXSZ

AZXRE   IXZDOXLS,   XBXUZTZY

YZTHXYEX   YLXZOXRDXY

YZMZXADYZEX   YTYZXHYYEX

XHZYEYXAZZVXEXYNXSY

~ Psalm 96:5

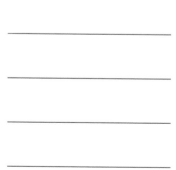

Prayer

Heavenly Father, you are my stronghold and my refuge. I will praise your name always. Amen.

God's Great Presence

The exalted One says…"I live in a high and holy place, but also with the one who is contrite and lowly in spirit.

– **Isaiah 57:15**

Kayla's Big Decision

"What's up, Kayla?" asked her mom. "You seem confused."

Kayla sighed. Avery had invited her to go on a picnic on Saturday, but Lily had called right then to ask if Kayla could go swimming on that day. Kayla wanted to do both. How could she decide what to do?

Kayla explained her problem. "I haven't done anything with Avery in a long time, and I want to see her," she said. "But swimming with Lily is a lot of fun too. Is there any way I can do both?"

Her mom smiled. "Let me ask you a question, Kayla. Do you know anyone who can be in two places at once?"

Kayla thought for a minute. "Yes, I do!" she answered triumphantly. "God!"

"Explain what you mean," said her mom.

"He lives in your heart and in my heart…and in anyone's heart who believes in him."

Her mom grinned. "Well, then here's the real question. Can you be in two places at once like God can?"

Kayla's face fell. "No. Only he can." She shrugged. "I guess I need to make a decision after all."

Your Turn

1. Name a time when you wanted to be in two places at the same time. What did you decide to do?
2. God is able to be many places at one time. How does that encourage you?

Prayer

God, I worship you. You have abilities no one and no thing can ever come close to. Amen.

God's Great Presence

The exalted One says…"I live in a high and holy place, but also with the one who is contrite and lowly in spirit.

– Isaiah 57:15

A Few Things to Learn

"Let's say that the soccer field measures 100 yards long by 60 yards wide," said Mrs. McDonnell, the math teacher. "How would you compute the total area?"

Madison groaned silently. Math was not her favorite subject.

Just behind her, Cody's hand shot up into the air. "You'd multiply 100 by 60," he said.

Madison growled to herself. Cody was her twin. Why did he always know all the answers? It just didn't seem fair that math was easy for Cody, but she had to work hard to understand it.

"And how would you label your answer, Cody?" asked Mrs. McDonnell.

"Yards," said Cody, "since that's what the field's measurements are in."

"Close," said Mrs. McDonnell. "It would be square yards because you're calculating area rather than length."

Looks like he's still got a few things to learn too, Madison thought.

Your Turn

1. How would you encourage Madison?
2. Everyone is unique and has special gifts or talents. What does that say about God?

_____

_____

_____

Prayer

God, I praise you. No one compares to you. Amen.

God's Great Presence

The exalted One says…"I live in a high and holy place, but also with the one who is contrite and lowly in spirit.

– Isaiah 57:15

A Discontinued Item

Laura and her mom stood in the cereal aisle of the grocery store looking for crispy rice puffs.

"I just don't see them anywhere," said Laura's mom.

Another shopper overheard their conversation. "You might want to check with the store manager. I've heard this store is discontinuing some items."

Laura's mom thanked the shopper. "Come on, Laura," she said.

They walked to the front of the store, and asked to speak with the manager.

Laura asked, "Can the manager help us?"

"Maybe," said Laura's mom. "But it could be a decision made by the head of all the managers for all the Food World grocery stores or by the leaders that own all the Food World grocery stores. If the leaders have decided to stop distributing crispy rice puffs, our manager must do what they say."

"I guess we can ask him ourselves if there's anything he can do," said Laura, as she spotted the manager walking toward them. "Here he comes."

Your Turn

1. Name the people who help you make good decisions, be responsible and live wisely.
2. Who advises those people?

Prayer

Thank you, God, that you are the Manager of all managers and the ultimate Leader in my life. I trust you. Amen.

God's Great Presence

The exalted One says…"I live in a high and holy place, but also with the one who is contrite and lowly in spirit.

– Isaiah 57:15

A Big Job

Katie moved the power washer hose back and forth across the concrete patio. Its stream of water removed debris and stains. She worked slowly; the patio hadn't been cleaned for several seasons, and stains had built up. Fast movements left splotchy streaks on the surface, but careful work made the patio look nearly new. At last she reached the patio's edge.

"Well done, Katie!" said her dad, walking over to the patio after cutting the lawn. "That was a big job."

"It looks a lot better, but it's still not totally clean," said Katie, pointing to three stains. "I went over those spots several times. I couldn't get them out."

"I'd say you cleaned it as well as anyone could," said her dad. "Some stains just can't be removed."

"But just yesterday, you told me that my mistakes are like stains," Katie reminded him. "You said that God can wipe all of them out when I tell him I'm sorry."

"That's right," said her dad. "God's forgiveness can clean anything. He's the ultimate power washer!"

Your Turn

1. Name a time when you felt stained and dirty on the inside from your mistakes.
2. What can God do to our inside stains?

Prayer

Thank you, Lord, that you can and will forgive my mistakes—all of them. Clean me up completely and make me feel new. Amen.

God's Great Presence

The exalted One says…"I live in a high and holy place, but
also with the one who is contrite and lowly in spirit.

– Isaiah 57:15

A Lot to Think About

The bus pulled to a stop in front of the school. Megan picked up her
backpack and got off. She had a lot to think about today—a big math
test this morning, a book report due tomorrow, tryouts for the softball
team. To top it off, she'd had a fight with her dad this morning. Megan
had asked if she could visit her aunt this weekend instead of next.
He'd misunderstood, thinking she didn't want to go with him to the
sportsman's show like they'd planned. Megan had just totally spaced it.

Megan made her way through the crowded halls, lost in her own
thoughts. Then she saw Emily leaning against the wall of lockers.

"Emily, I'm so sorry," she said, hurrying over to her friend. "I didn't
wait for you at the front of the school to walk to class together. I had a
lot on my mind this morning. I totally forgot."

Emily gave her an unpleasant look. "Whatever," she said, walking
away. "I guess I'll see you later."

Megan shook her head. *First Dad, now Emily. Am I that easy to*
misunderstand?

Your Turn

1. How do you feel when someone misunderstands you?
2. God understands all your thoughts and motives. What can you tell
   him when you're hurting?

Prayer

God, I'm grateful you can see into my heart and understand me. Amen.

God's Great Presence

How Does God Do It?

In the Bible, the term "heart" refers to a person's thoughts and feelings. How does God avoid misunderstanding your heart? Discover God's special technique by answering the questions after you read this verse:

The LORD searches every heart and understands every desire and every thought. If you seek him, he will be found by you (1 Chronicles 28:9).

I. What does the Lord do to every heart?

_____

2. What does he understand?

_____

3. When you seek him, what will happen?

_____

4. What does that mean to you?

_____

Prayer

Lord, I pray that as you search my heart you will weed out negative and destructive thoughts. I want to be right with you. Amen.

God's Great Presence

Make Your Home in My Heart

Fill in the blanks and then pray this prayer based on John 14:23 to God.

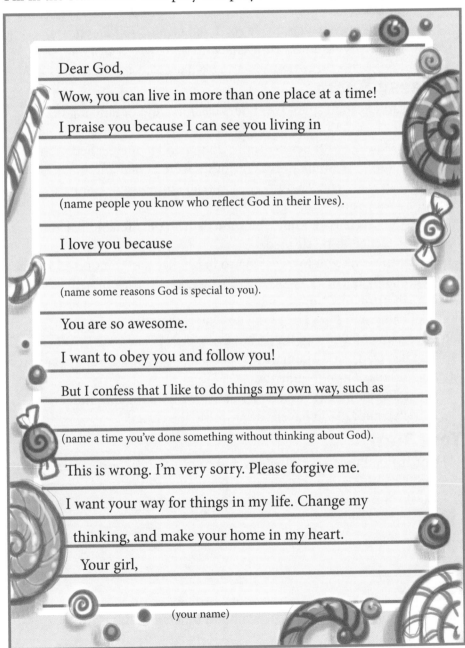

Dear God,

Wow, you can live in more than one place at a time!

I praise you because I can see you living in

_____

(name people you know who reflect God in their lives).

I love you because

_____

(name some reasons God is special to you).

You are so awesome.

I want to obey you and follow you!

But I confess that I like to do things my own way, such as

_____

(name a time you've done something without thinking about God).

This is wrong. I'm very sorry. Please forgive me.

I want your way for things in my life. Change my

thinking, and make your home in my heart.

Your girl,

_____
(your name)

Offering Encouragement

Let everything you say be good and helpful, so that your
words will be an encouragement to those who hear them.

– Ephesians 4:29 NLT

A Messy Room

Hannah smiled. She'd spent two hours cleaning and organizing her room.

Her dad knocked on her bedroom door, and Hannah called, "Come in." The bookshelves were in order, clothes were folded and put away, and the floor had been vacuumed. "I'm really impressed, Hannah," her dad said. "Your room looks great!"

She grinned. Hannah knew she wasn't a neat person, and her room had badly needed to be cleaned.

"I want to thank you for working so hard," her dad went on. "I realize this is probably not your favorite way to spend Saturday morning."

Hannah grinned. "No kidding!"

"Your mom and I are proud of you," her dad said. "You're showing lots of responsibility. Keep it up."

"Thanks, Dad," said Hannah. She paused. "It really helps to hear you say that because I'm not quite done yet."

"What do you mean?" asked Hannah's dad, looking around.

Hannah sighed. "You haven't seen inside the closet!"

Your Turn

1. Hannah's dad used special words and phrases to encourage her. What were they?
2. How do you encourage and build up people?

Prayer

God, show me what words to use to build others up today. Amen.

Offering Encouragement

Let everything you say be good and helpful, so that your words will be an encouragement to those who hear them.

– Ephesians 4:29 NLT

What's the Joke?

Travis and Michael were whispering as Lauren approached the bus stop. The two boys burst out laughing.

"Good one, Travis," said Michael, slapping his pal on the shoulder.

Travis smirked.

"Hi, guys," said Lauren. "What's up?"

They looked at her surprised. "Uh, hi, Lauren," said Travis. "We didn't see you coming."

"So, what's the joke?" she asked.

The boys looked at each other and laughed.

"Do you really want to know?" asked Michael.

"It sure seemed funny to you," said Lauren.

Travis leaned over and whispered a few words in Lauren's ear.

Lauren's face reddened as she turned away from him. "Next time, no thanks."

Your Turn

1. What kind of joke do you think Travis whispered to Lauren?
2. Why do some jokes and comments make people feel uncomfortable?

_____

_____

_____

_____

Prayer

Lord, I want to avoid words that are out of place, rude, and inappropriate. Amen.

Offering Encouragement

*Let everything you say be good and helpful, so that your
words will be an encouragement to those who hear them.*

– Ephesians 4:29 NLT

Lexi Loses Her Cool

Josh had followed his sister Lexi around all day, even when her friends
came over to listen to music. Now he stood in her bedroom doorway.

"Want to play a game with me?" Josh asked.

"You are so annoying!" Lexi yelled. "Can't you see that I want to be
alone?" She slammed her bedroom door.

Why did I do that? Lexi wondered. *He's not that bad. Even my friends
think he's fun.* She opened the door and ran to the stairs where Josh sat,
his head in his hands. "I'm sorry, Josh."

Josh looked at her suspiciously. "Okay," he said slowly. "But what
made you change your mind?"

Lexi hung her head. "You spent a lot of time with my friends and me,
so when you asked to spend more time, I lost my cool."

Josh patted her knee. "How about playing a game?"

Lexi smiled. "Good idea."

Your Turn

1. What better way could Lexi have responded to Josh and still get her
   alone time?
2. When are you most tempted to lose your cool? What can you do to
   calm down and stay in control?

_____

_____

Prayer

Lord, it can be hard to use good words, especially when things don't go
my way. Help me be respectful to others. Amen.

Offering Encouragement

*Let everything you say be good and helpful, so that your
words will be an encouragement to those who hear them.*

– **Ephesians 4:29 NLT**

What About God?

"Jeez, Samantha, do you have to take so long?" Kristy asked her twin.
Kristy was waiting outside the dressing room with their mom.

"I'm trying on the last pair of jeans right now," Samantha answered.
"Omigod, they look great! Let me show them to you."

"Lordy, they're terrific!" said Kristy as Samantha opened the door.

"Just a minute, girls," said their mom. They both turned to her.
"You've both been wonderful on this shopping trip, but there's one way
you've been very disrespectful."

They looked at her in surprise. "Mom, we've been very polite to you
and to each other all day," said Kristy.

"True," their mom agreed. "But what about to God?" She paused for
a moment. "How do you think he feels when you use his name and his
Son's name so casually? Words like 'Jeez,' 'Omigod,' and 'Lordy' are slang
terms derived from God's names."

"I never thought I could hurt God's feelings," said Samantha.

"Me neither," said Kristy. "But now I understand why he doesn't like
it."

Your Turn

1. How should you use God's names?
2. What do you do when your friends disrespect God?

_____

_____

Prayer

Lord, help me honor your name when I speak. Amen.

Offering Encouragement

Let everything you say be good and helpful, so that your words will be an encouragement to those who hear them.

– Ephesians 4:29 NLT

Helpful or Hurtful?

Jessica stood at the door of the church nursery, helping Mrs. Honeyman greet parents and children. One little boy clung to his mother's hand.

"Hi, Brandon," Jessica said to the two-year-old. "I'm really glad to see you! Let's read a book together." Brandon grinned. He let go of his mom and reached for Jessica.

"Won't it be fun to play together again?" said Jessica.

Brandon nodded and picked up a book. Soon he and Jessica were snuggled together reading about trains.

Chad pulled on Jessica's arm. "Me too," he said. "I wanna read!" Chad grabbed the book from Brandon.

"Stop, Chad. You can't read with us," said Jessica. Chad started crying.

Mrs. Honeyman picked up Chad and spoke to him with soothing words. "You know, Jessica, you're very special to these little ones."

"What do you mean?" asked Jessica.

"Your helpful words when welcoming Brandon made him feel safe and loved. But those hurtful words to Chad were upsetting to him. These children look up to you."

"I guess what I say is more powerful than I realized," she said.

Your Turn

1. How could Jessica have better handled the situation with Chad?
2. Share a time when you encouraged a friend or family member. How did you feel at the time?

Prayer

Lord, words are powerful. Let me use them to help others today. Amen.

Offering Encouragement

Choosing Your Words

Each phrase in the thought bubble has the power to help people or hurt them. Which ones should you let through? Circle the helpful words. Draw a line through the words that are hurtful.

Prayer

Heavenly Father, please help me think before I speak so I won't hurt people's feelings. Amen.

Offering Encouragement

Change Your Words

Speaking respectfully gets easier with practice. Below are several disrespectful phrases. Write down a different way to say each one. This way, you'll have some practice under your belt the next time you're tempted to lose your cool!

I'm not wearing that! _____

I don't care what you think. _____

That is so stupid. _____

You're such a brat! _____

Do I have to? _____

Prayer

Dear Lord, I will practice speaking respectfully so I will develop a good habit. Amen.

Communicating with Grace

Do not be quick with your mouth.

– Ecclesiastes 5:2

A Piece of Cake

Kelsey walked to her seat, set down her backpack, and unzipped it. Math was her first subject of the day, and she was good at it. She liked starting each morning feeling smart. As she pulled her math book out of her backpack, Caroline sat down in the seat next to her. "Did you understand the homework?" asked Caroline. "I'm totally confused."

"Oh, it was so easy!" said Kelsey. "Anyone can get it."

"Well, I sure didn't," answered Caroline. "I'm worried about the quiz today. I hope I don't fail."

"I'm not worried at all," said Kelsey. "It'll be a piece of cake."

Caroline looked away.

Ben sat down across from Caroline. "Everyone knows you're better than the rest of us at math, Kelsey," he said. "Do you always have to rub it in?"

Kelsey glanced at Caroline. *She looks really upset,* thought Kelsey, *and I sure didn't help.*

Your Turn

1. Did Kelsey stop to think about Caroline's feelings before she spoke?
2. How could Kelsey have responded differently?

Prayer

Lord, I want to help others with my words. Remind me to stop and think before I speak today. Amen.

Communicating with Grace

Do not be quick with your mouth.

– **Ecclesiastes 5:2**

Sensitive Megan

"Do you want to come over tomorrow after school?" Megan asked her best friend, Grace. "We can finish making the necklaces we started together last week."

"No, I don't want to come over to your house ever again!" Grace answered. Then she grinned. "Just kidding!"

But Megan looked hurt.

"What's wrong?" asked Grace. "That was a joke. You know I like to kid around."

"Well, I don't mean to be overly sensitive," said Megan. "But lately, it seems like everything you say is a 'joke.'"

"Yep, I'm a comedian, and you're a sourpuss," said Grace. "Just ki…" She paused.

Megan looked at her friend.

"I'm sorry, Megan. I didn't realize my jokes had become a habit," said Grace. "And I'm not kidding about that."

It was Megan's turn to grin.

Your Turn

1. When are jokes and teasing not fun?
2. Why does God want us to speak with sincerity to others?

_____

_____

_____

Prayer

God, help my words be fun yet but sincere to people around me. Amen.

Communicating with Grace

Do not be quick with your mouth.

– Ecclesiastes 5:2

Grouchy Erin

Erin stared gloomily out the window. She'd promised to clean out the attic with her brother, Steven, but she wanted to read a book instead.

"C'mon, Erin," said Steven. "Let's get going."

"Quit being so cheerful," Erin complained.

Erin got dressed, went out into the hall, and pulled the rope for the attic's drop-down stairs. "Ugh, this is heavy."

"I'll get the light," said Steven as they climbed up, but the light wouldn't turn on.

"Oh, great," said Erin sarcastically. "Now we have to replace the bulb." She shivered and drew her sweater around her. "Nothing is going right."

"Erin, are you going to keep saying grouchy things?" asked Steven, fitting a fresh light bulb into the socket. "It seems like you're only thinking about bad stuff."

"That's because I'm in a bad mood," said Erin.

"All you need to do is find one good thing to think about," said Steven, "like working with your wonderful brother."

Erin rolled her eyes. "Okay, I'll try to find something positive to say."

Your Turn

1. What do you usually do when you're in a bad mood?
2. How can focusing your thoughts on good things turn your mood around?

Prayer

God, help me find good things in my day, think about them, and talk about them. Amen.

Communicating with Grace

Do not be quick with your mouth.

– Ecclesiastes 5:2

The Group Collage

It was nearly the end of the scout meeting. The group collage hung on the wall. Girls scurried around the collage, adding final touches, and talking and sharing ideas.

Jocelyn leaned forward to press one last crepe paper flower onto the board. Over the noise, she heard their leader.

"Listen up, girls!" said Mrs. Nixon. There was so much noise that Jocelyn had to listen carefully. "Let me know if you're free on Saturday morning. I'd like for a few of you to come with me when we present this collage to the staff at the children's hospital."

The girls tidied up and prepared to leave. Jocelyn stopped to thank Mrs. Nixon for leading the meeting. "I can come on Saturday morning to the hospital," she said.

"Wonderful!" answered Mrs. Nixon. "I'm afraid everyone else was so busy talking that they didn't listen to the announcement."

"I'll be there," said Jocelyn, thinking how fun it would be to share the group's handiwork. "I hope the others don't miss out just because they didn't listen."

Your Turn

1. Why does listening to others take effort sometimes?
2. What are the benefits of listening carefully when people speak?

Prayer

Lord, help me take the time to listen to the people around me today. Amen.

Communicating with Grace

Do not be quick with your mouth.

– Ecclesiastes 5:2

Who Told You That?

Kate and Marissa passed the soccer ball back and forth while they waited for the rest of the team to arrive.

"I heard that you and Sarah aren't friends anymore," Kate said.

"Who told you that?" asked Marissa, feeling hurt and confused. The day before, she and Sarah had argued, but Sarah had called last night to apologize.

"Jamie," said Kate. "She told me yesterday after school."

"We worked it out…" Marissa began. Just then, she saw Jamie and Sarah get out of the car together.

"Looks like they rode together to practice," said Kate.

Marissa didn't know what to think. Could she have been mistaken about Sarah's apology?

"Hi, Marissa!" shouted Sarah, running over to greet her friend. "I'm glad we made it! My mom's car broke down on the way to practice. Jamie's dad recognized us on the road. He stopped and picked us up."

Marissa sagged with relief. "I'm glad you're okay," she said. *So much for listening to gossip, she thought.*

Your Turn

1. Gossip hurts a lot of people. Who got hurt in this story?
2. What would be a way to avoid all that hurt?

_____

_____

Prayer

God, help me never to talk behind someone's back. Remind me to speak directly to the person for accurate information. Amen.

Communicating with Grace

Think of These Things

Use the list of positive characteristics from Philippians 4:8 to solve the puzzle. Remember, these are the qualities to look for in anything and everything you are involved in. One letter is in place to get you started.

TRUE
NOBLE
RIGHT
PURE
LOVELY
ADMIRABLE
EXCELLENT
PRAISEWORTHY

Prayer

Lord, help me memorize and then think about the positive qualities in Philippians 4:8. Amen.

Communicating with Grace

How to Avoid Gossiping

Use the code to fill in the letters and find a sure way to avoid gossiping.

A	!
C	@
D	#
E	$
F	%
G	^
H	&
I	*
K	+
N	\
O	<
P	>
R	?
S	/
T	=

< \ =   / > ? $! #   ^ < / / * >   * \ / = $!

_ _ _ _ ,   _ _ _ _ _ _   _ _ _ _ _ _ ,   _ _ _ _ _ _ _

/ > $! +   % ! @ $ = <   % ! @ $

_ _ _ _ _   _ _ _ _   _ _   _ _ _ _ .

Prayer

Lord, help me to never gossip. When I'm tempted, please bring to my mind how awful I would feel if someone gossiped about me. Amen.

God's Family, God's House

Remember the Sabbath day by keeping it holy.

– Exodus 20:8

God's Day

Maya and her mom were in the car on the way to worship service. "So many people go to church just once in a while," said Maya. "Not week after week, each and every single time the doors are open, like we do." It wasn't that Maya didn't like church. In fact, she loved it. But it sure would be nice to skip it occasionally.

Maya's mom smiled. "I've got an idea," she said. "Why don't we skip your ice skating lesson on Tuesday afternoon and just stay home and relax?"

"What do you mean?" asked Maya, horrified. "No way! That's my coach's special time at the rink with her students—the only time she has reserved."

Her mother nodded. "That's kind of like God's day each week," she said. "It's a special time set apart for his people to meet together."

Maya never had considered that before. "Okay, that sounds like a standing reservation."

Maya's mom laughed. "That's a good way to put it, Maya!"

Your Turn

1. Are you ever tempted to skip church?
2. How does setting aside time with believers to worship God reveal your love for him?

Prayer

God, so many things want my time. Setting aside time with you is my top priority. Amen.

God's Family, God's House

Remember the Sabbath day by keeping it holy.

– Exodus 20:8

The Big Fire

It was Saturday morning. Julia stood on the sidewalk with her brother, her mom, and her dad. They were across the street from their church. By now, the fire trucks had turned off their sirens. Streams of water had doused the flames.

Julia had discovered the fire. Since her dad was the pastor, she and her family lived in the parsonage next door. That morning Julia looked out her window and saw smoke seeping out the back of the church building.

She'd woken up her parents right away, and they'd called 911.

Word of the fire had spread quickly. Julia noticed that dozens of friends from church had come to see how badly the sanctuary was damaged.

"What will we do tomorrow morning, Dad?" asked Philip, Julia's brother. "Where will we have church?"

Pastor Bob looked up at the skies. It was clear and beautiful. "Tomorrow we'll have worship right here, on the front lawn," he said. "A church is not just a building. A church is made up of people."

Your Turn

1. What is more important than a church building?
2. How does God make a church live and grow, through the building or the people?

_____

_____

Prayer

God, thank you for the people who make your church alive and vibrant. Amen.

God's Family, God's House

Remember the Sabbath day by keeping it holy.
– Exodus 20:8

Natalie Helps Out

"Time to get up!" Natalie's mom called from the hallway. "We don't want to be late for church."

Natalie rolled over and groaned. *I can't get up yet—not after what happened yesterday.*

Nearly a half hour later, she felt a hand shaking her. "Natalie, did you fall back asleep?" asked her mom. "We need to leave in five minutes."

I can't do this, thought Natalie during the car ride to church. The day before, her softball team had lost after 13 innings—all because she'd dropped a fly ball in the outfield. Nobody would ever want her to be a part of anything ever again.

Natalie stumbled into the sanctuary. The praise band was warming up.

"Natalie, I'm so glad to see you!" said Scott, the praise leader. "One of our singers is sick. Will you help us out and sing with us?"

"Sure," she answered, feeling nervous and excited at the same time. *Maybe everybody doesn't think I'm a total loser after all.*

Your Turn

1. Name some reasons why you sometimes want to skip church.
2. Scott encouraged Natalie. How can you encourage members of your church?

_____

_____

Prayer

God, help me experience joy in worshipping you with other believers. Amen.

God's Family, God's House

Remember the Sabbath day by keeping it holy.
– Exodus 20:8

The Church Offering

Jenna sat with her dad in church, waiting for the service to begin. Her friend Emma slipped into the pew beside her. "My mom said I could sit with you today," she whispered.

Emma reached into her pocket and pulled out a plastic bag full of coins. "I'm going to put these in the offering today."

"Wow! There must be 40 or 50 coins!" Jenna whispered in return.

Jenna's dad leaned forward, his finger on his lips. Quietly, the girls placed the bag on the pew between them and fingered the coins. The praise song ended, and the pastor called the congregation to silent prayer.

Jenna put her hands together on her lap and shut her eyes.

Emma closed the songbook. As she reached forward to place it in the pew rack, her sleeve caught the edge of the plastic bag. C-c-c-clunk! The coins scattered across the pew and onto the floor.

Heads turned. Jenna's dad glared. Jenna hid her face with her hands.

Emma scrambled to pick up the coins. *I wish I'd been thinking about God instead of coins. The bag would have been zipped closed, at least.*

Your Turn

1. What helps you stay focused on God when you're in church?
2. What helps us to develop a worshipful attitude?

_____

_____

Prayer

God, the church is your special place. Help me focus on you when I'm there. Amen.

God's Family, God's House

Remember the Sabbath day by keeping it holy.

– Exodus 20:8

Something New

"I'm trying something new today," said Pastor Mark just before the worship service began. "You'll notice that when you came in, you received a handout. It will help guide you through the morning message."

Audrey heard papers ruffling all around her. She reached for her handout.

"You'll notice that I've listed the day's Scripture verses at the top," Pastor Mark said. "I want to encourage you to take the time to read through the passage before the service begins. When you come in, you can sit down and prepare for worship."

Audrey flipped open her Bible to the day's verses.

"That way, you have time to think about what the day's message will be," continued Pastor Mark. "You'll have ideas and questions, even before we get to the sermon." He smiled. "And there's a better chance I won't bore you."

Audrey giggled as a ripple of laughter moved through the congregation.

Your Turn

1. See if you can remember a story you heard in a recent sermon. Can you do it?
2. Why is it important to discipline yourself to listen to Bible messages and understand them?

_____

_____

Prayer

Lord, help me listen carefully in church. I want to learn and understand more about you. Amen.

God's Family, God's House

God's Special Day

Unscramble the words to find out a good reason to worship God.

HSIT   IS   ETH   YDA

_____   ___   _____   _____

HET   LORD   SAH   DMEA.

_____   _____   ____   _____

EW   LIWL   ICERJEO   DNA

____   _____   _____   ____

EB   DLGA   NI   TI

____   _____   ____   ____. Psalm 118:24 NLT

Prayer

Dear Lord, thank you for my church. Help me really listen during the teaching. Amen.

God's Family, God's House

Different Names for God's House

The Bible and the church use several descriptive names for places God's people worship. Match the description with the correct name.

A tent of worship for the early Israelites: _____

A building set apart for worship: _____

Where local groups of Jews meet: _____

Assembly of Christians: _____

Christians meeting in homes: _____

church	tabernacle	house church
	temple	synagogue

Prayer

Thank you, Lord, for my church—the believers I worship and socialize with. Amen.

Parents and Home

Children, obey your parents in everything, for this pleases the Lord.
– Colossians 3:20

Devin's Decision

The phone rang. It was Devin's dad. "How much homework do you have tonight?" he asked.

Devin groaned. "A lot. A page of math problems and some sentences to write using spelling words. Plus, I have a social studies test tomorrow."

"It's four o'clock right now," her dad answered. "I'll be home at six. Get your homework done before that."

"Why?" asked Devin.

"It's a surprise," said her dad. "Trust me, you'll like it. Just make sure you've studied and completed all your assignments."

Devin poured a glass of milk and ate some cookies. *There's still plenty of time before six,* thought Devin. *I'll relax a few minutes before I start my homework.* Time slipped away.

At six o'clock, Devin's dad stood in the doorway with her brother Tyler. "Did you finish your homework?" he asked.

"Not exactly," said Devin. "But I have all evening."

Her dad frowned. "Yes, you do," he said, pulling some tickets out of his pocket. "Tyler, I guess it will just be you and me going to the game tonight."

Your Turn

1. What happened when Devin didn't do as her father asked?
2. What do you think Devin will do differently next time?

Prayer

God, help me obey my parents immediately. Amen.

Parents and Home

Children, obey your parents in everything, for this pleases the Lord.
– **Colossians 3:20**

Don't Give Up!

Caitlyn put her head in her hands. Tears trickled down her cheeks. The Explorers Project was just too much to handle.

Her dad walked through the kitchen and saw Caitlyn crying. "Caitlyn, what's wrong?" he asked. He noticed the books spread out across the kitchen table. "Are you having trouble with some schoolwork?"

Caitlyn looked up and nodded. "The project was just assigned today," she said. "But there's a bunch of different parts to it. I'm confused…and I'm scared I'm never going to get it done."

Her dad pulled up a chair to sit next to Caitlyn. He put his arm around her. "You know, I struggled in school. But I never gave up. God helped me find ways to learn. Let's look at your assignment together. We'll break it into parts so it's easier to understand."

Caitlyn wiped her face. "That would be great, Dad."

"Just don't give up," said Caitlyn's dad. "You'll get it done. Now, show me those instructions."

Your Turn

1. What problem did Caitlyn's dad have when he was young?
2. Name several ways Caitlyn's dad encouraged her.

_____

_____

_____

Prayer

God, you picked my parents just for me. Thank you for helping them raise me. Amen.

Parents and Home

Children, obey your parents in everything, for this pleases the Lord.
– Colossians 3:20

Four Baskets of Laundry

"Have you seen my red sweater?" Jasmine asked her older brother. She wanted to wear it to school the next day.

"Nope," said Johnny. He was sprawled out on the sofa in the living room watching TV. "Check in there," he said, nodding toward four baskets of washed laundry sitting in the middle of the floor.

"I guess Mom didn't get to the folding last night," said Jasmine. "She got home from work after I went to bed."

Johnny nodded. "She looks really tired lately. And she told me she wouldn't be home until nine tonight. Something about working overtime to save up some money for Christmas."

Jasmine had an idea. She plunked down on the floor next to the first basket and started folding jeans, stacking Johnny's in one pile and hers in another.

"What are you doing?" asked Johnny.

"Mom's working extra for us. I thought I'd help her out a little bit too," answered Jasmine.

Johnny rolled off the couch. "I'll give you a hand."

Your Turn

1. Why did Jasmine and Johnny fold laundry?
2. How do you show your parents consideration and love?

_____

_____

_____

Prayer

Lord, show me a way to help my parents without being asked. Amen.

Parents and Home

Children, obey your parents in everything, for this pleases the Lord.

– Colossians 3:20

Ebony's Attitude

Ebony had asked her parents for months if she could paint her room. They had set aside this Saturday morning to help her. She hadn't realized what a huge job it was. She was tired, and beads of sweat were trickling down her back. "It's so hot in here!"

"Open the window to let some air in," suggested her mom.

Ebony put down her brush and walked over to the window. She tugged, but it wouldn't budge. "This is such a pain," she groaned. "I can't get it!"

Her dad chuckled from the ladder. "Try unlocking it."

Ebony flipped back the lock and pushed the window open. "Do we have to paint anymore? It's so much work. I want to be outside, instead." She stood by the window, breathing deeply.

She noticed her mom had put down the roller.

Dad stepped off the ladder. "We do too," he said quietly.

They're working just as hard as I am—just so I'll have a pretty room, thought Ebony. *They're not complaining.* "I'm sorry for my crummy attitude."

Your Turn

1. Why did Ebony's parents help her?
2. How can Ebony's complaining attitude make the job harder for everyone?

Prayer

Lord, my parents do so much for me. Let me have a positive attitude when I'm around them. Amen.

Parents and Home

Children, obey your parents in everything, for this pleases the Lord.
– Colossians 3:20

Fruit in the Fridge

Taylor opened the refrigerator door and frowned. "Mom, I thought you said you went to the grocery store this afternoon. There's nothing good in here."

The fridge shelves were stacked with yogurts, oranges, and grapes. A bag of trail mix sat on the kitchen counter.

"Tell me what you mean by 'good,' " said her mom.

"Like, did you get any cookies or sodas?" Taylor answered.

"Nope," said her mom, grinning.

Taylor groaned. "You're still on that health kick, aren't you?" A few weeks ago, their family doctor had encouraged Taylor's mom to evaluate the foods she purchased, prepared, and served at home. After that, Taylor's mom had sorted through the kitchen pantry and cupboards, tossing out all the chips and candy. Now, it seemed all the family ate were salads and fresh fruit.

"Yes, I think we're all healthier since we made those changes," said Taylor's mom. "I want what's best for you, Dad, and your brother, even if it's hard for me too." Taylor's mom sighed. "I sure miss eating ice cream."

Your Turn

1. What are some ways your parents show they care for you?
2. What's a way you can show your parents you appreciate their love and care?

_____

_____

Prayer

God, you've given my parents a big job in raising me. Give them your wisdom and patience. Amen.

Parents and Home

The Maze of Life

God has given your parents a huge job—guiding you through life. As you complete the puzzle, notice the roadblocks they may face.

Prayer

Lord, when my parents make mistakes raising me, help me forgive them immediately. Amen.

Parents and Home

Your Obedient-O-Meter

Obeying your parents doesn't mean just following their directions. It also means behaving the way they've taught you. How are you doing in that department? Check it out!

I. Dad asked me to be ready to leave for softball practice on time.
☐ I do this ☐ I don't do this

2. I'm supposed to call home when I get home after school, so my parents know I'm safe.
☐ I do this ☐ I don't do this

3. Mom and Dad are talking with friends after church. I wait patiently.
☐ I do this ☐ I don't do this

4. I have to ask if my friend's parents will be home before I tell her I can sleep over.
☐ I do this ☐ I don't do this

5. There were two voice messages. I wrote then down for my brother and my mom.
☐ I do this ☐ I don't do this

Prayer

Heavenly Father, help me obey my parents and do chores cheerfully. Amen.

Love Reaches Out

Always strive to do what is good for each other and for everyone else.

– **1 Thessalonians 5:15**

Happy Birthday!

"Happy Birthday, Shawna!" Bethany shouted, placing a chocolate birthday cake in front of her friend. The cake had Shawna's name on it, and the top was covered with colorful sprinkles. Soon the entire lunchroom was singing "Happy Birthday." Bethany helped Shawna cut pieces of cake and pass them out to everyone at the table.

There was one piece left. Bethany produced two forks. "Let's share!"

Shawna felt her cheeks get hot. She was confused and embarrassed. "Bethany, you're my best friend, but I forgot your birthday last month," she whispered. "And now you've given me this wonderful surprise? I feel kind of bad. Why did you go to so much trouble?"

"Oh, Shawna, I was upset that you forgot my birthday," admitted Bethany. "But I wouldn't feel any better if I'd missed yours on purpose just to get back at you. I talked with my mom about forgiving you. Together, we came up with the idea of bringing a surprise cake to you at school."

"I'm really glad you did," said Shawna.

Your Turn

1. 1. Have you been hurt by a friend on purpose or by accident? What did you do?
2. 2. Why is showing kindness a choice you make?

_____

_____

_____

Prayer

Lord, help me to choose to be kind every time. Amen.

338

Love Reaches Out

Always strive to do what is good for each other and for everyone else.
– 1 Thessalonians 5:15

Leah Reaches Out

The party in the gym was sponsored by Leah's youth group, but the entire middle school had been invited. "The idea is to help everyone have a good time and feel comfortable," their youth pastor, Joe, had said.

The gym was packed by the time Leah and Amelia arrived. One corner was set up with games and prizes. Music blared over the sound system. Laughter filled the room.

"Do you know her?" Amelia asked, nudging Leah and pointing to a girl standing in the corner.

Zoe wore black jeans, a black shirt, and black fingernail polish. "As a matter of fact, I do," Leah answered.

"You're kidding!" said Amelia.

"Well, she sure dresses differently than I do," said Leah, "but she's really good at math. She helped me out a lot when we first studied decimals." Let's go over and say hi." She headed Zoe's way, with Amelia trailing a few steps behind her.

"Hey, Zoe!" said Leah. "This is my friend Amelia. It's good to see you!"

Your Turn

1. 1. Why did Amelia think Zoe was different in a negative way? Was Amelia right?
2. 2. How did Leah help welcome Zoe?

_____

_____

Prayer

Lord, help me welcome people even when they seem really different. Amen.

Love Reaches Out

Always strive to do what is good for each other and for everyone else.
— **1 Thessalonians 5:15**

Swim Practice

It was almost time for swim practice. Usually, Tasha was the first one on the team ready to go, but not today.

"Tasha, what's wrong?" Abby asked, walking over to her teammate.

Tasha shifted her swim bag from one hand to another. "I'm moving," she said flatly. "My dad got a job in another state. He starts next week."

Tasha sat down on the bench and buried her face in her hands. "What if there's no swim club in my new town?"

Abby couldn't imagine what it would feel like to have to move. "Here," she said, reaching into her locker and pulling out some tissues. She handed Tasha the tissue, and sat down next to her on the bench. As Tasha wiped her eyes, Abby realized she was going to miss her friend a lot. "I have an idea! After practice, come over to my house. We'll look up the name of your new town on the Internet and find the nearest swim club!"

Tasha threw her arms around Abby. "Thank you for caring!"

Your Turn

1. List several ways Abby showed Tasha she cared.
2. Why does it help to have a friend share your sadness?

Prayer

Lord, show me how to care for my friends when they are sad. Amen.

Love Reaches Out

Always strive to do what is good for each other and for everyone else.

– 1 Thessalonians 5:15

Letters

Dear Mrs. Barrett,

Thank you for helping me prepare for my piano contest. I got straight A marks! Plus, I felt totally ready because of your help. I actually had fun playing my pieces.

You are a wonderful piano teacher, and I really appreciate you.

Love, Felicia

P.S. Hope you enjoy the Firecracker Treat!

Dear Felicia,

Congratulations on your straight A's. I knew you'd do well. But what is even more wonderful is hearing how much you enjoyed performing.

I thought you'd like to know how much your gift and note meant to me. Recently, I have considered closing my piano studio. I realize I'm getting older, and I've started feeling that I'm not relating well with my students. After getting your letter, I'm inspired to keep teaching.

Thank you, Felicia!

Love, Mrs. Barrett

Your Turn

1. List several reasons why Felicia's letter meant so much to Mrs. Barrett.
2. Do you go out of your way to show your gratitude?

_____

_____

_____

Prayer

God, help me take time to thank the people I interact with. Amen

Love Reaches Out

Always strive to do what is good for each other and for everyone else.

– 1 Thessalonians 5:15

It's Not Safe

Shelby tugged at Aaron's jacket. "Sit down," she hissed. "It's not safe for you to be standing up while the bus is moving."

Aaron shrugged but dropped into the seat next to his sister. "The kids back there don't seem to be in mortal danger."

It was only the second week of school, but the party-like atmosphere on bus 29 made it feel like the last day. Three or four students stood in the aisles, hanging over seats and talking with friends. A paper airplane whizzed by Shelby's left ear.

Suddenly, the bus lurched to a halt. Two students stumbled. David Feathers fell into Aaron's lap.

Mrs. Fielding, the bus driver, had pulled over to the side of the road. Now she stood, faced the students, and spoke over the little PA system. "Boys and girls, you've each signed an agreement to behave properly on the bus." She held up a stack of bright-yellow papers. "You are not following the rules. Am I going to have any more problems?"

There was silence. As the bus resumed its route, Shelby heard several riders grumble, but by the time bus 29 arrived at the school, they were chattering happily once again—this time safely seated.

Your Turn

1. How did Shelby show respect to the bus driver?
2. List five things that might happen if you don't follow the rules at school.

_____

_____

Prayer

God, help me show respect to the people around me. Amen.

Love Reaches Out

Why Be Kind?

Does God expect you to be kind even when other people aren't? Solve the rebus to find out.

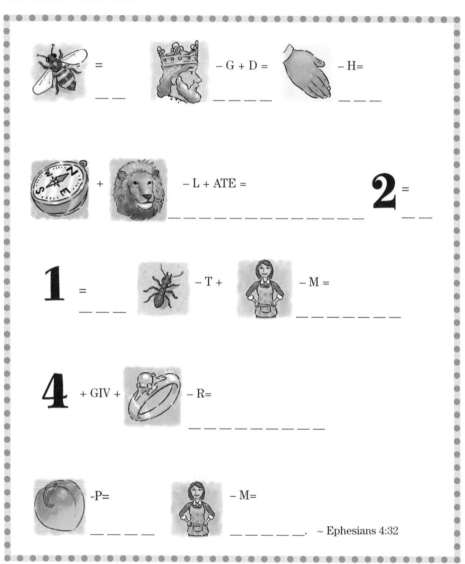

~ Ephesians 4:32

Prayer

Lord, help me be kind to everyone I meet—even those who aren't pleasant to be around. Amen.

Love Reaches Out

How Jesus Helped

Martha and Mary were sad because their brother, Lazarus, died. Figure out the ways Jesus supported them by identifying which caption goes with which picture.

Captions

A. Jesus prayed for them. _____

B. Jesus thought about them and cared about them. _____

C. Jesus helped them the best he could. _____

D. Jesus went to see them. _____

E. Jesus offered comforting words.

_____

Prayer

Lord, help me find ways to be kind to people who are in pain. Amen.

344

God-Given Relationships

Love one another deeply, from the heart.

– 1 Peter 1:22

It's Too Quiet

The apartment was quiet. Too quiet. Kristen wandered down the hall to the living room, where her stepmother worked at the computer.

"Doesn't it seem kind of boring around here?" Kristen asked.

Kristen's stepmother looked up. "It's nice and quiet," she said, smiling.

"But there's nothing to do," Kristen went on.

Kristen's stepmother's eyes twinkled. "You must be missing Joey."

Kristen paused. Her stepbrother was a year younger than she was. Even though Kristen and Joey didn't see eye to eye on everything, having Joey around meant lots of action. His friends came over almost every day. But now Joey's room was quiet and empty.

Kristen sighed. "Joey can be loud and annoying. But I never realized how much fun he is and what a commotion he creates."

"He's away at camp for another week," her stepmother said. "Write him a letter. I bet he misses you too."

"He'd never admit it," Kristen said with a giggle.

Your Turn

1. Make a list of your family members.
   `Write down three things you appreciate about each one.
2. Now do the same with your closest friends.

_____

_____

_____

Prayer

Lord, thank you for each one in my family. Help me to appreciate them each day. Amen.

God-Given Relationships

Love one another deeply, from the heart.
– 1 Peter 1:22

School Lunch

Alissa looked across the courtyard. She saw Brittany come in, joking and laughing with some girls from the school chorus. The group sat down at a picnic table together and began eating lunch.

Alissa opened her bag lunch, but she wasn't hungry. She fought back tears. She and Brittany had been in the homeschool group together since kindergarten. Then, last year, Brittany had entered public school.

"It's fun, Alissa," Brittany had told her. "You get to meet lots of new people."

So when Alissa's mom had to go back to work, Alissa wasn't too worried about starting up at school.

"It'll be great!" said Brittany. "We'll get to go to classes and eat lunch together!"

But it hadn't quite worked out that way. Brittany had a year's head start at making new friends. Alissa was still trying to find her way around the school.

Brittany told me she'd meet me here today for lunch, thought Alissa. *I guess she forgot again.* Alissa sighed.

Your Turn

1. Was Brittany being an inconsiderate friend on purpose? Explain.
2. What could Alissa have done that might have made her feel better?

_____

_____

_____

Prayer

God, help me remember and keep the promises I make. Amen.

God-Given Relationships

Love one another deeply, from the heart.

– 1 Peter 1:22

The Slumber Party

The scout meeting was in full swing as the girls busily cut and stamped greeting cards.

"What about you, Michelle? Can you spend the night at my house on Saturday?" Brianna asked as they worked. "Everyone else is."

The girls around the table turned and looked at Michelle, waiting for her to answer.

She felt awkward. Her parents didn't allow her to spend Saturday night at another friend's house unless the girl's family attended church the next morning—and promised to take Michelle with them. Michelle knew Brianna didn't go to church.

Amber leaned forward. "I think I have the same problem as you, Michelle," she whispered. "My mom is picking me up early on Sunday morning from the sleepover to go to church. I'm sure it would be fine if you went with us."

Michelle shot Amber a grateful look. "Thanks a lot. That would be great!" she whispered back. She turned to Brianna. "I'll check with my parents, but Saturday night sounds like fun!"

Your Turn

1. What did Michelle and Amber have in common?
2. How did Amber help out Michelle?

Prayer

Lord, thank you for putting believers in my life to help and be friends with. Amen.

God-Given Relationships

Love one another deeply, from the heart.

– 1 Peter 1:22

Bad Weather

Sammi climbed out of the backseat into the pouring rain.

"I'm surprised there are so many people here tonight," said Sammi's dad, as they hurried up the sidewalk to the church fellowship hall. "Even though our Church Family Suppers are just once a month, I had a feeling this weather would keep lots of people away."

"But it's always so much fun!" said Sammi. "The food, the games—it's like being home on a holiday."

"And it's a good way for some of our older members to get out for an evening," added Sammi's mom, shifting the casserole to keep water off the lid. "They can spend time with people in a fun and relaxing way."

As the threesome reached the door, they noticed one last car pull into the lot. It circled slowly, looking for a spot.

"That's Mrs. Gardner," said Sammi. "She can't find a close parking space and she uses a cane." Sammi turned to her parents. "Mom, may I use the umbrella? Dad, will you go with me and park Mrs. Gardner's car while I help her get inside?"

"Great idea, Sammi!" said her father.

Your Turn

1. Why did Sammi enjoy Church Family Supper nights?
2. How will Sammi and her dad help Mrs. Gardner feel like a loved member of her church family?

Prayer

God, thank you for giving me people who love me at home and at church. Amen.

God-Given Relationships

Love one another deeply, from the heart.

– 1 Peter 1:22

Hurt Feelings

Cody stormed into the house from the bus stop. Jocelyn, sitting at the kitchen counter munching on an apple, heard her younger brother slam his bedroom door. This was so unlike Cody. Normally he stopped to talk with Jocelyn after school, chattering away about his day, what he learned from the latest book he'd read, or things he'd noticed about people.

Jocelyn felt strange. *Usually I think Cody is such a pest. People always tell him to shut up–even I do sometimes. But he's a decent kid.* She crept upstairs and leaned her ear against Cody's door. She heard some quiet sniffling. *What should I do?*

Taking a deep breath, she tapped gently on the door and pushed it open.

Cody turned his face away. "Do you want to tell me I'm a know-it-all like everyone else does?"

Someone hurt his feelings, Jocelyn realized. "Well, you are pretty smart," she admitted with a smile. "I kind of missed you telling me stuff today...even though you probably don't know everything."

"Well, duh," Cody answered. He wiped his face...and started talking.

Your Turn

1. When you see someone hurting, what can you do?
2. Share a time when you encouraged your sibling or good friend.

_____

_____

Prayer

Lord, thank you for kids for me to know and interact with—even when they are siblings. Amen.

God-Given Relationships

Names for Believers

People who follow Jesus are given lots of different names in the Bible. Fit all the names into the puzzle. You can do it!

ADOPTED SONS HIS CHILDREN
BROTHERS HOUSEHOLD OF FAITH
CHRISTIANS PEOPLE OF GOD
DISCIPLES SAINTS
FAMILY OF BELIEVERS SISTERS
FELLOW CITIZENS THOSE OF THE WAY
GOD'S FAMILY

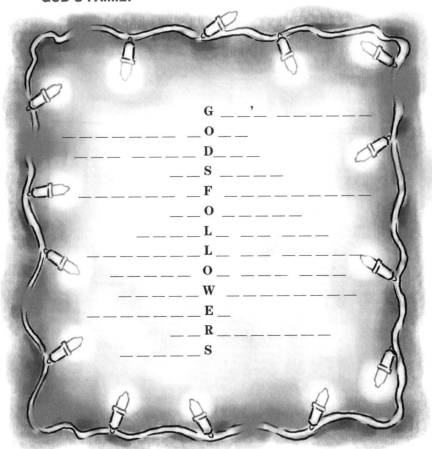

Prayer

Lord, thank you for adopting me! I love being your child. Amen.

God-Given Relationships

Your Church Family

In what ways are your church family members special to you? Next to each position, write the member's name(s). List what each member does and what you learn or appreciate about him or her.

MY SPECIAL CHURCH FAMILY

MY PASTOR _____

MY SUNDAY SCHOOL TEACHER _____

MY YOUTH LEADER _____
_____

MY MUSIC DIRECTOR _____
_____

MY ADULT FRIENDS _____
_____

MY CLASS FRIENDS _____
_____

MY OTHER FRIENDS _____
_____

Prayer

Lord, help me remember to pray for the leaders of my church family. Amen.

Life Wisdom

See to it...that none of you has a sinful, unbelieving heart that turns away from the living God.

– Hebrews 3:12-13

Nikki's Double Standard

Luke, the youth group leader, had asked Nikki and Faith to help him at the Community Summer Camp Fair. Both girls had attended church camp last summer, so they agreed to hand out brochures and encourage students to sign up for the coming summer.

Faith handed out information and talked a mile a minute. Nikki sat at the back of the booth. *She's totally embarrassing me,* thought Nikki, scowling. *I know she had a good time at camp, but does she have to be so excited about it?*

The crowd thinned out, and Faith came back for more brochures. "Nikki, what's wrong? Why aren't you out here talking with students?"

Nikki frowned. "You're doing enough talking for both of us."

Luke overheard. "Does her enthusiasm bother you that much?"

Nikki nodded, sinking further into the chair. "She's so open about her feelings. It's...too revealing."

Luke smiled. "The same way you're being open about being embarrassed and irritated with her by sitting back here?"

Nikki sat up, surprised.

Your Turn

1. How could Nikki encourage Faith instead of acting irritated?
2. What can discouragement do to people?

Prayer

Lord, when people around me are excited, help me encourage their enthusiasm rather than discourage it. Amen.

Life Wisdom

*See to it…that none of you has a sinful, unbelieving heart
that turns away from the living God.*

– Hebrews 3:12-13

God's Great Work

As Mr. Arnold, the head usher, walked to the front of the sanctuary, the church grew silent. Everyone knew what was written on the slip of paper in his hand. It was the total figure of the offerings and pledges for the new church building fund.

Jane's hands felt sweaty. *This has been so hard for Mom and Dad,* Jane thought.

Jane's dad, Pastor Bill, took the slip of paper from Mr. Arnold. "Friends," Pastor Bill said, "The total amount given or pledged this day for the new church building…exceeds our need."

Cheers and amens broke out across the sanctuary. Jane looked to the front of the church and saw her father wipe tears from his face.

"Let's give praise to God right now that his people have given back to him for his work," said Pastor Bill.

Jane looked at her mom, who was beaming. "God is doing a great work here, Jane," she said.

Your Turn

1. Why does God own all that we have and all that we are?
2. How might failing to give your time, skills, gifts, and offerings to God be the same as stealing from him?

_____

_____

_____

Prayer

Lord, show me how to honor you with my prayers, worship, and service. Amen.

Life Wisdom

See to it…that none of you has a sinful, unbelieving heart that turns away from the living God.

– **Hebrews 3:12-13**

Caught

Sophie studied the Parcheesi board. Her cousin Ryan was winning. As soon as he got two more of his red markers to home, he'd be done. Ryan's brother, Jeff, didn't look too happy about it.

One of Ryan's markers was near the finish line. Sophie took her turn, setting up a blockade of two of her blue markers right in front of Ryan's.

"What are you doing, Cuz?" Ryan teased. "Trying to make me lose?"

Ryan and Sophie were so busy laughing that they didn't notice Jeff moving one of his markers ahead of Ryan's, close to the finish line.

"Your turn, Ryan," said Jeff, with a smirk.

Sophie felt uneasy. Suddenly, she knew why. "Jeff, your turn comes after Ryan's," she said. "Are you stealing an extra turn?"

"His marker is stuck behind your blockade anyway," said Jeff.

"But is that fair?" Sophie asked.

Jeff rolled his eyes.

Ryan rolled the dice. "Better not celebrate your victory so soon," he said to Jeff, looking at the number on the dice and reaching for his free marker. "Looks like I just got your man out."

Your Turn

1. Would you have called Jeff on his cheating?
2. Have you thought of cheating as "stealing"? Why or why not?

Prayer

God, help me play fair and give people the opportunities that belong to them. Amen.

Life Wisdom

*See to it...that none of you has a sinful, unbelieving heart
that turns away from the living God.*

– Hebrews 3:12-13

Miss Goody-Goody

Savannah was one of those girls, Kari reasoned, who was goody-goody.
She always turned in her homework on time. She was polite to everyone.
She even loaned her new glitter pencils to Brigit Brady. Kari decided it
was time to toughen up Miss Goody-Goody.

On Thursday morning when Mrs. Ryan stood in front of the class
with a sad face, Kari saw her opportunity. "Class, I have some bad news,"
said Mrs. Ryan "The envelope that contained our field trip money is
gone. If you have any information about the money, come talk with me
privately."

Kari had seen Savannah going through papers on Mrs. Ryan's desk
yesterday after lunch. She hadn't actually seen Savannah take anything,
but did that matter? Kari approached Mrs. Ryan and told her that
Savannah was the thief.

"Kari, the envelope was missing yesterday morning—hours before
you say Savannah took it," Mrs. Ryan replied. "You're telling me that
Savannah tried to steal something, but do you realize you just tried to
steal her reputation? A person's good name is a precious possession."

Your Turn

1. How did Savannah earn a good reputation?
2. Do you think Kari's reputation with Mrs. Ryan changed?

_____

_____

Prayer

God, let me build a good name by living as your girl. Help me respect
the reputations of people around me. Amen.

Life Wisdom

*See to it…that none of you has a sinful, unbelieving heart
that turns away from the living God.*

– Hebrews 3:12-13

Gifts from God

It was the first day of school. Keisha waved to the Ernst twins and high-fived Brad and Tyler on her way to homeroom. She noticed new sixth graders studying their schedules and searching for room numbers, trying to locate their next class. *It's a relief to be in seventh grade—no longer the youngest at the school,* she thought.

She recalled her own embarrassment on her first day last year. On the way to orchestra, she slipped on her shoelace going upstairs and fell flat on her face. No one stopped to help her. *That felt terrible,* thought Keisha as she rounded the corner to the seventh-grade wing. Just then, two young boys next to Keisha collided in the hallway. Papers and notebooks flew everywhere. Several students laughed and pointed. Others, in a hurry to get to class, simply ignored the mess and kept walking. *I can help, even if others don't,* thought Keisha.

"Here, let me help," she said to the two boys as she knelt down and began collecting stray papers and pencils. They looked at her gratefully.

Your Turn

1. How did Keisha feel about what happened to her on her first day of school?
2. Other students withheld help. That's sometimes called a "sin of omission." What were they leaving out?

_____

_____

Prayer

God, help me recognize opportunities to do good and follow through. Amen.

Life Wisdom

Jesus' Reputation

During his time on earth, Jesus traveled from place to place, healing people, performing miracles, and showing compassion to those in need. What kind of reputation did he earn? Look up 9:18-20, and then answer these questions.

1. Jesus wanted to know what kind of reputation he had with the people. Whom did he ask?

   _____

2. Whom did the crowds think Jesus was?

   _____

3. A prophet is a person who shares God's message with people. Why do you think people thought Jesus was a prophet?

   _____

4. What kind of reputation did Jesus have with Peter and the disciples?

   _____

5. Who had spent more time with Jesus: the disciples or the crowds?

   _____

6. Who would have been in a better situation to know who Jesus was?

   _____

Prayer

Lord, my reputation is important. Help me live in such a way that people see me and know I am your child. Amen.

Life Wisdom

Who Gets What?

Jesus taught people to give to God but also to respect their earthly leaders and obey the rules of the land. Some of the people were confused about what he taught and some didn't like it. Use the list of captions to label each scene as Jesus explains the truth about "who gets what." The story is in Matthew 22:15-22.

a. "It's got our emperor's face."

b. "Let's ask Jesus!"

c. "Pay your taxes to the emperor, and give God what's his, too."

d. "Show me the coin. Whose face is on it?"

e. "They're trying to trap me right now."

f. "Wow, Jesus really surprised us with that answer."

Prayer

Lord, help me to understand your teachings in your Word. I love you. Amen.

Faith and Integrity

The crooked heart will not prosper;
the lying tongue tumbles into trouble.

– Proverbs 17:20 NLT

Any Homework Tonight?

The book report isn't due until Monday. It's Thursday, and I haven't even started reading the book. But I have all weekend to get it done, thought Ellie. There was no way she wanted to plunge into 168 pages right now. Instead, Ellie flipped on the TV and settled onto the couch.

"Any homework tonight, Ellie?" asked her mom, looking around her computer screen.

"Nope, not tonight," Ellie answered. *Nothing is actually due tomorrow,* she rationalized.

"So, how's your book report coming along? Is it finished then?" asked Ellie's mother.

"Oh, how did you know I have a book report assignment?" asked Ellie. "It's right here on the daily e-mail from your English teacher," said Ellie's mom.

Ellie turned her head away.

"I take it you're still working on it," said Ellie's mom, frowning. She got up and turned off the TV. "Why don't you show me the book you're reading, and tell me what the story is about?"

Ellie cringed. *This is going to get ugly.*

Your Turn

1. Do you think Ellie's decisions were a big deal? Why or why not?
2. Have you ever been confronted when trying to deceive someone? What happened?

Prayer

God, when I'm tempted to deceive someone, remind me that dishonesty seldom succeeds and always hurts someone. Amen.

Faith and Integrity

The crooked heart will not prosper;
the lying tongue tumbles into trouble.

– Proverbs 17:20 NLT

Chess Club

"Are you coming to the Chess Club this afternoon?" Jacob asked Marie as they stood in the lunch line waiting to fill their trays.

At first, Marie had thought Chess Club would be fun. She'd attended twice, but each time, she'd been matched against players who had a lot more experience, so she lost miserably. *What should I say to Jacob?* "I can't come to the meeting today," Marie lied. "I have to go right home after school and watch my stepsister until my stepmom gets home from work."

"That's a lie!" said Andrea, reaching for an empty lunch tray. She was standing in line behind Jacob and had overheard the conversation. "You told me your stepsister goes to Kids Connection every day, and you're free to attend after-school activities."

Jacob reached for a bowl of butterscotch pudding and set it on his tray. "So, Marie, what's the real reason you're not coming to Chess Club today?"

Marie felt her face burn with embarrassment.

Your Turn

1. Why did Marie lie?
2. What could have happened if she'd told the truth?

_____

_____

_____

Prayer

God, give me the courage to tell the truth even if it injures my pride. Amen.

Faith and Integrity

The crooked heart will not prosper;
the lying tongue tumbles into trouble.

– Proverbs 17:20 NLT

The Quandary

Jennifer felt trapped.

Tomorrow she was having a birthday party for Lisa, but Lisa just had a fight with Anna and didn't want Anna to come to her party.

If Anna comes, Jennifer thought, *Lisa will make a scene. But how can I tell Anna not to come? That would be too rude.*

Jennifer reached for the phone. "Who are you calling?" asked Jennifer's mother as she walked in the room.

Jennifer moaned. "I can only think of one way out, Mom," she said. "I'll call Anna and tell her that Lisa is sick and that the party is canceled."

"You're forgetting the second choice you have," said her mom.

"What's that?" asked Jennifer.

"Call Anna, explain how uncomfortable you feel, and ask her to find a way to resolve things with Lisa."

"You mean tell her the truth?" asked Jennifer. "That's so hard! It's a touchy subject."

Her mom nodded. "Yes, it is, but don't you think it's the best way?"

Jennifer sighed. "I think you're right."

Your Turn

1. Why did Jennifer think she had only one option?
2. Why is telling the truth to friends and family so hard sometimes?

Prayer

God, help me tell the truth with grace and kindness—even when it's hard. Amen.

361

Faith and Integrity

The crooked heart will not prosper;
the lying tongue tumbles into trouble.

– Proverbs 17:20 NLT

False Accusations

Catherine stood with three other girls in the guidance counselor's office. "I'd like to know who is responsible for the graffiti on the bathroom wall," said Mrs. Yates. "The four of you were the last ones in there after lunch. The custodian found the graffiti shortly after that."

The girls looked at each other. Catherine shifted her feet. Debbie wiped her hands on her jeans. Suzanne and Leah stood like statues.

"It was Debbie!" Leah blurted out.

"Thank you, Leah," said Mrs. Yates. "Debbie, please stay here. The rest of you may go back to class."

Catherine filed out of the office with the other girls, her stomach in knots. She knew the charge against Debbie was wrong. It was actually Leah and her best friend, Suzanne, who had written the graffiti. *It's wrong for Debbie to take the blame for something she didn't do,* Catherine thought.

She stopped, turned around, and knocked on Mrs. Yates' door. The counselor poked her head out into the hall. Debbie stood behind the counselor.

"May I speak to you privately, Mrs. Yates?" asked Catherine. "There's something I need to tell you."

Your Turn

1. Do you think it was hard for Catherine to tell the truth?
2. What consequences (good *and* bad) might Catherine face for telling the truth?

Prayer

God, help me not withhold truth. I want to stick up for what is right. Amen.

Faith and Integrity

The crooked heart will not prosper;
the lying tongue tumbles into trouble.

– Proverbs 17:20 NLT

You're Not My Friend

"You're not my friend anymore," Kelsey said to Ming in front of the rest of the girls in the playground.

Ming couldn't believe Kelsey would hurt and embarrass her so badly. She stood with her hand over her mouth, tears forming in her eyes.

"Ming, if I were you, I'd never speak to her again," said Amber, who had been standing nearby during the exchange.

"No, I've got a better idea," Katie chimed in. "Let's share some good dirt we've got on her!"

What's the true and right way for me to respond? Ming wondered. Just this past week her Sunday-school class had discussed what Jesus said to do in this type of situation. "If your brother or sister sins, go and point out their fault, just between the two of you" (Matthew 18:15). She knew what she needed to do.

Ming turned, ran, and caught up with Kelsey. "May I talk with you for a minute alone?" she asked.

Your Turn

1. How did Ming figure out what to do?
2. Why can reviewing God's truths help you live your life with integrity?

_____

_____

_____

_____

Prayer

Lord, help me to turn to you for advice and follow your truths. Amen.

Faith and Integrity

Where to Find the Truth

Where can you find truth? Start at the magnifying glass and work your way through the maze to find the One Person who will give you straight and true advice.

Prayer

Lord, you are the way and the truth and the life. I want to live in a way that pleases you. Amen.

Faith and Integrity

Jacob's Deception

Esau and Jacob were twins. As the eldest, Esau would receive their father's blessing and inheritance. Jacob tricked Esau and their father, Isaac, to get what he wanted. The deception forced him to leave his family and home. To find out what happened, fill in the correct caption with each scene. The story is found in Genesis 27.

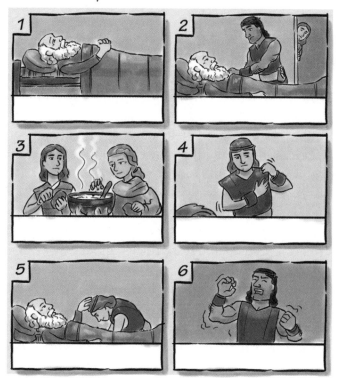

Captions

a. Esau finds out and Jacob must leave
b. While Esau is away in the field, Jacob puts on his brother's clothes
c. Isaac, Esau and Jacob's father, is blind and dying
d. The twins' mother secretly helps Jacob
e. Jacob pretends to be Esau, and receives his father's blessing
f. Jacob finds out that Isaac wants to give Esau a special blessing

Prayer

Lord, sometimes I'm tempted to compromise my integrity. I want to honor you with a pure heart, so I'll stick to the truth. Amen.

Walk in Gratitude

Life does not consist in an abundance of possessions.
– Luke 12:15

The Empty House

"C'mon up to my room," said Christine. Ellie followed her up the beautiful curved staircase.

Ellie walked into the bedroom and felt the soft, plush carpet beneath her feet. "Wow, you have your own entertainment system in your room!"she exclaimed.

"Yeah," said Christine, "but to tell you the truth, I enjoy watching TV downstairs. At least that way I have the chance to see my mom and dad if they walk through the living room."

I'd love the chance to get away from my sisters and watch TV by myself, thought Ellie. She sank onto the velvet cushions in the window seat that overlooked the pool, flower garden, and backyard. "This is so cool, Christine. You can pretend you're a princess hidden away in a castle up here."

"That's about right," said Christine, sighing. "Sometimes I feel locked away from everybody."

Ellie then noticed how empty the house felt—almost cold. *I should be jealous of Christine,* thought Ellie. *But maybe my busy family and my little bedroom aren't so bad after all. Even if I have to share everything.*

Your Turn

1. Ellie was a bit envious of Christine. What changed her mind?
2. Why is it easy to take your life and possessions for granted sometimes?

_____

_____

Prayer

Lord, thank you for what you've given me. Help me walk in an attitude of gratitude. Amen.

Walk in Gratitude

Life does not consist in an abundance of possessions.

– Luke 12:15

A Big Help

Caroline shifted the home-economics book higher on her desk, and slid lower into her seat to disappear from the teacher's view. *I'm just not the homemaking type,* Caroline thought in despair. *I like sports and being outside.*

"The recipe says to blanch the vegetables to prepare them for canning," said Mrs. Moore. "Can anyone tell me what that means?"

The class was silent until Jill raised her hand. "Isn't it easier to just get them at the grocery store?"

Caroline recalled the hot, sunny days last August when she'd helped her grandfather in his garden. Together, they'd picked bushels of tomatoes, green beans, okra, cucumbers, and squash. Suddenly Caroline sat up straight. Her hand shot in the air.

"I help my grandparents with their canning in the summer. They put tomatoes in boiling water just for a minute or two to remove the skins. I think that's called blanching."

"That's exactly right, Caroline," said Mrs. Moore. "I bet you were a big help to them."

Maybe I'm not hopeless in the kitchen after all! thought Caroline.

Your Turn

1. What were Caroline's gifts and strengths?
2. What are some of your gifts and strengths?

_____

_____

Prayer

God, thank you for giving me talents and strengths I can use to help people and share your love. Amen.

Walk in Gratitude

Life does not consist in an abundance of possessions.

– Luke 12:15

Emily's Jacket

It was 7:55 a.m. "Mom, have you seen my navy-blue jacket?" Emily called downstairs. Her ride to school was due any minute.

"I saw something blue in the driveway last night," her mom called back.

Emily threw open the front door and ran out into the blustery cold. It had rained the night before, so ice on the driveway crackled under her feet. Emily saw her jacket right where she'd left it yesterday afternoon. It was frozen and heavy when Emily picked it up and hurried inside.

"Mom, wh-wh-wh-what should I d-d-d-do?" she asked, her teeth chattering.

"Well, for one thing, don't let your jacket get water all over the kitchen floor!" answered her mom. "Put it in the bathtub. Get your brother's red jacket from the hall closet."

"But I c-c-can't w-w-wear a g-g-guy's coat to school!" Emily wailed.

Her mother looked out the window and noticed a car pulling into the driveway. "This experience will help you remember to take care of your things," she said. "Now put on the jacket and get going. Your ride is here."

Your Turn

1. What do you think Emily will do with her jacket the next time she plays basketball in the driveway?
2. How can keeping track of your belongings help you be content with what you have?

Prayer

Lord, show me how to be faithful to you with all you give me. Amen.

Walk in Gratitude

Life does not consist in an abundance of possessions.

– Luke 12:15

Ashley's Big Disappointment

It was the "end of the year" awards ceremony, and every seat in the auditorium was full. Ashley was sure she'd walk away with the Physical Education Achievement Award. After all, she was the most skilled athlete in the school, particularly in softball.

As Mr. Martinez, the physical education teacher, walked to the platform, Ashley tingled with anticipation. "It's my pleasure to present this year's physical education award to one of the hardest-working students I've ever known."

Something didn't feel quite right to Ashley. Mr. Martinez never complimented her on her hard work. In fact, he often challenged her to try harder to reach her potential.

"There are many students who may have more natural athletic ability than this person," Mr. Martinez went on. "But this young lady took every opportunity that was presented to her as a challenge to improve her skills. I have no doubt she will succeed not only as next year's softball team captain, but also in life. This year's physical education award goes to Grace Wilson!"

Ashley bowed her head in disappointment.

Your Turn

1. Do you think Ashley made the most of every opportunity that was presented to her?
2. What kinds of opportunities did Grace make the most of?

Prayer

Lord, help me recognize the opportunities you send my way each day. Amen.

Walk in Gratitude

Life does not consist in an abundance of possessions.
– Luke 12:15

Spanish Spoken Here

Isabelle opened the car door, got in, and put on her seat belt. "Good to see you, honey," said her mom, still in her nurse's scrubs. Isabelle had gone to Lakisha's house after school, and her mom was picking her up.

Her mom hummed as she signaled a turn at a stoplight.

"You always seem so happy after you get off work, Mom," Isabelle said. "Lakisha's dad is getting ready to change jobs because he's not happy."

Her mom nodded. "It just shows you that the best future for you may be something that surprises you," she answered.

"What do you mean?" asked Isabelle.

"When I was young, I always felt a little embarrassed that my parents never spoke English at home," her mom answered. "I didn't realize that God wanted me to know Spanish for a good reason! Now that I'm a nurse, I can communicate with patients who don't speak English and are scared and confused."

She turned the car into their driveway. "Won't it be fun to see where God leads Lakisha's dad?"

Your Turn

1. How did God prepare Isabelle's mom for her future?
2. How does knowing God has a future planned for you give you hope and excitement?

Prayer

Thank you, God, that you have a plan for my future! Amen.

Walk in Gratitude

Keeping Track of Your Things

Use this list to help you keep track of your things. Circle the items on the list you are responsible for. On the blank lines, write down other things you are responsible for.

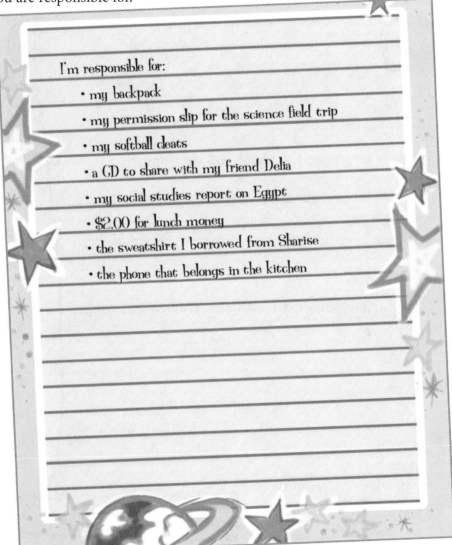

I'm responsible for:

- my backpack
- my permission slip for the science field trip
- my softball cleats
- a CD to share with my friend Delia
- my social studies report on Egypt
- $2.00 for lunch money
- the sweatshirt I borrowed from Sharise
- the phone that belongs in the kitchen

Prayer

Heavenly Father, I want to develop the habit of taking care of my possessions to show my gratitude. Amen.

Walk in Gratitude

God's Plans for You

God has plans for your future! Find out what those plans are by thinking about Jeremiah 29:11. Refer to that verse to fill in the lists.

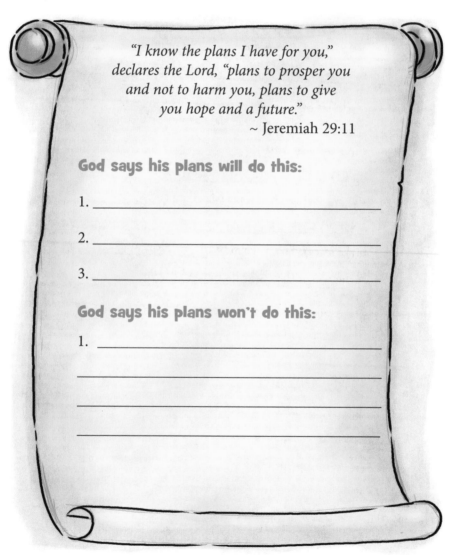

"I know the plans I have for you,"
declares the Lord, "plans to prosper you
and not to harm you, plans to give
you hope and a future."

~ Jeremiah 29:11

God says his plans will do this:

1. _____

2. _____

3. _____

God says his plans won't do this:

1. _____

_____

_____

_____

_____

Prayer

Heavenly Father, thank you for the plans You have for me. I'm excited to see what comes next! Amen.

Answer Key

Page 21: Family Love

Page 22: Family Album

Jesse
Ruth
David
Esau
Jesus

Page 28: Fruit of the Spirit

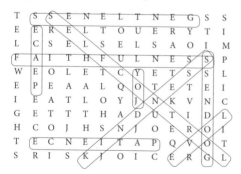

Page 29: Heaven is...

Forever	Perfect
Joyful	Peaceful
Angels	Magnificent
Jesus	Saints
Praise	

Page 35: Ancient Worriers

People Clues—
Across
1. Jehoshaphat
3. Zacchaeus
Down
2. Martha   4. Rachel
5. Moses

Solutions Clues—
Across
1. Enemies   3. Sycamore
Down
2. Mary   4. Son   5. Aaron

Page 36: Worry Advice

Trust God

Page 42: A Message for You

Island
Over
Every
Tour

    I love you

Page 49: Who Stayed Committed?

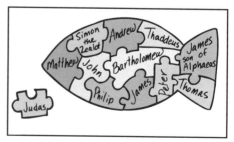

Page 50: Weird Words

1. Joy in times of sadness
2. Falling down
3. A hole in one
4. Over the hill
Bonus: A second helping

Page 57: Trust God

I trust in God's unfailing love for ever and ever. Psalm 52:8

Page 63: The Secret of Loyalty

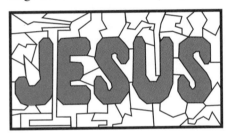

Page 70: A Good Verse

Surely your goodness and love will follow me all the days of my life.

Page 78: Something to Avoid

A lying tongue

Page 84: Ripe or Not

David [circle]   Barak [square]
Joshua [circle]   Mary [circle]
Moses [square]   Deborah [circle]
Gideon [square]

Page 85: Courage Under Fire

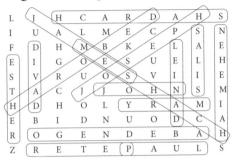

Page 91: A Promise for a Friend

Across
1. Mephibosheth   4. Land
5. Saul   6. Lame
Down
2. Ziba   3. Jerusalem

Page 98: Everyone Is Special

Sinners   Tax
Men   Deaf
Lame   Lepers
Blind   Poor
Sick   Insane

Page 99: The Least of These

Hungry   Fed
Thirsty   Drink
Stranger   Invited
Home   Naked
Clothing   Sick
Cared   Prison
Visited

Page 105: Prayer Power

1. Desert of Shur; drinkable water
2. the sun and moon to hold still
3. a son; the Lord's house
4. inside a fish
5. at home; three times a day
6. a mountainside
7. the leper; to be made clean/healed
8. Paul and Silas, prison

Page 106: Command Code

Whoever has my commands and keeps them is the one who loves me.

Page 112: Psalm 100

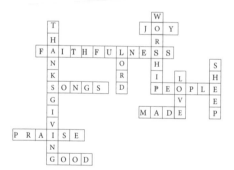

Page 119: Read the Rebus

Live in harmony with one another. Be compassionate.

Page 126: An Abundance of Animals

T	C	Z	E	B	R	A	R	B	M	A	L
N	R	N	I	H	P	L	O	D	O	G	A
A	H	E	A	O	S	T	R	I	C	H	E
H	I	P	P	O	P	O	T	A	M	U	S
P	N	E	I	R	H	O	L	I	O	N	T
E	O	A	G	A	A	T	S	Y	N	O	P
L	C	C	A	G	W	E	H	B	K	T	T
E	E	O	L	N	K	E	A	E	E	N	A
L	R	C	A	Q	R	R	R	A	Y	A	O
K	O	K	O	K	A	Y	K	R	H	O	G
O	S	R	K	N	U	M	P	I	H	C	T

Page 127: Bible Plants

1. cucumbers and onions
2. melons, leeks, garlic
3. grapes
4. barley
5. pomegranate
6. dates, raisins
7. cedar
8. apple
9. rose of Sharon, lily of the valley
10. figs, pine, palm
11. juniper
12. fig, pomegranate, apple tree
13. lilies
14. wheat
15. mustard
16. sycamore-fig, olive
17. thistles (thorns)
18. fig tree, olives, grapevines

Page 133: Living in Unity

1. May 2. Each
3. In 4. Help
5. God 6. Romans
7. Complete 8. With
9. 15 10. Other
11. 5 12. You
13. Harmony 14. Live

May God . . . help you live in complete harmony with each other. Romans 15:5 (NLT).

Page 134: Letting God Work

Acts 3:1-10— a lame beggar asked Peter and John for money; the man was healed and praised God.
Acts 12:1-17— Peter was thrown into prison and then freed by an angel; the church had prayed for him. But they were surprised to see him free.

Page 140: Plans for the Future

Page 141: Future Fears

Jesus Christ is the same yesterday and today and forever.

Page 154: Love in Action

God wants us to be loyal to him and his Word.

Page 155: A Change of Heart

Message: You can too

Page 162: The Greatest Gift

Today in the town of David a Savior has been born to you; he is the Messiah, the Lord. (Luke 2:11)

Page 168: Following and Obeying

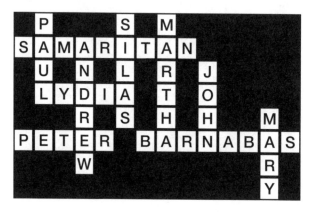

Page 183: Jesus' Friends

Sinners   Tax collectors
Blind   Lame
Poor   Lepers
Children   Beggars

Page 196: A Sincere Need

Page 176: Trust

	P		S	M		
S	A	M	A	R	I	T	A	N
	U		N	L	R	J
	L	Y	D	I	A	T	O
	R		S	H	H	M
P	E	T	E	R	B	A	R	N	A	B	A	S
	W					R
						Y

Page 182: A Way to Accept

Jesus has your best interests at heart.

Page 197: The Pledge

Be devoted to one another in love. Honor one another above yourselves. (Romans 12:10)

Page 211: A Word from Our Sponsor

Show mercy and compassion to one another.

Page 217: Kindness Ingredients

Goodness
Knowledge
Self-control
Perseverance
Godliness
Mutual affection
Love

Page 218: Godly Appeal

1. I
2. 1; one
3. all
4. to
5. appeal
6. agree
7. of
8. with
9. 10
10. another
11. that
12. you
13. 1 Corinthians

I appeal to you...that all of you agree with one another. 1 Corinthians 1:10

Page 224: Who Deserves Fairness?

Every answer about who deserves fairness is "Yes."

Page 225: Forgiveness Formula

1. As the Lord forgave you
2. Anyone you hold anything against (everyone)
3. So God will also forgive you
4. Seven times in a day (everytime)
Blanks: your name; forgives; forgive

Page 231: Free Advice

Think of others instead of yourself

Page 238: Cross Out

Instead of thinking sad thoughts, rejoice!

Page 245: The Courage to Trust

The LORD is my strength and my shield; my heart trusts in him, and he helps me. (Psalm 28:7)

Page 246: Loads of Confidence

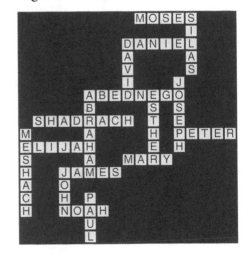

Page 253: A Verse to Live By

Be joyful in hope, patient in affliction, faithful in prayer. Romans 12:12

Page 259: God, the Teacher

It is by grace you have been saved. (Ephesians 2:5)

Page 266: The Way to Wisdom

Your word is a lamp for my feet, a light on my path. (Psalm 119:105)

Page 267: A Walk to the Park

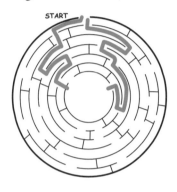

Page 273: David's Plea

O God you are my God. I seek you. My soul thirsts for you.

Page 280: Famous Promises

Genesis: God, Noah, Noah's sons, all living creatures; never again will a flood destroy the earth

1 Samuel: Jonathan, David; friendship

Hebrews: Jesus Christ, those who are called (believers); free from sin, receive eternal inheritance (life)

Page 281: Moses' Big Meeting

Wash — Their clothes
Touch — The mountain
Sky — Thunder & lightning
Mountain — Clouds & smoke
Heard — Trumpet blast

Page 287: Name the Six

Exodus 20:12	Honor your father and your mother
Exodus 20:13	You shall not murder
Exodus 20:14	You shall not commit adultery
Exodus 20:15	You shall not steal
Exodus 20:16	You shall not give false testimony against your neighbor
Exodus 20:17	You shall not covet

Page 294: Look for the Hearts

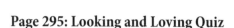

Page 295: Looking and Loving Quiz

"B" is the loving response to each situation

Page 301: What It Means to Be Holy

Heart
Only
Lives
You

Page 302: Worthy of Worship

For all the gods of the nations are idols, but the LORD made the heavens.

Page 308: How Does God Do It?

1. Searches
2. Every desire and every thought
3. You will find him
4. (write your own thoughts)

Page 315: Choosing Your Words

Circled words
great; good job; excellent; way to go; thank you; can I help?; you're awesome; I love you

Crossed out words
jerk; cheater!; you're not one of us; I don't care; I hate you; you're stupid

Page 322: Think of These Things

Page 323: How to Avoid Gossiping

Don't spread gossip, instead speak face to face.

Page 329: God's Special Day

This is the day the LORD has made. We will rejoice and be glad in it.

Page 330: Different Names for God's House

Tabernacle
Temple
Synagogue
Church
House church

Page 336: The Maze of Life

Page 343: Why Be Kind?

Be kind and compassionate to one another, forgiving each other.

Page 344: How Jesus Helped

A. 4; B. 1; C. 5; D. 2; E. 3

Page 350: Names for Believers

```
              God'sfamily
    adoptedsOns
     hischilD'ren
        siSters
    familyoFbelievers
        brOthers
       peopLeofGod
    househoLdoffaith
      thoseOftheway
     felloWcitizens
      disciplEs
        chRistians
       saintS
```

Page 357: Jesus' Reputation

1. The disciples
2. John the Baptist, Elijah, or one of the old prophets
3. Jesus shared God's love with them
4. Peter said Jesus is "the Christ of God"
5. The disciples
6. The disciples

Page 358: Who Gets What?

1. b; 2. e; 3. d; 4. a; 5. c; 6. f

Page 364: Where to Find the Truth

Page 365: Jacob's Deception

1. c; 2. f; 3. d; 4. b; 5. e; 6. a

Page 372: God's Plans for You

Will – prosper you; give you hope; give you a future.
Will not – harm you.

THE GiRL'S GUiDE TO . . .

Encourage girls with these fun and creative books covering issues that matter most to them: fashion, being their best, making friends, understanding the Bible, getting along with Mom, dealing with money, and LIFE! **Ages 10–12.**

176-208 pages, Paperback, Illustrated

The Girl's Guide to . . .

Being Your Best!	L48211	ISBN: 9781584110354
Friendship!	L48212	ISBN: 9781584110439
The Bible	L48213	ISBN: 9781584110446
Your Mom	L48214	ISBN: 9781584110453
Money	L48215	ISBN: 9781584110675
Change: Inside & Out!	L48216	ISBN: 9781584110866
Style	L48217	ISBN: 9781584110903
Me: The Quiz Book	L48218	ISBN: 9781584110873
Your Dream Room	L48219	ISBN: 9781584111436
Life.	L48220	ISBN: 9781584111498
Manners	L48221	ISBN: 9781584111511

THE GOD AND ME!® BIBLE

Designed to capture the vivid imaginations of growing girls, *The God and Me! Bible* puts God's Word inot the hearts and minds. The bright illustrations, creative activities, puzzles, and games that accompany each Bible story make learning important Bible truths both fun and easy. **Ages 6–9.**

192 pages, Paperback, Full Color Illustrations

The God and Me! Bible	L48522	ISBN: 9781584110897

JUST FOR ME! FOR GIRLS

Through stories, crafts, and fun activities, younger girls will discover what they need to grow closer to God! **Ages 6–9.**   152 pages, Paperback, Illustrated

Friends	L48411	ISBN: 9781584110828
My Family	L48413	ISBN: 9781584110958

TRUE HEART GIRLS DEVOTIONALS

Through relatable stories, Bible connections, and interactive pages, girls will discover promises that will make a difference in their lives and help them deal with the sometimes overwhelming emotions that come with growing up. From learning to make new friends to not stressing out about that math test, the tween years can be a rollercoaster time!—but when girls focus on God's promises for them, it's so much more fun!
Packed with 15 weeks of devotions, stories, Scriptures, and over 50 fun activities & crafts, girls get a godly foundation for growing up that they will treasure for the rest of their lives. **Ages 8-12.**

224 pages, Paperback, Full Color Illustrations

| God's Promises for Me! | L50019 | ISBN: 9781628627701 |
| Joyful Me! | L50023 | ISBN: 9781628627848 |

Each empowering devotional features—

- A short, relatable story & Bible connection

- Key Scripture to memorize and a short prayer to read

- Exciting Bible activities, puzzles, and crafts

- Space for journaling

These devotionals are filled with several Key Bible Promises for Girls, such as:

- God Saves

- God Takes Care of Every Need

- God Is with You

- God Loves You

- God Is Faithful

- And much more!

SUPER INCREDIBLE FAITH SERIES
FOR GIRLS AND BOYS

Help your children better understand how much God takes care of them! In these 100 devotions, Michelle Howe encourages kids to develop character traits including unconditional love, the fruits of the Spirit, the blessedness of the Beatitudes, and more. Each reflection includes a story, a Scripture verse, a prayer, and an activity page. **Ages 6 to 9.**

320 pages, Paperback, Full Color Illustrations

| Living Bravely | L50020 | ISBN: 9781628627800 |
| Conquering Fear | L50021 | ISBN: 9781628627824 |

GUIDED JOURNALS FOR GIRLS AND BOYS

Preteen boys and girls will love these daily devotional journals that really encourage them to dig into the Bible. **Ages 10–12.**

136–160 pages, Paperback, Illustrated

| My Bible Journal | L46911 | ISBN: 9781885358707 |
| My Prayer Journal | D46731 | ISBN: 9781885358370 |

Find more great stuff by visiting our website: **www.hendricksonrose.com**